Lincoln Christian College

D1230268

LETTERS

OF

FELIX MENDELSSOHN BARTHOLDY

LETTERS

OF

FELIX MENDELSSOHN BARTHOLDY,

FROM 1833 TO 1847.

EDITED BY
PAUL MENDELSSOHN BARTHOLDY,
OF BERLIN;

AND

DR. CARL MENDELSSOHN BARTHOLDY,
OF HEIDELBERG:

WITH
CATALOGUE OF ALL HIS MUSICAL COMPOSITIONS
COMPILED BY
DR. JULIUS RIETZ.

𝔗𝔯𝔞𝔫𝔰𝔩𝔞𝔱𝔢𝔡

BY

LADY WALLACE.

BOOKS FOR LIBRARIES PRESS
FREEPORT, NEW YORK

First Published 1864
Reprinted 1970

STANDARD BOOK NUMBER:
8369-5272-3

LIBRARY OF CONGRESS CATALOG CARD NUMBER:
73-114867

PRINTED IN THE UNITED STATES OF AMERICA

927.8
M53
c.1.

Books for Libraries

15 00

11 Feb 71

PREFACE.

THE Letters of Felix Mendelssohn Bartholdy from Italy and Switzerland have amply fulfilled the purpose of their publication, by making him *personally known* to the world, and, above all, to his countrymen.

Those Letters, however, comprise only a portion of the period of Mendelssohn's youth; and it has now become possible, by the aid of his own verbal delineations, to exhibit in a complete form that picture of his life and character which was commenced in the former volume.

This has been distinctly kept in view in the selection of the following letters. They commence directly after the termination of the former volume, and extend to Mendelssohn's death. They accompany him through the most varied relations of his life and vocation, and thus lay claim, at least partially, to another kind of interest from that of the period of gay, though not insignificant, enjoyment, depicted by him in the letters written during his travels. For example, the negotia-

38282

tions on the subject of his appointment at Berlin take
up a large space ; but this is inevitable, so characteristic are they of the manner in which he conceived and
conducted such matters, while they reveal to us much
that lies outside his own personal character, and thus
possess a more than merely biographical value.

On the other hand, the minute details of the pure and
elevated happiness which Mendelssohn enjoyed in his
most intimate domestic relations are expressly with-
held, as being the peculiar treasure of his family, and a
few passages only have been selected for publication
from these letters, which, however, are sufficiently clear
on the point. In conclusion, it should be observed,
that no letter addressed to any living person has been
published without express permission readily accorded.

A Catalogue of all Mendelssohn's compositions, compiled by Herr Kapellmeister Dr. Julius Rietz, is added
as a supplement, which, by its classification and arrangement, will no doubt prove an object of interest both to
musicians and amateurs of music.

Berlin and Heidelberg,
  June, 1868.

LETTERS.

To Pastor Bauer, Beszig.

Berlin, March 4th, 1833.

Since I set to work again, I feel in such good spirits
that I am anxious to adhere to it as closely as possible,
so it monopolizes every moment that I do not spend
with my own family. Such a period as this last half-
year having passed away makes me feel doubly grateful. It is like the sensation of going out for the first
time after an illness; and, in fact, such a term of uncertainty, doubt, and suspense really amounted to a
malady, and one of the worst kind too.* I am now,
however, entirely cured; so, when you think of me,
do so as of a joyous musician, who is doing many things,
who is *resolved* to do many more, and who would *fain*
accomplish all that can be done.

For the life of me I cannot rightly understand the
meaning of your recent question and discussion, or
what answer I am to give you. Universality, and
everything bordering on æsthetics, makes me forth-

---

* At the period to which Mendelssohn here refers, owing to the
advice of his friends, he had applied for the situation of Director of the
Singing Academy, but was not chosen.

with quite dumb and dejected. Am I to tell you how
you ought to feel? You strive to discriminate between
an excess of sensibility and genuine feeling, and say
that a plant may bloom itself to death.

But no such thing exists as an excess of sensibility;
and what is designated as such is, in fact, rather a
dearth of it. The soaring, elevated emotions inspired
by music, so welcome to listeners, are no excess; for
let him who can feel do so to the utmost of his power,
and even more if possible; and if he dies of it, it will
not be in sin, for nothing is certain but what is felt or
believed, or whatever term you may choose to employ;
moreover, the bloom of a plant does not cause it to
perish save when forced, and forced to the uttermost;
and in that case, a sickly blossom no more resembles
a healthy one, than sickly sentimentality resembles
true feeling.

I am not acquainted with Herr W——, nor have I
read his book; but it is always to be deplored when
any but genuine artists attempt to purify and restore
the public taste. On such a subject words are only
pernicious; deeds alone are efficient. For even if people
do really feel this antipathy towards the present, they
cannot as yet give anything better to replace it, and
therefore they had best let it alone. Palestrina effected
a reformation during his life; he could not do so now
any more than Sebastian Bach or Luther. The men
are yet to come who will *advance* on the straight road,
and who will lead others onwards, or back to the ancient and right path, which ought, in fact, to be termed
the onward path; but they will write no books on the
subject.

To Pastor Bauer, Beszig.

Berlin, April 6th, 1833.

My work, about which I had recently many doubts, is finished; and now, when I look it over, I find that, quite contrary to my expectations, it satisfies myself. I believe it has become a good composition; but, be that as it may, at all events I feel that it shows progress, and that is the main point. So long as I feel this to be the case, I can enjoy life and be happy; but the most bitter moments I ever endured, or ever could have imagined, were during last autumn, when I had my misgivings on this subject. Would that this mood of happy satisfaction could but be hoarded and stored up! But the worst of it is, that I feel sure I shall have forgotten it all when similar evil days recur. and I can devise no means of guarding against this, nor do I believe that you can suggest any. As, however, a whole mass of music is at this moment buzzing in my head, I trust that it will not, please God, quickly pass away.

Strange that this should be the case at a time in other respects so imbued with deep fervour and earnestness, for I shall leave this place feeling more solitary than when I came. I have found my nearest relatives, my parents, my brother and sisters, alone unchanged; and this is a source of happiness for which I certainly cannot be too grateful to God; indeed, now that I am (what is called) independent, I have learned to love and honour and understand my parents better than ever; but then I see many branching off to the right and to the left, who I had hoped would always go along with me ; and yet I could not follow them on their path, even if I wished to do so.

The longer I stay in Berlin, the more do I miss Rietz, and the more deeply do I deplore his death. X——declares that the fault lies very much with myself, because I insist on having people exactly as I fancy they ought to be, and that I have too much party spirit for or against a person ; but it is this very spirit the want of which I feel so much here. I hear plenty of opinions given ; but where there is no fervour there can be no sound judgment ; and where it does exist, though it may indeed not unfrequently lead to error, still it often tends towards progress too, and then we need not take refuge in past times, or anywhere else, but rather rejoice in the present, if only for bringing with it in its course a spring or an Easter festival.

To Pastor Julius Schubring, Dessau.

Coblenz, September 6th, 1833.

Dear Schubring,

Just as I was beginning to arrange the sheets of my oratorio,* and meditating on the music that I intend to write for it this winter, I received your letter enclosing your extracts, which appeared to me so good that I transcribed the whole text so far as it has gone, and now return it to you with the same request as at first, that you will kindly send me your remarks and additions. You will perceive various annotations on the margin as

---

* "St. Paul."

to the passages I wish to have from the Bible or the Hymn Book. I am anxious also to have your opinion —1st. As to the form of the whole, especially the narrative part, and whether you think that the *general* arrangement may be retained,—the blending of the narrative and dramatic representation. I dare not adopt the Bach form along with this personified recital; so this combination seems to me the most natural, and not very difficult, except in such passages, for example, as Ananias, owing to the length of the continuous narration. 2d. Whether you are of opinion that any of the principal features in the history or the acts, and also in the character and teaching, of St. Paul, have been either omitted or falsified. 3d. Where the divisions of the first and second parts should be marked. 4th. Whether you approve of my employing chorales. From this I have been strongly dissuaded by various people, and yet I cannot decide on giving it up entirely, for I think it must be in character with any oratorio founded on the New Testament. If this be also your opinion, then you must supply me with all the hymns and passages. You see I require a great deal from you, but I wish first to enter fully into the spirit of the words, and then the music shall follow; and I know the interest you take in the work.

If you will do all this for me, write me a few lines immediately to Berlin, for I am obliged to go there for three or four days with my father, who went to England with me, and was dangerously ill there. Thank God, he is now quite restored to health; but I was under such dreadful apprehension the whole time, that I shall leave nothing undone on my part to see him once more safe at home. I must, however, return forthwith and proceed to Düsseldorf, where you are probably aware that I directed the Musical Festival, and subsequently decided on taking up my abode there for two or three years, nominally in order to direct the church music, and the Vocal Association, and probably also a new theatre which is now being built there, but in reality for the purpose of securing quiet and leisure for composition. The country and the people suit me admirably, and in winter " St. Paul " is to be given. I brought out my new symphony in England, and people liked it; and now the " Hebrides " is about to be published, and also the symphony. This is all very gratifying; but I hope the things of real value are yet to come. I trust it may be so. It is not fair in me to have written you such a half-dry and wholly serious letter, but such has been the character of this recent period, and so I am become in some degree like it.-

To I. Moscheles, London.

Berlin, 1833.

. . . Do you suppose that I have not gone to hear Madame B—— because she is not handsome, and wears wide hanging sleeves ? This is not the reason, although there are undoubtedly some physiognomies which can never, under any circumstances, become artistic,—from which such icy cold emanates that their very aspect freezes me at once. But why should I be forced to listen for the thirtieth time to all sorts of variations by

Herz? They cause me less pleasure than rope-dancers or acrobats. In their case we have at least the barbarous excitement of fearing that they may break their necks, and of seeing that nevertheless they escape doing so. But those who perform feats of agility on the piano do nbt even endanger their lives, but only our ears. In such I take no interest. I wish I could escape the annoyance of being obliged to hear that the public demands this style; I also form one of the public, and I demand the exact reverse. Moreover, she played in the theatre between the acts, and that I consider most obnoxious. First, up goes the curtain, and I see before me India, with her pariahs and palm-trees and prickly plants, and then come death and murder, so I must weep bitterly; then up goes the curtain again, and I see Madame B—— with her piano, and a concert ensues in every variety of minor key, and I must applaud with all my might; then follows the farce of "Ein Stündchen vor dem Potsdamer Thor," and I am expected to laugh. No! This I cannot stand, and these are the reasons why I do not deserve your censure. I stayed at home because I like best to be in my own room, or with my own family, or in my own garden, which is wonderfully beautiful this year. If you will not believe me, come and judge for yourself, I cannot resist always reverting to this,

To Rebecca Dirichlet, Berlin.

Düsseldorf, October 26th, 1833.

My dear Sister,

The history of my life during the last few weeks is long and pleasant. Sunday, Maximilian's day, was my first Mass; the choir crammed with singers, male and female, and the whole church decorated with green branches and tapestry. The organist flourished away tremendously, up and down. Haydn's Mass was scandalously gay, but the whole thing was very tolerable. Afterwards came a procession, playing my solemn march in E flat,—the bass performers repeating the first part, while those in the treble went straight on; but this was of no consequence in the open air; and when I encountered them later in the day, they had played the march so often over that it went famously; and I consider it a high honour that these itinerant musicians have bespoken a new march from me for the next fair.

Previous to that Sunday, however, there was rather a touching scene. I must tell you that really no appropriate epithet exists for the music which has been hitherto given here. The chaplain came and complained to me of his dilemma; the Burgomaster had said that though his predecessor was evangelical, and perfectly satisfied with the music, he intended himself to form part of the procession, and insisted that the music should be of a better class. A very crabbed old musician, in a threadbare coat, was summoned, whose office it had hitherto been to beat time. When he came, and they attacked him, he declared that he neither could nor would have better music; if any improvement was required, some one else must be employed; that he knew perfectly what vast pretensions some people made now-a-days, everything was expected to sound so beautiful; this had not been the case in his day, and he played just as well now as formerly. I was really very reluctant to take the affair out of his hands, though there could be no doubt that others would do infinitely better; and I could not help thinking how I should myself feel, were I to be summoned some fifty years hence to a town-hall, and spoken to in this strain, and a young greenhorn snubbed me, and my coat was seedy, and I had not the most remote idea why the music should be better; and I felt rather uncomfortable.

Unluckily, I could not find among all the music here even one tolerable solemn Mass, and not a single one of the old Italian masters; nothing but modern dross. I took a fancy to travel through my domains in search of good music; so, after the Choral Association on Wednesday, I got into a carriage and drove off to Elberfeld, where I hunted out Palestrina's "Improperia," and the Misereres of Allegri and Bai, and also the score and vocal parts of "Alexander's Feast," which I carried off forthwith, and went on to Bonn. There I rummaged through the whole library alone, for poor Breidenstein is so ill that it is scarcely expected he can recover; but he gave me the key, and lent me whatever I chose. I found some splendid things, and took away with me six Masses of Palestrina, one of Lotti and one of Pergolesi, and Psalms by Leo and Lotti, etc., etc. At last, in Cologne I succeeded in finding out the best old Italian pieces which I as yet know, particularly two motetts of Orlando Lasso, which are

1*

wonderfully fine, and even deeper and broader than the two " Crucifixus" of Lotti. One of these, · " Populus meus," we are to sing in church next Friday.

The following day was Sunday : so the steamboat did not come, and, knowing that my presence was necessary in Düsseldorf, I hired a carriage and drove here. People were crowding along the *chaussée* from every direction ; a number of triumphal arches had been erected, and the houses all adorned with lamps. I arrived with my huge packet, but not a single person would look at it ; nothing but "the Crown Prince," " the Crown Prince," again and again. He arrived safely at the Jägerhof on Sunday evening, passing under all the triumphal arches during the time of the illuminations, and amidst the pealing of bells and firing of cannon, with an escort of burgher guards, between lines of soldiers, and to the sound of martial music. Next day he gave a dinner, to which he invited me, and I amused myself famously, because I was very jovial at a small table with Lessing, Hübner, and a few others. Besides, the Crown Prince was as gracious as possible, and shook hands with me, saying that he was really quite angry at my forsaking both him and Berlin for so long a time,—listened to what I had to say, called me forward from my corner as " dear Mendelssohn :" in short, you see I am thought infinitely more precious when I am a little way from home.

I must now describe to you the fête that was given in his honour, and for which I suggested the employment of some old transparencies, to be connected, by appropriate verses for " Israel in Egypt," with *tableaux vivants*. They took place in the great Hall of the Academy, where a stage was erected. In front was the double chorus (about ninety voices altogether), standing in two semicircles round my English piano; and in the room seats for four hundred spectators. R——, in mediæval costume, interpreted the whole affair, and contrived very cleverly, in iambics, to combine the different objects, in spite of their disparity.

He exhibited three transparencies:—first, "Melancholy," after Dürer, a motett of Lotti's being given by men's voices in the far distance; then the Raphael, with the Virgin appearing to him in a vision, to which the "O Sanctissima" was sung (a well-known song, but which always makes people cry); thirdly, St. Jerome in his tent, with a song of Weber's "Hör' uns, Wahrheit." This was the first part. Now came the best of all. We began from the very beginning of "Israel in Egypt." Of course you know the first recitative, and how the chorus gradually swells in tone; first the voices of the *alti* are heard alone, then more voices join in, till the loud passage comes with single chords, "They sighed," etc. (in G minor), when the curtain rose, and displayed the first tableau, "The Children of Israel in bondage," designed and arranged by Bendemann. In the foreground was Moses, gazing dreamily into the distance in sorrowful apathy; beside him an old man sinking to the ground under the weight of a beam, while his son makes an effort to relieve him from it; in the background some beautiful figures with uplifted arms, a few weeping children in the foreground, —the whole scene closely crowded together like a mass of fugitives. This remained visible till the close of the first chorus; and when it ended in C minor, the curtain at tne same moment dropped over the bright picture. A finer effect I scarcely ever saw.

The chorus then sang the plagues, hail, darkness, and the first-born, without any tableau; but at the chorus, " He led them through like sheep," the curtain rose again, when Moses was seen in the foreground with raised staff, and behind him, in gay tumult, the same figures who in the first tableau were mourning, now all pressing onwards, laden with gold and silver vessels; one young girl (also by Bendemann) was especially lovely, who, with her pilgrim's staff, seemed as if advancing from the side scenes and about to cross the stage. Then came the choruses again, without any tableau, " But the waters," " He rebuked the Red Sea,' " Thy right hand, O Lord," and the recitative, "And Miriam, the Prophetess," at the close of which the solo soprano appeared. At the same moment the last tableau was uncovered,—Miriam, with a silver timbrel, sounding praises to the Lord, and other maidens with harps and citherns, and in the background four men with trombones, pointing in different directions. The soprano solo was sung behind the scene, as if proceeding from the picture; and when the chorus came in *forte*, real trombones, and trumpets, and kettle-drums, were brought on the stage, and burst in like a thunder-clap. Handel evidently intended this effect, for after the commencement he makes them pause till they come in again in C major, when the other instruments recommence.   And thus we concluded the second part.

This last tableau was by Hübner, and pleased me exceedingly.   The effect of the whole was wonderfully fine.   Much might possibly have been said against it

had it been a pretentious affair, but its character was
entirely social, and not public, and I think it would
scarcely be possible to devise a more charming fête.
The next that followed was a *tableau vivant*, designed
and arranged by Schadow, " Lorenzo de' Medici, surrounded by the Geniuses of Poetry, Sculpture, and
Painting, leading to him Dante, Raphael, Michael Angelo, and Bramante," with a complimentary allusion to
the Crown Prince, and a final chorus. The second division consisted of the comic scenes from the "Midsummer Night's Dream," represented by the painters here;
but I did not care so much for it, having been so absorbed by the previous one.

How would you translate in the same measure the
following line:—

" So Love was crowned, but Music won the cause" ? *

Ramler, with the genuine dignity of a translator, says,
"Heil, Liebe, dir! der Tonkunst Ehr' und Dank" (All
hail to thee, O Love! to Music thanks and honour),
which has no point, and is anything but a translation;
the first part of the Ode closes with these lines, so the
whole sense would be lost, for the pith of the sentence
lies in the word " *won.*" Give me some good hint about
this; for on the 22d of November, we come before the
public with " Alexander's Feast," the overture to "Egmont," and Beethoven's concerto in C minor. I am told
that an orchestra is to be constructed in Becker's Hall,
for two hundred persons. All who can sing, or play, or
pay, are sure to be there. Tell me if I shall resume my

* From " Alexander's Feast."
2

Greek here.*   I feel very much disposed to do so, but
fear it will not go on very swimmingly.   Could I
understand Æschylus? tell me this honestly.   Further,
do you attend to my advice about pianoforte playing
and singing?   If you want any songs, as Christmas
draws near, you can get them from me if you wish it.
Send for the " Hebrides" arranged as a duett; it is, no
doubt, published by this time.   I think, however, that
the overture to " Melusina" will be the best thing 1
have as yet done; as soon as it is finished I will send
it to you.   Adieu.   FELIX.

To HIS FATHER.

Bonn, December 28th, 1883.

Dear Father,
    First of all, I must thank you for your kind, loving
letter, and I rejoice that even before receiving it I had
done what you desired.†   Strange to say, my official
acceptance, I must tell you, was sent last week to
Schadow ; the biography was enclosed, so I expect the
patent next week ; but I must thank you once more for
the very kind manner in which you write to me on the
subject, and I feel proud that you consider me worthy
of such a confidential tone.
    The people in Düsseldorf are an excitable race !   The

---

    * Mendelssohn's sister had learned Greek along with him.
    † The subject in question was Mendelssohn's nomination (which
afterwards ensued) as a member of the musical class of the Academy of
Art in Berlin, as to the acceptance of which he had been doubtful.

" Don Juan" affair amused me, although riotous enough, and Immermann had a sharp attack of fever from sheer vexation.* As you, dear Mother, like to read newspapers, you shall receive in my next letter all the printed articles on the subject, which engrossed the attention of the whole town for three long days. After the *grand scandale* had fairly begun, and the curtain three times dropped and drawn up again,—after the first duett of the second act had been sung, entirely drowned by whistling, shouting, and howling,—after a newspaper had been flung to the manager on the stage, that he might read it aloud, who on this went off in a violent huff, the curtain being dropped for the fourth time,—I was about to lay down my *bâton*, though I would far rather have thrown it at the heads of some of these fellows, when the uproar suddenly subsided. The shouting voices were hoarse, and the well-conducted people brightened up; in short, the second act was played in the midst of the most profound silence, and much applause at the close. After it was over, all the actors were called for, but no one came, and Immermann and I consulted together in a shower of fiery rain and gunpowder smoke—among the black demons—as to what was to be done. I declared that until the company and I had received some apology, I would not again conduct the opera; then came a deputation of several members of the orchestra, who in turn said that

* Immermann and Mendelssohn had agreed to give a certain number of performances in the theatre, which they termed " classical." A certain portion of the public considered this to be arrogance on their part, and as the prices were also raised on the occasion, at the first performance the tumult ensued that Mendelssohn here describes.

if I did not conduct the opera they would not play; then the manager of the theatre began to lament, as he had already disposed of all the tickets for the next perform- ance. Immermann snubbed everybody all round, and in this graceful manner we retreated from the field.

Next day in every corner appeared, " Owing to ob- stacles that had arisen," etc. etc. ; and all the people whom we met in the streets could talk of nothing but this disturbance. The newspapers were filled with articles on the subject; the instigator of the riot justi- fied himself, and declared that in spite of it all he had had great enjoyment, for which he felt grateful to me and to the company, and gave his name; as he is a Government secretary, the president summoned him, blew him up tremendously, and sent him to the direc- tor, who also blew him up tremendously. The soldiers who had taken part in the tumult were treated in the same manner by their officers. The Association for the Promotion of Music issued a manifesto begging for a repetition of the opera, and denouncing the disturb- ance. The Theatrical Committee intimated that if the slightest interruption of the performance ever again occurred, they would instantly dissolve. I procured also from the committee full powers to put a stop to the opera in case of any unseemly noise. Last Monday it was to be given again; in the morning it was uni- versally reported that the manager was to be hissed, on account of his recent testiness; Immermann was seized with fever, and I do assure you that it was with feelings the reverse of pleasant that I took my place in the orchestra at the beginning, being resolved to stop the performance if there was the slightest disorder. But the moment I advanced to my desk the audience received me with loud applause, and called for a flourish of trumpets in my honour, insisting on this being three times repeated, amid a precious row; then all were as still as mice, while each actor received his share of applause; in short, the public were now as polite as they formerly were unruly. I wish you had seen the performance: individual parts could not, I feel sure, have been better given; the quartett, for instance, and the ghost in the finale at the end of the opera, and almost the whole of " Leporello," went splendidly, and caused me the greatest pleasure. I am so glad to hear that the singers who at first, I am told, were prejudiced against me personally, as well as against these classical performances, now say they would go to the death for me, and are all impatience for the time when I am to give another opera. I came over here for Christmas, by Cologne and the Rhine, where ice is drifting along, and have passed a couple of quiet pleasant days here.

And now to return to the much-talked-of correspondence between Goethe and Zelter. One thing struck me on this subject: when in this work Beethoven or any one else is abused, or my family unhandsomely treated, and many subjects most tediously discussed, I remain quite cool and calm; but when Reichardt is in question, and they both presume to criticize him with great arrogance, I feel in such a rage that I don't know what to do, though I cannot myself explain why this should be so. His " Morgengesang" must unluckily rest for this winter; the Musical Association is not yet sufficiently full fledged for it; but the first musical festival to which I go it shall be there. It is

said they will not be able to have it at Aix-la-
Chapelle, and that it is to be given at Cologne, and
many of my acquaintances urge me strongly to pay my
court to one or the other, in which case I should be
selected; but this I never will do. If they should choose
me without this, I shall be glad; but if not, I shall
save a month's precious time (for it will take that at
least), and remain as I am. Having been obliged to give
three concerts this winter, besides the " Messiah" and
the " Nozze di Figaro," I think I have had nearly enough
of music for the present, and may now enjoy a little
breathing-time. But how is it, Mother, that you ask
whether I *must* conduct all the operas? Heaven forbid
there should be any *must* in the case, for almost every
week two operas are given, and the performers consider themselves absolved by one rehearsal. I am only
one of the members of the Theatrical Association,
chosen to be on the select committee, who give six or
eight classical performances every year, and elect a
council for their guidance, this council consisting of
Immermann and myself; we are therefore quite independent of the rest, who consequently feel increased
respect for us.

When the great Theatrical Association is fairly established, and the theatre becomes a settled and civic institution, Immermann is resolved to give up his situation in the Justiciary Court, and to engage himself for
five years as director of the theatre. Indeed, I hear
that most of the shareholders have only given their
signatures on condition that *he* should undertake the
plays, and *I* the operas; how this may be, lies close
hidden as yet in the womb of time, but in any event I

will not entirely withdraw from the affair. I have composed a song for Immermann's "Hofer," or rather, I should say, arranged a Tyrolese popular melody for it, and also a French march; but I like the thing, and mean to send it to Fanny. We think of giving " Hofer" this winter, and perhaps also " Das laute Geheimniss," and " Nathan," or the " Braut von Messina," or both. You also advise me, Mother, to acquire the habit of dictation; but in the mean time I can get through by the use of my own pen, and intend only to have recourse to such a dignified proceeding in the greatest possible emergency.* Thank you very much for the letter you send me from Lindblad.† It gave me great pleasure, and made me like my concerto far better than I did before, for I know few people whose judgment I respect more than his. I can as little explain this, or give any reason for it, as for many another feeling; but it is so; and when I have finished a thing, whether successful or a failure, he is the first person, next to yourself, whose opinion I should be glad to hear. That a piece so rapidly sketched as this pianoforte concerto should cause pleasure to so genuine a musician, enhances mine; and so I thank you much for the letter. But it is high time to close this letter and this year, to which I am indebted for many blessings and much happiness, and which has been another bright year for me.

I thank you also, dear Father, now as ever, for having gone with me to England for my sake; and though my

---

* He never had recourse to it. Mendelssohn wrote invariably everything, without exception, himself.

† Music Director in Stockholm.

.

advice, which you followed for the first time, proved so unfortunate, and caused us all so much anxiety and uneasiness, you never once reproached me. Still I think, since you write that you are now perfectly well and in good spirits, the journey may have contributed to this. May these happy results be still further increased during the approaching year, and may it bring you all every blessing. Farewell.

FELIX.

To HIS FAMILY.

Düsseldorf, January 16th, 1834.

We are leading a merry life here just now, casting aside all care; every one is full of fun and jollity. I have just come from the rehearsal of " Egmont," where, for the first time in my life, I tore up a score from rage at the stupidity of the *musici*, whom I feed with 6–8 time in due form, though they are more fit for babes' milk; then they like to belabour each other in the orchestra. This I don't choose they should do in my presence : so furious scenes sometimes occur. At the air, " Glücklich allein ist die Seele die liebt," I fairly tore the music in two, on which they played with much more expression. The music delighted me so far, that I again heard something of Beethoven's for the first time; but it had no particular charm for me, and only two pieces—the march in C major, and the movement in 6–8 time, where Klärchen is seeking Egmont—are quite after my own heart. To-morrow we are to have another rehearsal; in the evening the Prince gives a ball, which will last till four in the morning, from which I could excuse myself if I were not so very fond of dancing. I must now tell you about my excursion to Elberfeld. Sunday was the concert: so in the morning I drove there in a furious storm of thunder and rain. I found the whole musical world assembled in the inn, drinking champagne at twelve in the forenoon, instead of which I ordered chocolate for myself. A pianoforte solo of mine had been announced, after which I intended to have come away immediately; but, hearing that there was to be a ball in the evening, I resolved not to set off till night, and as they had introduced music from "Oberon" in the second part, feeling myself in a vein for extemporizing, I instantly took up their last *ritournelle*, and continued playing the rest of the opera. There was no great merit in this: still it pleased the people wonderfully, and at the end I was greeted with plaudits loud enough to gratify any one. As the room was crowded, I promised to return in the course of the winter to play for the benefit of the poor. The Barmers sent me a deputation of three Barmer ladies to persuade me to go there on Monday; and, as my travelling companion had both time and inclination for this, I played extempore on the Monday afternoon in the Barmer Musical Association, and then a quartett in Elberfeld, travelled through the night, and arrived at home at four on Tuesday morning, as my hour for receiving people is from eight to nine. The Barmer fantasia was well designed; I must describe it for Fanny.

A poem had been sent me anonymously, at the end of which I was advised to marry (of course this was said in good poetry, interwoven with laurel leaves and *immortelles*); and, wishing to respond to this compliment, I began with my " Bachelor's Song" (though, unluckily, no one found out its meaning, but that was no matter), continuing to play it gayly for some time ; I then brought in the violoncello with the theme, " Mir ist so wunderbar," and so far it was very successful. I was anxious, however, before closing, to introduce some matrimonial felicity, but in this I utterly failed, which spoiled the conclusion. I wish, however, you had been present at the beginning, for I believe you would have been pleased. I think I already wrote to you that my fantasia in F sharp minor, Op. 28,* is about to be published. I have introduced a fine massive passage in octaves in my new E flat rondo ; I am now going to work at my *scena* for the Philharmonic, to edit the three overtures, to compose another trio or a symphony, and then comes " St. Paul." Addio.

FELIX.

To I. MOSCHELES, LONDON.

Düsseldorf, February 7, 1834.

My own poverty in novel passages for the piano struck me very much in the *Rondo brillant*† which I wish to dedicate to you; these are what cause me to demur, and to torment myself; and I fear you will remark this. In other respects there is a good deal in it that I like, and some passages please me exceedingly; but

---

* This fantasia and the E flat rondo (with orchestra), Op. 29, are both dedicated to Moscheles.

† E flat (with orchestra), Op. 29.

how I am to set about composing a methodical *tranquil* piece (and I well remember you advised me strongly to do this last spring) I really cannot tell. All that I now have in my head for the piano is about as *tranquil* as Cheapside,* and even when I control myself, and begin to extemporize very soberly, I gradually break loose again. On the other hand, the *scena* which I am now writing for the Philharmonic is, I fear, becoming much too tame; but it is needless to carp so much at myself, and I work hard : by saying this you will see that I am well, and in good spirits. Dear Madame Moscheles, when you, however, advise me to remain quite indifferent towards the public and towards critics, I must in turn ask, Am I not, in my profession, an *anti-public-caring* musician, and an *anti-critical* one into the bargain ? What is Hecuba to me, or critics either ? (I mean the press, or rather pressure) ; and if an over-ture to Lord Eldon were to suggest itself to me, in the form of a reversed canon, or a double fugue with a *cantus firmus*, I should persist in writing it, though it would certainly not be popular,—far more, therefore, a " lovely Melusina," who is, however, a very different object; only it would be fatal indeed were I to find that I could no longer succeed in having my works per-formed ; but as you say there is no fear of this, then I say, long live the public and the critics ! but I intend to live too, and to go to England next year if possible.

Your observations on Neukomm's music find a com-plete response in my own heart. What does astonish me is, that a man of so much taste and cultivation

---

* Well known as the most crowded street in London.

should not, with such qualifications, write more elegant and refined music; for, without referring to the ideas or the basis of his works, they appear to me most carelessly composed, and even commonplace. He also employs brass instruments recklessly, which ought, through discretion even, to be sparingly used, to say nothing of artistic considerations. Among other things, I am particularly pleased by the mode in which Handel, towards the close, rushes in with his kettle-drums and trumpets, as if he himself were belabouring them. There is no one who would not be struck by it; and it seems to me far better to *imitate* this, than to over-excite and stimulate the audience, who before the close have become quite accustomed to all this Cayenne pepper. I have just looked through Cherubini's new opera,* and though I was quite enchanted with many parts of it, still I cannot but deeply lament that he so often adopts that new corrupt Parisian fashion, as if the instruments were nothing and the effect everything,— flinging about three or four trombones, as if it were the audience who had skins of parchment instead of the drums: and then in his finales he winds up with hideous chords, and a tumult and crash most grievous to listen to. Compare with these some of his earlier pieces, such as " Lodoiska" and " Medea," etc., etc., where there is as much difference in brightness and genius as between a living man and a scarecrow; so I am not surprised that the opera did not please. Those who like the original Cherubini cannot fail to be provoked at the way in which he yields to the fashion of

---

* " Ali Baba."

the day, and to the taste of the public; and those who do not like the original Cherubini find far too much of his own style still left to satisfy them either, no matter what pains he may take to do so,—he always peeps forth again in the very first three notes. Then they call this *rococo, perruque*, etc., etc.

To his Father.

Düsseldorf, March 28, 1834.

Dear Father,

A thousand thanks for your kind letter on my Mother's birthday. I received it in the midst of a general rehearsal of the " Wasserträger," otherwise I should have answered it, and thanked you for it, the same day. Pray do often write to me. Above all, I feel grateful to you for your admonitions as to industry, and my own work. Believe me, I intend to profit by your advice; still I do assure you that I have not an atom of that philosophy which would counsel me to give way to indolence, or even in any degree to palliate it. During the last few weeks, it is true, I have been incessantly engaged in active business, but exclusively of a nature to teach me much that was important, and calculated to improve me in my profession; and thus I never lost sight of my work.

My having composed *beforehand* the pieces bespoken by the Philharmonic and the English publishers, was owing not only to having received the commission, but also to my own inward impulse, because it is really

3

very long since I have written or worked at anything steadily, for which a certain mood is indispensable. But all this tends to the same point; so I certainly do not believe that these recreations will dispose me to become either more careless or more indolent; and, as I said before, they really are not mere amusements, but positive work, and pleasant work often, too. A good performance in the Düsseldorf theatre does not find its way into the world at large,—indeed, scarcely perhaps beyond the *Düssels* themselves; but if I succeed in thoroughly delighting and exciting both my own feelings and those of all in the house in favour of good music, that is worth something, too!

The week before the "Wasserträger" was given was most fatiguing; every day two great rehearsals, often from nine to ten hours each on an average, besides the preparations for the church music this week: so that I was obliged to undertake the regulation of everything, —the acting, the scenery, and the dialogue,—or it would all have gone wrong. On Friday, therefore, I came to my desk feeling rather weary; we had been obliged to have a complete general rehearsal in the forenoon, and my right arm was quite stiff. The audience, too, who had neither seen nor heard of the "Wasserträger" for the last fifteen or twenty years, were under the impression that it was some old forgotten opera, which the committee wished to revive, and all those on the stage felt very nervous. This, however, gave exactly the right tone to the first act; such tremor, excitement, and emotion pervaded the whole, that at the second piece of music the Düsseldorf opposition kindled into enthusiasm, and applauded and shouted

and wept by turns. A better Wasserträger than Gün-
ther I never saw; he was most touching and natural,
and yet with a shade of homeliness, too, so that the
noblesse might not appear too factitious. He was immensely applauded, and twice called forward; this
rather spoiled him for the second performance, when
he overacted his part, and was too confident; but I
wish you could have seen him the first time! It is long
since I have had such a delightful evening in the theatre,
for I took part in the performance like one of the spectators, and laughed, and applauded, and shouted
"bravo!" yet conducting with spirit all the time; the
choruses in the second act sounded as exact as if fired
from a pistol. The stage was crowded between the
acts, every one pleased, and congratulating the singers.
The orchestra played with precision, except some plaguy
fellows who, in spite of all my threats and warnings,
could not be prevailed on to take their eyes off the
stage during the performance, and to look at their
notes. On Sunday it was given again, and did not go
half so well; but I had my full share of enjoyment the
first time, though the house on this second occasion
was far more crowded, and the effect the same. I write
you all these details, dear Father, for I know that you
are interested in this opera, and in our provincial
doings. We really have as much music, and as good
music, as could be expected during my first winter
here. To-morrow evening (Good Friday) we are to
sing in church the "Last Seven Words" of Palestrina,
which I found in Cologne, and a composition of Lasso,
and on Sunday we give Cherubini's Mass in C major.

The Government order prohibiting the celebration of

the Musical Festival on Whitsunday is a bad business; the news came yesterday, and has inflicted such a blow on the festival that here we have no idea how it can be arranged, for on no other day can we reckon on so much support from strangers. The first meeting of the Theatrical Association took place recently; the matter has been very sensibly begun, and may turn out well; but I keep out of the way, because, in spite of the pleasure that the opera, for instance, lately caused me, I can feel no sympathy for actual theatrical life, or the squabbles of the actors and the incessant striving after effect; it also estranges me too much from my own chief purpose in Düsseldorf, which is to work for myself. I am the chief superintendent of the musical performances, the arrangements of the orchestra, and the engagement of the singers, and about every month I have an opera to conduct (but even this is to depend on my own convenience); of course I still have my three months' vacation: in short, I wish to be entirely independent of the theatre, and only to be considered a friend, but with no official duties; on this account I have given up all claim to any salary, which is to be transferred to a second conductor, on whom the chief trouble will devolve. A circumstance that occurred yesterday will amuse you. During the Carnival there was a pretty girl here who played the piano, the daughter of a manufacturer near Aix-la-Chapelle, and whose relations, though strangers to me, asked me to allow her to play to me occasionally, to benefit by my advice,—in fact, to give her a few lessons. This I accordingly did, and read her some severe lectures on all her Herz music and so forth, and on the day of her

departure she left this with a quantity of newly-pur-
chased Mozart and Beethoven; so yesterday arrived a
large parcel for me, with a very polite letter of thanks
from her father, saying he had sent me a piece of cloth
from his manufactory, as an acknowledgment. I could
scarcely believe this at first, but the parcel really contained enough of the finest black cloth to make an entire suit. This savours of the Middle Ages; the painters
are mad with envy at my good luck.

Last week I had a great pleasure, for Seydelmann,
from Stuttgart, was here, and enchanted us all. I have
not felt such unalloyed delight since I saw Wolff; so
artistic, so elevated: such acting prôves what a noble
thing a play may be. I saw him first in the "Essig-
händler" and "Koch Vatel." People compare him to
Iffland; but I never in my life heard so thrilling a voice,
or such pure harmonious German. I then saw him as
Cromwell, in Raupach's "Royalisten;" it was the first
piece I had seen of Raupach's, and I am not the least
anxious to see a second, for I thought it quite odious;
incongruous, tiresome, and full of theatrical phrases, so
that even Seydelmann could not give it dignity in spite
of his stern and gloomy countenance and costume; but
then came "Nathan," which went off admirably, and
Seydelmann, as Nathan, could not be excelled. I
thought of you, and wished you were here, a hundred
times at least; when he told the story of the rings, it was
just as if you saw a broad tranquil stream gliding past,
so rapid and flowing, and yet so smooth and unruffled;
the words of the discreet judge were most exciting. It
is indeed a splendid piece! It is good to know that
there is such clearness in the world. It, however, of-

fends many; and when we were next day on the Gra-
fenberg we had war to the knife, because Schadow was
so irritable on the subject, and a gentleman from Berlin
declared, that "viewed in a dramatic aspect . . ." I
did not argue the point at all, for where there is such a
total difference of opinion on any subject, and about
first principles, there is nothing to be done.

I must now ask your advice on a particular subject.
I have long wished to ride here, and when Lessing
lately bought a horse, he advised me strongly to do the
same. I think the regular exercise would do me good,
—this is in favour of the scheme ; but against it there
is the possibility of its becoming an inconvenient and
even tyrannical custom, as I should think it my duty to
ride, if possible, every day. Then I also wished to
ask you whether you don't think it rather too *genteel*
for me, at my years, to have a horse of my own. In
short, I am undecided, and beg now, as I have ofien
done before, to hear your opinion, by which mine will
be regulated. Farewell, dear Father.—Your

FELIX.

To FANNY HENSEL, BERLIN.

Düsseldorf, April 7th, 1834.

Dear Fanny,

You are no doubt very angry with such a lazy *non-
writing* creature as myself ? but pray remember that I
am a town music director, and a beast of burden like
that has much to do. Lately on my return home I
found two chairs standing on my writing-table, the

guard of the stove lying under the piano, and on my bed a comb and brush, and a pair of boots (Bendemann and Jordan had left these as visiting-cards). This was, or rather is, the exact state of musical life in Düsseldorf; and before things become more orderly here, it will cost no little toil. So you must now more than ever excuse my indolence about letter-writing, and, indeed, write yourself oftener to stir me up, and heap coals of fire on my head. Your letter to which I am now replying, was inimitable; a few more such I beg. You say, by the by, that you speak of "Melusina" just like X———. I only wish this was true, and then, instead of a meagre *Hofrath*, we should have a solid fellow; but listen! I must fly into a passion. Oh, Fanny, you ask me *what* legend you are to read? How many are there, pray? and how many do I know? and don't you know the story of the "lovely Melusina"? and would it not be better for me to hide myself, and to creep into all sorts of instrumental music without any title, when my own sister (my wolf sister!) does not appreciate such a title? Or did you really never hear of this beautiful fish? But when I remember how you might grumble at me for waiting till *April* to grumble at your letter of *February*, I plead guilty and apologize. I wrote this overture for an opera of Conradin Kreuzer's, which I saw this time last year in the Königstadt Theatre. The overture (I mean Kreuzer's) was encored, and I disliked it exceedingly, and the whole opera quite as much; but not Mlle. Hähnel, who was very fascinating, especially in one scene, where she appeared as a mermaid combing her hair; this inspired me with the wish to write an overture which the people might not *encore*, but which would cause them more solid pleasure ; so I selected the portion of the subject that pleased me (exactly corresponding with the legend), and, in short, the overture came into the world, and this is its pedigree.

You intend, no doubt, to take me to task also on account of the four-part song in my " Volks Lieder ;" but I have a good deal of experience on this point. It seems to me the only mode in which *Volks Lieder* ought to be written ; because every pianoforte accompaniment instantly recalls a room and a music-desk, and also because four voices can give a song of this kind in greater simplicity without an instrument ; and if *that* reason be too æsthetic, then accept *this* one, that I was anxious to write something of the kind for Woringen, who sings these things enchantingly. Seriously, however, I find that the four-part songs do " suit the text (as a *Volks Lied*) and also my conception," and so you see we differ very widely.

By the by, I quite forgot to say that I wished to introduce a *Waldteufel* into the "Passion." It is a good idea. Don't whisper it to any one, or to a certainty they will really attempt it next year ; and Pölchau declares the Romans were familiar with them, under the name of *diabolus nemoris*. Only fancy, they have sent me my Academy patent in a formidable red case (carriage paid), and in it a very ancient statute of the "Academy for the fine arts and mechanical sciences," along with a complimentary letter, hoping I would return to Berlin, where my "productions" were as highly prized as elsewhere. An excellent reason ; had they only said " because, respected Sir, you can nowhere feel so happy as in the Leipziger Strasse, No. 3," or even given any hint about parents and brother and sisters—but not a word of this!

One of my Düsseldorf troubles is at this moment beginning; I mean my next-door neighbour, who has placed her piano against the wall just on the other side of mine, and to my sorrow practises two hours a day, making every day the same mistakes, and playing all Rossini's airs in such a desperately slow, phlegmatic *tempo*, that I certainly must have played her some malicious trick, had it not occurred to me that she was probably at all hours more tormented by my piano than I by hers. Then I sometimes hear the teacher or the mother (I can't tell which) strike the right note distinctly seventeen times in succession; and when she is playing at sight, and gradually out of the darkness developes some old barrel-organ tune, which could be recognized by a single note,—it is hard to bear. I know all her pieces by heart now, the moment she strikes the first chord.—Farewell, dear Sister. Ever your

FELIX.

To HIS MOTHER.

Düsseldorf, May 23d, 1834.

. . . Yesterday week I drove with the two Woringens to Aix-la-Chapelle, as a ministerial order was issued, only five days before the festival, sanctioning the celebration of Whitsunday, and expressed in such a manner that it is probable the same permission may be

2*

given next year also.   The diligence was eleven hours
on the journey, and I was shamefully impatient, and
downright cross when we arrived.   We went straight
to the rehearsal, and, seated in the pit, I heard a movement or two from "Deborah;" on which I said to
Woringen, "I positively will write to Hiller from here,
for the first time for two years, because he has performed his office so well."   For really his work was un-
pretending and harmonious, and subordinate to Handel,
from whom he had cut out nothing; so I was rejoiced to
see that others are of my opinion, and act accordingly.
In the first tier was seated a man with a moustache,
reading the score; and when, after the rehearsal, he
went downstairs, and I was coming up, we met in the
passage, and who should stumble right into my arms
but Ferdinand Hiller, who almost hugged me to death
for joy !   He had come from Paris to hear the oratorio,
and Chopin had left his scholars in the lurch and come
with him, and thus we met again.   I had now my full
share of delight in the Musical Festival, for we three
lived together, and got a private box in the theatre
(where the oratorio is performed), and of course next
morning we betook ourselves to the piano, where I had
the greatest enjoyment.   They have both improved
much in execution, and, as a pianist, Chopin is now one
of the very first of all.   He produces new effects, like
Paganini on his violin, and accomplishes wonderful passages, such as no one could formerly have thought
practicable.   Hiller, too, is an admirable player—vigorous, and yet playful.   Both, however, rather toil in the
Parisian spasmodic and impassioned style, too often
losing sight of time and sobriety and of true music ; I,

again, do so perhaps too little : thus we all three mutually
learn something and improve each other, while I feel
rather like a school-master, and they a little like *mirli-
flors* or *incroyables*. After the festival we travelled
together to Düsseldorf, and passed a most agreeable day
there, playing and discussing music ; then I accompanied them yesterday to Cologne. Early this morning
they went off to Coblenz *per* steam,—I in the other direction,—and the pleasant episode was over.

To Pastor Julius Schubring, Dessau.

Düsseldorf, July 15th, 1834.

Dear Schubring,

It is now nearly a year since I ought to have written to you. I shall not attempt to ask your forgiveness
at all, for I am too much to blame, or to excuse myself,
for I could not hope to do so. How it occurred I cannot myself understand. Last autumn, when I first established myself here, I got your letter with the notices
for " St. Paul ;" they were the best contributions I had
yet received. and that very same forenoon I began to
ponder seriously on the matter, took up my Bible in the
midst of all the disorder of my room, and was soon so
absorbed in it that I could scarcely force myself to attend to other works which I was absolutely obliged to
finish. At that time I intended to have written to you
instantly, to thank you cordially for all you had done ;
then it occurred to me it would be better to wait till I
could tell you that the work was fairly begun ; and

when I really did commence in spring, so many anxieties about my composition ensued, that they unsettled me. To-day, however, I cannot rest satisfied with merely thinking of you, but must write and ask how you and yours are ; for I know that since then you have had an increase to your family ; it was scarcely fair in you not to write me a single word on the subject, nor even to send me a formal card, but to allow me to hear of the event by chance, through a third person ; for, though I grant that I well deserved this, still a pastor like you should be the last to take revenge on any one, or to bear them a grudge. Now, pray don't do so with me, and let me hear something of you.

Your contributions for "St. Paul" were admirable, and I made use of them all without exception ; it is singular, and good, that, in the course of composition, all the passages that from various reasons I formerly wish to transpose or to alter, I have replaced exactly as I find them in the Bible—it is always the best of all ; more than half of the first part is ready, and I hope to finish it in autumn, and the whole in February. How are you now living in Dessau? I hope you will be able to say, "Just as we used to do." No doubt you retain your enjoyment of life, and your cheerfulness, and still play the p'ano, and still love Sebastian Bach, and are still what you always were. I ought not to feel such anxiety on the subject, but we are surrounded here by disagreeable specimens of pastors, who embitter every pleasure, either of their own or of others ; dry, prosaic pedants, who declare that a concert is a sin, a walk frivolous and pernicious, but a theatre the lake of brimstone itself, and the whole spring, with its leaves and blossoms and bright weather, a Slough of Despond. You have no doubt heard of the Elberfeld tenets; but when in contact with them, they are still worse, and most grievous to witness. The most deplorable thing is the arrogance with which such people look down on others, having no belief in any goodness but their own.

Our musical life here goes on slowly, but still it does go on. This summer we executed in church a Mass of Beethoven, one of Cherubini, and cantatas of Sebastian Bach, an "Ave Maria" from "Verleih' uns Frieden," and next month we are to give Handel's "Te Deum" (Dettingen).

Of course there is yet much to be wished for, but still we hear these works, and both the performance and the performers will be gradually improved by them. Hauser, in Leipzig, has arranged the score (from manuscript parts) of a cantata in E minor of Sebastian Bach, which is one of the finest things of his I know. When I can find an opportunity, I will sent you a copy of it, but now my paper and my letter are done. Farewell, my dear friend, and write soon.—Your

FELIX MENDELSSOHN BARTHOLDY.

To I. FÜRST, BERLIN.

Düsseldorf, July 20th, 1834.

Dear Fürst,

I know only too well that I have neither written to you, nor thanked you, since I received your passages for

4

"St. Paul;" * but I assure you that every day, when I return to my work, I do feel sincerely grateful to you. I certainly, however, ought to have written; for if the work, which since the spring entirely absorbs and monopolizes me, turns out good, I shall have chiefly to thank your friendly aid for it, because I never otherwise could have procured the groundwork of the text. When I am composing, I usually look out the Scriptural passages myself, and thus you will find that much is simpler, shorter, and more compressed than in your text; whereas at that time I could not get words enough, and was constantly longing for more. Since I have set to work, however, I feel very differently, and I can now make a selection. The first part will probably be finished next month, and the whole, I think, by January. Since last autumn, when I came here, I have written many other works which brought me into a happy vein, and I cannot wish for a more agreeable position than mine here, where I have both leisure in abundance, and a cheerful frame of mind, and so I succeed better than formerly.

This is, indeed, a pleasant, concentrated life, but still not so much so as you may perhaps imagine, for, unluckily, just as I came here, Immermann and Schadow, whose combined efforts first imparted life and animation to this place, had a violent quarrel, aggravated still further by religious, political grounds, and by wranglings, misunderstandings, and petulance. As I live in the same house with Schadow, and am engaged along with Immermann in regulating the new theatre, I do

---

* For the text of "St. Paul."

all I can to smooth over matters; but in vain,—which is a great misfortune. When, however, this is rectified (and, in spite of everything, I do not despair of it), then all will be delightful, for the way in which we young people associate is really enjoyable. The painters are entirely devoid of the slightest arrogance or envy, and live together in true friendship, and among them are some of the most admirable persons, who are examples to the others, such as Hildebrand, and Bende-mann, and between them the δαιμόνιος,—the tall, quiet Lessing. All this is cheering; and if you could only hear in our church music the bass of the choir, it would do your heart good to see one capital fellow of a painter standing next another, and all shouting like demons. This very morning we had some very good music in the church, in which all took part; and when Immer-mann gives a new piece, they paint the decorations for it gratis, and when they have a feast, he composes a poem for them, which I set to music,—and all this is pleasant, and in good-fellowship.

But there is a fair to-day, which means that the whole of Düsseldorf are drinking wine,—not as if this were not the case every day, but they walk about besides; not as if they did not do this also every day, but they dance besides (in this frightful heat), and shout, and get tipsy; and wild beasts are exhibited, and puppet-shows, and cakes baked in the public streets. So now you know what a fair means. As a curious spectator, I must go there late in the evening, but, first, I intend to plunge into the Rhine with a lot of painters. Fare-well, till we meet in Berlin, in September.—Ever yours,

FELIX MENDELSSOHN BARTHOLDY.

To his Parents.

Düsseldorf, August 4th, 1834.

My dear Parents,

For a week past, during which we have had heavy storms and a very sultry atmosphere, I felt so jaded that I was unable to do anything all day long; more especially I cannot compose, which vexes me exceedingly. I seem to care for nothing beyond eating and sleeping, and perhaps bathing and riding. My horse is a favourite with all my acquaintances, and deserves their respect from his good temper; but he is very shy; and when I was riding him lately during a storm, every flash made him start so violently, that I felt quite sorry for him. Lately we made an excursion on horseback to Saarn, for Madame T——'s birthday, which was celebrated by wreaths of flowers, fireworks, shooting, a large society, a ball, etc. etc. The route was as charming as ever, though different from what it was in spring; the apple-tree in the bowling-green, which was then in blossom, was now loaded with unripe green apples; and sometimes I was able to ride across the stubble-fields and to get into the thick shady wood by a side path. We met several *diligences* at the very same places, and even the very same flocks of sheep, and there was the same noisy, merry life going on in the blacksmith's forge, and a burgher in Rathingen was shaving himself just the same,—thus reviving my old philosophy, which you, dear Father, always ignore.

The next day I rode on to Werden, a charming retired spot, where I wished to inquire about an organ; the whole party drove with me there; cherry tarts

were handed to me on horseback out of the carriages.
We dined in the open air at Werden; I played fantasias and Sebastian Bachs on the organ to my heart's
content; then I bathed in the Ruhr, so cool in the
evening breeze that it was quite a luxury, and rode
quietly back to Saarn. The bathing in the Ruhr was
peculiarly agreeable; first of all, a spot close to the
water with high grass, in which large hewn stones were
lying, as if placed there by some Sultan to shade him
and his clothes; then close to the shore the water
comes up to your chin, and the green hills opposite
were brightly lighted up by the evening sun; and the
little stream flowing very quietly along, and so cool and
shady. I felt myself in Germany indeed when, as I
was swimming across, a man on the opposite bank suddenly stood still, and began a regular conversation with
me while I lay in the water puffing,—whether I could
touch the ground where I was? and if swimming was
very difficult? Then, too, I felt myself, alas! quite in
Germany when the wife of the organist, to whom I paid
a visit, offered me a glass of *schnapps*, and regretted so
much that her husband was absent just at this time,
for he had so many enemies, who all maintained that he
could not play the organ, and he might have played to
me, and then by my judgment (like Solomon) I could
have put to shame all these talkers. Wrangling and
discord are to be found everywhere. A handsome new·
organ has just been put up at considerable expense in
a large roomy choir, and there is no way to reach it but
by narrow dark steps, without windows, like those in a
poultry-yard, and where you may break your neck in
seventeen different places; and on my asking why this

was, the clergyman said it had been left so purposely, in order to prevent any one who chose, running up from the church to see the organ. Yet, with all their cunning, they forget both locks and keys: such traits are always painful to me.

The evening before this Saarn excursion (a week since) I had a very great pleasure. I had received the proof-sheets of my rondo in E flat, from Leipzig, and, as I was unwilling to have it published without at least trying it over once with the orchestra, I invited all our musicians here to come to the music hall, and played it over with them. As I could not offer them any payment for this, which they would have taken highly amiss, I gave them a *souper* of roast veal and bread-and-butter, and let them get as tipsy as they could desire. This was not, however, the great pleasure I alluded to, but my overture to "Melusina," which was played there for the first time, and pleased me extremely. In many pieces I know from the very beginning that they will sound well, and be characteristic, and so it was with this one as soon as the clarionet started off into the first bar. It was badly played; and yet I derived more pleasure from it than many a finished performance, and came home at night with a gladness of heart that I have not known for a long time. We played it over three times, and the third time, immediately after the last soft chord, the trumpets broke in with a flourish in my honour, which had a most laughable effect. It was very pleasant, too, when we were all seated at dinner, and one of the company commenced a long oration, with an introduction and all sorts of things, but, beginning to flounder, he wound

up by giving my health, on which the trumpet and
trombone players jumped up like maniacs, and ran off
for their instruments to give me another grand flourish;
then I made a vigorous speech, worth of Sir Robert
Peel, in which I strongly enforced unity, and Christian
love, and steady time, and with a toast to the progress
of music at Düsseldorf I closed my oration. Then
they sang four-part songs, and, among others, one that
I gave to Woringen last year at the Musical Festival,
called "Musikantenprügelei," the transcriber (one of
the players and singers present) having copied it for his
own benefit at the time, and coolly produced it on this
occasion, which, indeed, I could not myself help laughing at. Then they all vowed that this was the most
delightful evening of their whole lives; then they
began to wrangle again a little, as a proof of the strong
effect my Peel speech had made on them; then the
sober ones of the party, *videlicet*, fat Schirmer and I,
pacified them once more, and towards midnight we
separated; they having enjoyed the wine, and I still
more "the lovely Melusina," and next morning at six
o'clock I was on horseback on my way to Saaran. A
couple of charming days they were!

Dear mother, I saw the Queen of Bavaria, but not in
state. I was seated in a boat, and just going to jump
into the Rhine with two friends, when her Majesty
arrived in her steamboat. As none of us possessed any
swimming attire, so were not in a very fit state to
appear at Court, we sprang just *a tempo* into the water
as she came nearer, and thence saw all the ceremonies,
and how Graf S—— presented the clergy and the Gene-
rals, and how the *senatus populusque Düsseldorfiensis*

stood on shore and made music. I had no opportunity
of seeing the Queen again ; but now I must really conclude, having gossiped at a great rate. Farewell, my
dear parents!

FELIX M. B.

<hr>

TO PASTOR SCHUBRING, DESSAU.

Düsseldorf, August 6th, 1834.

How could you for one moment imagine that I was
annoyed by your showing the text to Schneider ? Why
should I take umbrage at that ? I hope you do not
consider me one of those who, when once they have an
idea in their heads, guard it as jealously as a miser does
his gold, and allow no man to approach till they produce it themselves. There is certainly nothing actually
wrong in this, and yet such jealous solicitude is most
odious in my eyes ; and even if it were to occur that
some one should plagiarize my design, still I should
feel the same ; for one of the two must be best, which
is all fair, or neither are good, and then it is of no
consequence. Moreover, I feel very melancholy to-day,
and indeed for some days past have been lying here,
completely knocked up and unable to write a line,
whether from feverishness or the sultriness of the
weather, or from what, I know not. The first part of
"St. Paul" is now nearly completed, and I stand before
it ruminating like a cow who is afraid to go through a
new door, and I never seem to finish it ; indeed, the
overture is still wanting, and a heavy bit of work it will

be. Immediately after the Lord's words to St. Paul on his conversion I have introduced a great chorus, "Arise and go into the city" (Acts of the Apostles, ix. 6), and this I, as yet, consider the best moment of the first part.

I don't know what to say as to your opinion of X——. I think you are rather hard on him; and yet there is a good deal of truth in what you assert, too, and quite in accordance with what I find in his compositions. But my belief is, that you do him great injustice in pronouncing him to be a flatterer, as he never *intends* to flatter, but always fully believes in the truth and propriety of what he is saying; but when such an excitable temperament is not mitigated by some definite, energetic, and creative powers, or when it can bring forth nothing but a momentary assimilation to some foreign element, then it is indeed unfortunate; and I almost begin to fear that this is his case, for his compositions I exceedingly disapprove of. For a long time past I have reluctantly come to this conclusion, and it pained me as much to admit the truth of it to myself, as to you now.

I grieve also to hear what you write to me of the —— family, for I know no feeling more distressing than that of having enemies; and yet it seems impossible to be avoided; at all events, I can say, to my great joy, that even now, when I am brought into contact (and disagreeable contact, too) with so many different people, no one can say that there is one single person with whom I am not on friendly terms, if they will at all permit me to be so; and I don't doubt that it is the same in your case.

Your remarks about the theatre are quite as unlucky as Bretschneider's criticisms; for though I am not myself director, I am what is still worse,—a kind of Honorary Intendant (or whatever you choose to call it) of the new theatre here *in spe;* and therefore my official zeal prompts me take up the cause of the stage. But, to speak seriously, I am by no means of your opinion that the theatre is pernicious to three-fourths of mankind, and I believe that those who are injured by it would find the same detriment, or perhaps worse, elsewhere, without any theatre. For there at least we do not find the vapid reality that exists in the world; and, as a general rule, I do not consider anything wrong in itself because it *may* possibly lead to bad results, but only when it *must* inevitably produce them. In a theatrical public, such as you describe, there are only depraved people, and no healthy ones who visit the theatre to see a piece as a work of art. I know that to myself it always was either tiresome or elevating (more commonly the former, I own) but *pernicious* it never appeared to me; and to prohibit it on that account . . . but this would involve a wide sphere and a very serious subject, and politics, tiresome as they are, must have their say in the matter; and all this cannot be thoroughly discussed in so small a sheet of paper as this: perhaps in conversation,—but scarcely even then.

I intended to have sent you some of my works, but prefer doing so from Berlin; the "Meeresstille" I have entirely remodelled this winter, and think it is now some thirty times better. I have also some new songs and pieces for the piano. You say that the newspapers extol me; this is always very gratifying, though I seldom read them, either the musical ones or any others; only occasionally English papers, in which there are some good articles. But my paper is becoming by degrees shorter and shorter, so my letter is done. Fare-well.—Your FELIX M. B.

To his Mother.

Düsseldorf, November 4th, 1834,

Dear Mother,

At last I have leisure to thank you for your kind letters; you know the great delight your writing always causes me, and I would fain hope that it does not fatigue you, for you write in as distinct and classical characters at the end of the letter as at the beginning of the first line, as you always do; therefore I do entreat you frequently to bestow this pleasure on me; that I am truly grateful for it you will readily believe.

You always take me at once back to my own home, and while I am reading your letters I am there once more; I am in the garden rejoicing in the summer; I visit the Exhibition, and dispute with you about Bendemann's small picture; I rally Gans on his satisfaction at being invited by Metternich, and almost think I am again paying court to the pretty Russians. To be thus transported home is most pleasant to me just at this time, when during the last few weeks I have been fuming and fretting in a rare fashion at Düsseldorf and its art doings, and Rhenish *soaring impulses*, and new efforts! I had fallen into a terrible state of confusion

and excitement, and felt worse than during my busiest
time in London. When I sat down to my work in the
morning, at every bar there was a ringing at the bell;
then came grumbling choristers to be snubbed, stupid
singers to be taught, seedy musicians to be engaged;
and when this had gone on the whole day, and I felt
that all these things were for the sole benefit and advantage of the Düsseldorf theatre, I was provoked; at
last, two days ago, I made a *salto mortale*, and beat a
retreat out of the whole affair, and once more feel myself a man. This resignation was a very unpleasant
piece of intelligence for our theatrical autocrat, *alias*
stage mufti; he compressed his lips viciously, as if he
would fain eat me up; however, I made a short and
very eloquent speech to the Director, in which I spoke
of my own avocations as being of more consequence to
me than the Düsseldorf theatre, much as I, etc.: in
short, they let me off, on condition that I would occasionally conduct; this I promised, and this I will certainly perform. I began a letter to Rebecca long ago,
containing the details of three weeks in the life of a
Düsseldorf Intendant, which I have not yet finished,
and I upbraid myself for it.

I have just arrived at that point with "St. Paul"
when I should be so glad to play it over to some one;
but I can find no eligible person. My friends here are
very enthusiastic with regard to it, but this does not
prove much in its favour. The *cantor** is wanting,
with her thick eyebrows and her criticism. I have the
second part now nearly all in my head, up to the

* Cantor (leader of a choir), a term Mendelssohn often applied to his
sister Fanny.

passage where they take Paul for Jupiter, and wish to offer sacrifices to him, for which some five choruses must be found; but as yet I have not the faintest conception what . . . it is difficult. You ask me, dear Mother, whether I have made any arrangements with publishers in Leipzig; Breitkopf and Härtel lately informed me that they would purchase every work I chose to publish, and also a future edition of my collected works (does not that sound very grand?), and mention that they have been very much annoyed by an announcement of another publisher. So you see possibly I may oblige these people! Besides this, I have had six applications for my music from other publishers in various places. This savours rather of *renommage;* but I know you like to read of such things, and will forgive me for it.

To FANNY HENSEL, BERLIN.

Düsseldorf, November 14th, 1834.

My dear Fanny,

May every happiness attend you on this day, and in the year about to commence, and may you love me as well as ever. I should like this year also to have sent you some piece or other, underneath which I could have written November 14th; but the "weeks of the life of an Intendant" have swallowed up everything, and I am only slowly becoming myself again. A few days ago I sketched the overture of "St. Paul," and thought I should at least contrive to get it finished; but it is still

5

a long way behind. If we could only be together now, in the evening, at all events; for when candles are lighted I feel a much greater longing to be at home than in the morning; and now here are candles, and the days from November 11th and December 11th, up to Christmas and the New Year,* are certainly not the best to be far from home, even if the evenings were not so long. But we must be very busy, and next summer set off on our travels again, and visit each other. My wish at this moment is, that the time were come!

I wonder what you are doing this evening? Music and society? or the Government newspaper read aloud? (in which, I am told, Henzel's school is much extolled, and considered in many respects preferable to ours here!)

But, my birthday child! we are not likely to agree on this occasion in our opinions about pictures; for one of the most repugnant to my feelings that I ever saw was that of S——. When a work of art aspires to represent factitious misery, like the famine in the wilderness, I take no interest in it, if ever so well painted,—which this is not. The whole thing seems to me nothing but a variation on Lessing's "Royal Pair," only this time with dead horses. The tone of art in it is very commonplace, and even if decked out twenty times over with bright colours, that does not make it better! I don't at all approve, either, of your taking the opportunity of hearing Lafont to speak of the *revolution* in the violin since Paganini, for I don't admit

---

* A number of birthdays occurred at this particular period in the family.

that any such thing exists in art, but only in people themselves; and I think that very same style would have displeased you in Lafont, if you had heard him *before* Paganini's appearance, so you must not, on the other hand, do less justice to his good qualities *after* hearing the other. I was lately shown a couple of new French musical papers, where they allude incessantly to a *révolution du goût* and a musical transition, which has been taking place for some years past, in which I am supposed to play a fine part; this is the sort of thing I do detest. Then I think that I must be industrious, and work hard, "above all, hate no man, and leave the future to God,"—finish the oratorio completely by March, compose a new A minor symphony and a pianoforte concerto, and then set off again on my travels and visit No. 3, Leipziger Strasse. My second concert took place yesterday, and afterwards a fashionable *soirée*, with no end of Excellencies and fine titles. The day after to-morrow I am again to conduct "Oberon," and shall drive on the orchestra full cry, like an evil spirit. I have fallen into a very splenetic tone, by no means in keeping with a birthday tone, but I now resume the latter, and wish you all possible good fortune; and may 1835 prove a happy year to you, and may you, and all at home, thoroughly enjoy the day.— Your

FELIX.

To Rebecca Dirichlet, Berlin.

Düsseldorf, November 23d, 1834.

My dear, dear Rebecca,

Can I still expect you to read anything that I write? I have been remiss, very remiss, in fact behaved shamefully, and I heartily wish it were not so; but I can't help it now! Would that I had an opportunity to make up for it; but unluckily this is not the case; I can therefore only say that I hope I am still in your good graces, and that I was very foolish. I ought indeed to have said this to you long since, but I could not, for I was resolved to write you a long confidential letter the first day I could find leisure, and this is the very first leisure day. Now that it is getting dark, and the shutters closed, and lights brought in at five o'clock, I thought that I must write to you, and, as it were, pull your door-bell and ask if you are at home. Do look kindly on me.

How things have been going on with me for some time past it would not be easy to say, all has been so detestable. But you really must listen to a little grumbling from me, that you may never take it into your head to become director of a theatre, nor to permit any one belonging to you to accept the office of an intendant. Immediately on my return here* the Intendant breezes were wafted towards me. In the statute it is set forth:—The *intendancy* is to consist of an intendant and a music director. The Intendant pro-

---

* Mendelssohn had made an expedition through part of Germany for the benefit of the theatre, in order to engage singers.

posed that I should be the musical intendant, and he the theatrical intendant. Then the question arose, which was to take precedence of the other: so here was forthwith a fine piece of work. I wished to do nothing but conduct and direct the musical studies, but this was not enough for Immermann. We exchanged desperately uncivil letters, in which I was obliged to be very circumspect in my style, in order to leave no point unanswered, and to maintain my independent ground and basis; but I think I did credit to Herr Heyse.* We came to an agreement after this, but quarrelled again immediately, for he required me to go to Aix, to hear and to engage a singer there, and this I did not choose to do. Then I was desired to engage an orchestra,—that is, prepare two contracts for each member, and previously fight to the death about a dollar more or less of their monthly salary; then they went away, then they came back and signed all the same, then they all objected to sit at the second music desk, then came the aunt of a very wretched performer, whom I could not engage, and the wife and two little children of another miserable musician, to intercede with the Director; then I allowed three fellows to play on trial, and they played so utterly beneath contempt that I really could not agree to take any of them; then they looked very humble, and went quietly away, very miserable, having lost their daily bread; then came the wife again, and wept. Out of thirty persons there was only one who said at once, "I am satisfied," and signed his contract; all the others bargained and haggled for an hour

---

* Professor Heyse, Mendelssohn's teacher.

5*

at least, before I could make them understand that I
had a *prix fixe*. The whole day I was reminded of
my father's proverb, "Asking and bidding make the
sale;" but they were four of the most disagreeable
days I ever passed. On the fourth, Klingemann arrived in the morning, saw the state of things, and was
horrified. In the mean time Rietz studied the "Templar," morning and evening; the choruses got drunk,
and I was forced to speak with authority; then they
rebelled against the manager, and I was obliged to
shout at them like the Boots at an inn; then Madame
Beutler became hoarse, and I was very anxious on her
account (a new sort of anxiety for me, and a most
odious one); then I conducted Cherubini's "Requiem"
in the church, and this was followed by the first concert. In short, I made up my mind to abdicate my Intendant throne three weeks after the reopening of the
theatre. The affair goes on quite as well as we could
expect in Düsseldorf: Rietz's playing is admirable,—
he is studious, accurate, and artistic, so that he is
praised and liked by every one. The operas we have
hitherto given are, the "Templar" twice, "Oberon"
twice, which I conducted, "Fra Diavolo," and yesterday the "Freischütz." We are about to perform the
"Entführung," the "Zauberflöte," the "Ochsen-
menuett," the "Dorf Barbier," and the "Wasserträger." The operas are well attended, but not the plays,
so that the shareholders are sometimes rather uneasy;
five of the company up to this time have actually run
away, two of them being members of the orchestra.

The Committee gave a supper to the company,
which was very dull, and cost each member of the

Council (including myself) eleven dollars; but pray refrain from all tokens of sympathy, in case of causing my tears to flow afresh. But since I have withdrawn from this sphere, I feel as if I were a fish thrown back into the water; my forenoons are once more at my own disposal, and in the evenings I can sit at home and read. The oratorio daily causes me more satisfaction, and I have also composed some new songs; the Vocal Association gets on well, and we intend shortly to give the " Seasons," with a full orchestra. I mean soon to publish six preludes and fugues, two of which you have already seen; this is the sort of life I like to lead, but not that of an intendant. How vexatious it is, that at the close of such well-spent days we cannot all assemble together to enjoy each other's society !*

---

* The mode, however, in which Mendelssohn treated this affair of the theatre was by no means approved of by his father; on the contrary, some time afterwards he wrote to him as follows:—

" I must once more resume the subject of the dramatic career, as I feel very anxious about it on your account. You have not, according to my judgment, either in a productive or administrative point of view, had sufficient experience to decide with certainty that your disinclination towards it proceeds from anything innate in your talents or character. I know no dramatic composer, except Beethoven, who has not written a number of operas, now totally forgotten, before attaining the right object at the right moment, and gaining a place for himself. You have only made one public effort, which was partly frustrated by the text, and, in fact, was neither very successful nor the reverse. Subsequently you were too fastidious about the words, and did not succeed in finding the right man, and perhaps did not seek him in a right manner; I cannot but think that by more diligent inquiries and more moderate pretensions you would at length attain your object. With regard to the administrative career, however, it gives rise to another series of reflections which I wish to impress on you. Those who have the opportunity and the inclination to become more closely and intimately ac-

I inclose my translation of "Alexander's Feast;"
you must read it aloud to the family in the evening,

---

quainted with you, as well as all those to whom you have the opportunity and the inclination to reveal yourself more fully, cannot fail to
love and respect you. But this is really far from being sufficient to
enable a man to enter on life with active efficacy; on the contrary,
when you advance in years, and opportunity and inclination fail, both
in others and yourself, it is much more likely to lead to isolation and
misanthropy. Even what we consider faults will be respected, or at
least treated with forbearance, when once firmly and thoroughly established in the world, while the individual himself disappears. He has
least of all arrived at the ideal of virtue who exacts it most inexorably
from others. The most stern moral principle is a citadel, with outworks,
in defence of which we are unwilling to expend our strength, in order
to maintain ourselves with greater certainty in our stronghold, which
indeed ought only to be surrendered with life itself. Hitherto it· is
undeniable that you have never been able to divest yourself of a tendency to austerity and irascibility, to suddenly grasping an object and
as suddenly relinquishing it, and thus creating for yourself many
obstacles in a practical point of view. For example, I must confess
that, though I approved of your withdrawing from any active partici-
pation in the management of details in the Düsseldorf theatre, I by no
means did so of the manner in which you accomplished your object, as
you undertook it voluntarily, and, to speak candidly, rather heedlessly.
From the beginning you, most wisely, declined any positive compact,
but only agreed to undertake the studying and conducting of particular operas, and, in accordance with this resolution, very properly insisted on another music director being appointed. When you came here
some time ago with the commission to engage Krethi and Plethi, I did
not at all like the idea; I thought, however, that, as you were coming
here at all events, you could not through politeness decline this service.
But on your return to Düsseldorf, after wisely refusing to undertake
another journey for the purpose of making engagements for the theatre, instead of persevering in your duties in this sense, and getting rid
of all *odiosa*, you allowed yourself to be overwhelmed by them; and
as they naturally became most obnoxious to you, instead of quietly
striving to remedy them, and thus generally to get rid of them, you at
one leap extricated yourself, and by so doing you undeniably subjected
yourself to the imputation of fickleness and unsteadiness, and made a
decided enemy of a man whom at all events policy should have taught

and in various passages where the rhymes are rugged
or deficient, if you will let me have your amendments
I shall be grateful. One stipulation, however, I must
make, that Ramler, or rather, I should say, the English
text, should not be sacrificed. *Apropos*, since then I
have once more mounted Pegasus, and translated Lord
Byron's poem, the first strophe of which, by Theremin,
is incomprehensible, and the second false. I find, however, that my lines halt a little ; perhaps, some evening,
you may discover something better.

> Schlafloser Augensonne, heller Stern !
> Der du mit thränenvollem Schein, unendlich fern,
> Das Dunkel nicht erhellst, nur besser zeigst,
> O wie du ganz des Glücks Erinn'rung gleichst !
> So funkelt längst vergangner Freuden Licht,
> Es scheint, doch wärmt sein matter Schimmer nicht,
> Der wache Gram erspäht die Nachtgestalt,
> Hell, aber fern, klar—aber ach ! wie kalt !

The poem is very sentimental, and I think I should
have set it to music repeatedly in G sharp minor or B
major (but, at all events, with no end of sharps), had it
not occurred to me that the music of Löwe pleases you
and Fanny ; so this prevents my doing so, and there is
an end of it, and my letter also. Adieu, love me as
ever.—Your

FELIX.

---

you not to displease, and most probably offended and lost the friendliness of many members of the *Comité* also, among whom there are, no
doubt, most respectable people. If I view this matter incorrectly,
then teach me a better mode of judging."

This letter will show what an impartial and incorruptible judge
Mendelssohn possessed in his father.

To CARL KLINGEMANN, LONDON.

Düsseldorf, December 16th, 1834.

. . . So now in these lines you have read my whole life and occupations since I came here; for that I am well and happy, and often think of you, is included in them, and that I am also diligent and working hard at many things, is the natural result. I really believe that Jean Paul, whom I am at this moment reading with intense delight, has also some influence in the matter, for he invariably infects me for at least half a year with his strange peculiarities. I have been reading 'Fixlein' again; but my greatest pleasure in doing so, is the remembrance of the time when I first became acquainted with it, by your reading it aloud to me beside my sickbed, when it did me so much good. I also began 'Siebenkäs' again, for the first time for some years, and have read from the close of the prologue to the end of the first part, and am quite enchanted with this noble work. The prologue itself is a masterpiece such as no one else could write, and so it is with the whole book, the friends, and the school-inspector, and Lenette. It revives my love for my country, and makes me feel proud of being a German, although in these days they all abuse each other. Yet such people do sometimes rise to the surface, and I do believe that no country can boast of such a sterling fellow as this.

To Rebecca Dirichlet, Berlin.

Düsseldorf, December 23d, 1834.

Dear Rebecca,

Why should we not, like established correspondents, exchange repeated letters on any particular subject about which we differ ? I on my part will represent a methodical correspondent, and must absolutely resume the question of *révolution*. This is chiefly for Fanny's benefit; but are not you identical? Can you not, therefore, discuss the subject together, and answer me together, if you choose ? And have I not pondered and brooded much over this theme since I got your letter, which now prompts me to write ? You must, however, answer me in due form, till not one jot or tittle more remains to be said in favour of *révolution*. Observe, I think that there is a vast distinction between reformation or reforming, and revolution, etc. Reformation is that which I desire to see in all things, in life and in art, in politics and in street-pavement, and Heaven knows in what else besides. Reformation is entirely negative against abuses, and only removes what obstructs the path; but a revolution, by means of which all that was formerly good (and really good) is no longer to continue, is to me the most intolerable of all things, and is, in fact, only a fashion. Therefore, I would not for a moment listen to Fanny, when she said that Lafont's playing could inspire no further interest since the *revolution* effected by Paganini; for if his playing ever had the power to interest me, it would still do so, even if in the mean time I had heard the Angel Gabriel on the violin. It is just this, however,

that those Frenchmen I alluded to can form no conception of; that what is good, however old, remains always new, even although the present must differ from
the past, because it emanates from other and dissimilar
men. *Inwardly* they are only ordinary men like the
former, and have only *outwardly* learned that something new must come; so they strive to accomplish
this, and if they are even moderately applauded or
flattered they instantly declare that they have effected
a *révolution du goût.* This is why I behave so badly
when they do me the honour (as you call it) to rank
me among the leaders of this movement, when I well
know that, for thorough self-cultivation, the whole of
a man's life is required (and often does not suffice);
and also because no Frenchman, and no newspaper,
knows or ever can know what the future is to give or
to bring; and, in order to guide the movements of
others, we must first be in motion ourselves, while such
reflections cause us to look back on the past, not forward.   Progress is made by work alone, and not by
talking, which those people do not believe.

But, for Heaven's sake, don't suppose that I wish to
disown either reformation or progress, for I *hope* one
day myself to effect a reform in music; and this, as you
may see, is because I am simply a musician, and I wish
to be nothing more.   Now answer me, I beg, and
preach to me again.

To-day I have completed and transcribed an entire
chorus for "St. Paul."   I may as well at once reply
here to a letter I received this morning, dictated by my
father to Fanny, and to which my mother added a
postscript.   First of all, I thank you for writing, and

then, dear Father, I would entreat of you not to withhold from me your valuable advice, for it is always clear gain to me; and if I cannot rectify the old faults, I can at least avoid committing new ones. The non-appearance of St. Paul at the stoning of Stephen is certainly a blemish, and I could easily alter the passage in itself; but I could find absolutely no mode of introducing him at that time, and no words for him to utter in accordance with the Scriptural narrative; therefore it seemed to me more expedient to follow the Bible account, and to make Stephen appear alone. I think, however, that your other censure is obviated by the music; for the recitative of Stephen, though the words are long, will not occupy more than two or three minutes, or—*including* all the choruses—till his death, about a quarter of an hour; whereas subsequently, at and after the conversion, the music becomes more and more diffuse, though the words are fewer.

To Pastor Bauer, Beszig.

Düsseldorf, January 12th, 1835.

[About a proposal as to some words for sacred music.]

. . . What I do not understand is the purport—musical, dramatic, or oratorical, or whatever you choose to call it—that you have in view. What you mention on the subject—the time before John, and then John himself, till the appearance of Christ—is to my mind equally conveyed in the word 'Advent,' or the birth of Christ. You are aware, however, that the music must

6

represent one particular moment, or a succession of moments; and how you intend this to be done you do not say. Actual church music—that is, music during the Evangelical Church service, which could be introduced properly while the service was being celebrated—seems to me impossible; and this, not merely because I cannot at all see into *which* part of the public worship this music can be introduced, but because I cannot discover that *any* such part exists. Perhaps you have something to say which may enlighten me on the subject. . . . But even without any reference to the Prussian Liturgy, which at once cuts off everything of the kind, and will neither remain as it is nor go further, I do not see how it is to be managed that music in our Church should form an integral part of public worship, and not become a mere concert, conducive more or less to piety. This was the case with Bach's "Passion;" it was sung in church as an independent piece of music, for edification. As for actual church music, or, if you like to call it so, music for public worship, I know none but the old Italian compositions for the Papal Chapel, where, however, the music is a mere accompaniment, subordinate to the sacred functions, co-operating with the wax candles and the incense, etc. If it be this style of church music that you really mean, then, as I said, I cannot discover the connecting link which would render it possible to employ it. For an oratorio, one principal subject must be adopted, or the progressive history of particular persons, otherwise the object would not be sufficiently defined; for if all is to be only contemplative with reference to the coming of Christ, then this theme has already been more grandly and beautifully treated in Handel's "Messiah," where he begins with Isaiah, and, taking the Birth as a central point, closes with the Resurrection.

When you, however, say "our poor Church," I must tell you what is very strange; I have found, to my astonishment, that the Catholics, who have had music in their churches for several centuries, and sing a musical Mass every Sunday if possible, in their principal churches, do not to this day possess one which can be considered even tolerably good, or in fact which is not actually distasteful and operatic. This is the case from Pergolese and Durante, who introduce the most laughable little trills into their "Gloria," down to the opera finales of the present day. Were I a Catholic, I would set to work at a Mass this very evening; and, whatever it might turn out, it would at all events be the only Mass written with a constant remembrance of its sacred purpose. But for the present I don't mean to do this; perhaps at some future day, when I am older.

To Herr Conrad Schleinitz, Leipzic.

Düsseldorf, January 26th, 1835.

Sir,

Pray receive my thanks for your kind letter, and the friendly disposition which it evinces towards myself. You may well imagine that it would be a source of infinite pleasure to me to find in your city the extensive sphere of action you describe, as my sole wish is to advance the cause of music on that path which I consider the right one; I would therefore gladly comply with a summons which furnished me with the means of doing so. I should not like, however, by such acceptance to injure any one, and I do not wish, by assuming this office, to be the cause of supplanting my predecessor. In the first place, I consider this to be wrong; and, moreover, great harm ensues to music from such contentions. Before, then, giving a decided answer to your proposal, I must beg you to solve some doubts:—namely, at whose disposal is the appointment you describe? with whom should I be in connection,—with a society, or individuals, or a Board? and should I by my acceptance injure any other musician? I hope you will answer this last question with perfect candour, imagining yourself in my place; for, as I previously said, I have no wish to deprive any one, either directly or indirectly, of his situation.

Further, it is not quite clear to me, from your letter, how the direction of an academy for singing can be combined with my six months' summer vacation; for you must be well aware how indispensable continual supervision is to such an institution, and that anything which can be accomplished in one half-year may be easily forgotten in the next; or is there another director for the purpose of undertaking the duties instead of me? Finally, I must also confess that, in a pecuniary point of view, I do not wish to accept any position that would be less profitable than my present one; but, as you mention a benefit concert, no doubt this is a matter that might be satisfactorily arranged, and we should have no difficulty in coming to an agreement on this point.

I have been quite candid with you, and hope, in any event, you will not take it amiss; be so good as to oblige me by sending an answer as soon as possible, and to believe that I shall ever be grateful to you for your kind letter, as well as for the honour you have done me

---

To Capellmeister Spohr, Cassel.

Düsseldorf, March 8th, 1835.

Respected Capellmeister,

I thank you much for your friendly communication. The intelligence from Vienna was most interesting to me; I had heard nothing of it. It strongly revived my feeling as to the utter impossibility of my ever composing anything with a view to competing for a prize. I should never be able to make even a beginning; and if I were obliged to undergo an examination as a musician, I am convinced that I should be at once sent back, for I should not have done half as well as I could. The thoughts of a prize, or an award, would distract my thoughts; and yet I cannot rise so superior to this feeling as entirely to forget it. But if you find that you are in a mood for such a thing, you should not fail to compose a symphony by that time, and to send it, for I know no man living who could dispute the prize with you (this is the second reason), and then we should get another symphony of yours (first reason). With regard to the members of the Judicial Committee in Vienna, I have my own thoughts, which, however, are not very legitimate, but, on the contrary, somewhat rebellious. Were I one of the judges, not a single member of the *Comité* should obtain a prize, if they competed for one.

You wish me to write to you on the subject of my works, and I cordially thank you for asking about them. I began an oratorio about a year ago, which I expect to finish next month, the subject of which is St. Paul. Some friends have compiled the words for me from the Bible, and I think that both the subject and the compilation are well adapted to music, and very solemn,—if the music only prove as good as I wish; at all events, I have enjoyed the most intense delight while engaged in writing it. I also composed some time since, a new overture to the "Lovely Melusina." and have another in my head at this moment. How gladly would I write an opera! but far and near I can find no libretto and no poet. Those who have the genius of poetry cannot bear music, or know nothing of the theatre; others are neither acquainted with poetry nor with mankind, only with the boards, and lamps, and side scenes, and canvas. So I never succeed in finding the opera which I have so eagerly, yet vainly striven to procure. Each day I regret this more ; but I hope at last to meet with the man I wish for this purpose. I have also written a good deal of instrumental music of late, chiefly for the piano, but others besides; perhaps you will permit me to send you some of these as soon as I have an opportunity to do so. I am, with the highest esteem and consideration, your devoted

FELIX MENDELSSOHN BARTHOLDY.

To Felix Mendelssohn Bartholdy,
from his Father.*

Berlin, March 10th, 1835.

This is the third letter I have written to you this week, and, if this goes on, reading my letters will become a standing article in the distribution of the budget of your time; but you must blame yourself for this, as you spoil me by your praise. I at once pass to the musical portion of your last letter.

Your aphorism, that every room in which Sebastian Bach is sung is transformed into a church, I consider peculiarly appropriate; and when I once heard the last movement of the piece in question, it made a similar impression on myself; but I own I cannot overcome my dislike to figured chorales in general, because I cannot understand the fundamental idea on which they are based, especially where the contending parts are maintained in an equal balance of power. For example, in the first chorus of the "Passion,"—where the chorale forms only a more important and consistent part of the basis; or where, as in the above-mentioned movement of the cantata (if I remember it rightly, having only heard it once), the chorale represents the principal building, and the individual parts only the decorations, —I can better comprehend the purpose and the conception; but not so certainly where the figure, in a certain

---

* The following letter from Mendelssohn's father will certainly not be read without interest, as it throws so clear a light on the intellectual relations between father and son ; a place may therefore be appropriately found for it here. It has been selected from a large collection of letters of a similar tendency.

manner, carries out variations on the theme. No
liberties ought ever assuredly to be taken with a chorale. Its highest purpose is, that the congregation
should sing it in all its purity to the accompaniment of
the organ ; all else seems to me idle and inappropriate
for a church.

At Fanny's last morning's music the motett of Bach,
"Gottes Zeit ist die allerbeste Zeit," and your " Ave
Maria," were sung by select voices. A long passage in
the middle of the latter, as well as the end also, appeared to me too learned and intricate to accord with the
simple piety, and certainly genuine catholic spirit,
which pervades the rest of the music. Rebecca remarked that there was some confusion in the execution
of those very passages which I considered too intricate ;
but this only proves that I am an ignoramus, but not
that the conclusion is not too abstrusely modulated.
With regard to Bach, the composition in question
seems to me worthy of the highest admiration. It is
long since I have been so struck or surprised by anything as by the Introduction, which Fanny played most
beautifully ; and I could not help thinking of Bach's
solitary position, of his isolated condition with regard to
his associates and his contemporaries, of his pure, mild,
and vast power, and the transparency of its depths.
The particular pieces which at the time were for ever
engraved on my memory were " Bestelle dein Haus,"
and " Es ist der alte Bund." I cared less for the bass
air, or the alt solos. What first, through his " Passion,"
seemed quite clear to me—that Bach is the musical type
of Protestantism—becomes either negatively or positively more apparent to me every time that I hear a

new piece of his; and thus it was recently with a Mass that I heard in the Academy, and which I consider most decidedly anti-Catholic; and, consequently, even all its great beauties seemed as unable to reconcile the inward contradiction, as if I were to hear a Protestant clergyman performing Mass in a Protestant Church. Moreover, I felt more strongly than ever what a great merit it was on Zelter's part to restore Bach to the Germans; for, between Forkel's day and his, very little was ever said about Bach, and even then principally with regard to his "wohltemperirte Clavier." He was the first person on whom the light of Bach clearly dawned, through the acquisition of his other works, with which, as a collector of music, he became acquainted, and, as a genuine artist, imparted this knowledge to others. His musical performances on Fridays were indeed a proof that no work begun in earnest, and followed up with quiet perseverance, can fail ultimately to command success. At all events, it is an undoubted fact, that without Zelter, your own musical tendencies would have been of a totally different nature.

Your intention to restore Handel in his original form has led me to some reflections on his later style of instrumentation. A question is not unfrequently raised as to whether Handel, if he wrote in our day, would make use of all the existing musical facilities in composing his oratorios,—which, in fact, only means whether the wonted artistic form to which we give the name of Handel would assume the same shape now that it did a hundred years ago; and the answer to this presents itself at once. The question, however, ought to be put in a different form,—not whether Handel would compose his oratorios now as he did a century since, but, rather, whether he would compose any oratorios whatever; hardly—if they must be written in the style of those of the present day.

From my saying this to you, you may gather with what eager anticipations and confidence I look forward to your oratorio, which will, I trust, solve the problem of combining ancient conceptions with modern appliances; otherwise the result would be as great a failure as that of the painters of the nineteenth century, who only make themselves ridiculous by attempting to revive the religious elements of the fifteenth, with its long arms and legs and topsy-turvy perspective. These new resources seem to me, like everything else in the world, to have been developed just at the right time in order to animate the inner impulses which were daily becoming more feeble. On the heights of religious feeling on which Bach, Handel, and their contemporaries stood, they required no numerous orchestras for their oratorios; and I can remember perfectly in my earliest years the "Messiah," "Judas," and "Alexander's Feast" being given exactly as Handel wrote them, without even an organ, and yet to the delight and edification of every one.

But how is this to be managed nowadays, when vacuity of thought and noise in music are gradually being developed in inverse relation to each other? The orchestra, however, is now established, and is likely long to maintain its present form without any essential modification. Riches are only a fault when we do not know how to spend them. How, then, is the wealth of the orchestra to be applied? What

guidance can the poet give for this, and to what re-
gions? or is music to be entirely severed from poetry,
and work its own independent way? I do not believe
it can accomplish the latter, at least, only to a very
limited extent, and not available for the world at large;
to effect the former, an object must be found for music
as well as for painting, which, by its fervour, its
universal sufficiency and perspicuity, may supply the
place of the pious emotions of former days. It seems
to me that both the oratorios of Haydn were, in their
sphere, also very remarkable phenomena. The poems
of both are weak, regarded as poetry; but they have
replaced the old positive and almost metaphysical religious impulses, by those which nature, as a visible
emanation from the Godhead, in her universality, and
her thousandfold individualities, instils into every susceptible heart. Hence the profound depth, but also
the cheerful efficiency, and certainly genuine religious
influence of these two works, which hitherto stand
alone; hence the combined effect of the playful and
detached passages, with the most noble and sincere
feelings of gratitude produced by the whole; hence is
it, also, that I individually could as little endure to
lose in the "Creation" and in the "Seasons" the crow-
ing of the cock, the singing of the lark, the lowing of
the cattle, and the rustic glee of the peasants, as I
could in nature herself; in other words, the "Creation"
and the "Seasons" are founded on nature and the
visible service of God; and are no new materials for
music to be found there?

The publication of Goethe's "Correspondence with a
Child" I consider a most provoking and pernicious

abuse of the press, through which, more and more rapidly, all illusions will be destroyed, without which life
is only death. You, I trust, will never lose your illusions, and ever preserve your filial attachment to your
father.

To his Father.

Düsseldorf, March 23d, 1835.

Dear Father,

I have still to thank you for your last letter and my
" Ave." I often cannot understand how it is possible
to have so acute a judgment with regard to music,
without being yourself technically musical; and if I
could *express* what I assuredly feel, with as much clearness and intuitive perception as you do, as soon as you
enter on the subject, I never would make another obscure speech all my life long. I thank you a thousand
times for this, and also for your opinion of Bach. I
ought to feel rather provoked that after only one very
imperfect hearing of my composition you at once discovered what, after long familiarity on my part, I have
only just found out; but then, again, it pleases me to
see your definite sense of music, for the deficiencies in
the middle movement and at the end consist of such
minute faults, which might have been remedied by a
very few notes (I mean struck out), that neither I nor
any other musician would have been aware of them
without repeatedly hearing the piece, because we in fact
seek the cause much deeper. They injure the simpli-

city of the harmony, which at the beginning pleases
me; and though it is my opinion that these faults
would be less perceptible if properly executed, that is,
with a numerous choir, still some traces of them will
always remain. Another time I shall endeavor to do
better. I should like you, however, to hear the Bach
again, because there is a part of it which you care less
for, but which pleases me best of all. I allude to the
alto and bass airs; only the chorale must be given by
a number of alto voices, and the bass very well sung.
However fine the airs "Bestelle dein Haus" and "Es
ist der alte Bund" may be, still there is something very
sublime and profound in the plan of the ensuing movements, in the mode in which the alto begins, the bass
then interposing with freshness and spirit, and continuing the same words while the chorale comes in as a
third, the bass closing exultantly, but the chorale not
till long afterwards, dying away softly and solemnly.
There is one peculiarity of this music,—its date must
be placed either very early or very late, for it entirely
differs from his usual style of writing in middle age,—
the first choral movements and the final chorus being
of a kind that I should never have attributed to Sebastian Bach, but to some other composer of his day;
while no other man in the world could have written a
single bar of the middle movements.

My mother does not judge Hiller rightly, for, in spite
of his pleasures and honours in Paris, and the neglect
he met with in Frankfort, he writes to me that he
envies me my position here on the Rhine, even with
all its drawbacks; and as, no doubt, a similar one may
still be met with in Germany, I do not give up the

7

hope of prevailing on him to forsake the Parisian atmosphere of pleasures and honours and return to his studio. Now farewell, dear Father. I beg you will soon let me hear from you again.—Your

FELIX.

To HIS FATHER.

Düsseldorf, April 3d, 1835.

Dear Father,

I am delighted to hear that you are satisfied with the programme of the Cologne Musical Festival. I shall not be able to play the organ for "Solomon," as it must stand in the background of the orchestra and accompany almost every piece, the choruses and other performers here being accustomed to constant beating of time. I must therefore transcribe the whole of the organ part in the manner in which I think it ought to be played, and the cathedral organist there, Weber, will play it; I am told he is a sound musician and first-rate player. This is all so far well, and only gives me the great labour of transcribing, as I wish to have the performance as perfect as possible. I have had a good deal of trouble, too, with the "Morgengesang,"* as there is much in it that requires alteration, owing to the impossibility of executing it as written, with the means we have here. In doing so, however, it again caused me extreme pleasure, especially the stars, the moon, the elements, and the whole of the admirable

---

* By Reichardt. Compare the passage in reference to Reichardt in the letter of December 28th, 1833.

finale. At the words "und schlich in dieser Nacht," etc., it becomes so romantic and poetical, that each time I hear it I feel more touched and charmed; it therefore gratifies me to be of any use to so noble a man. The *Comité* were very much surprised when I maintained that it was a fine composition, and scarcely would consent to have it; but at that moment they were in a mood to be persuaded to anything. I would also have insisted on their giving an overture of Bach's, if I had not dreaded too strong a counter-revolution. There is to be nothing of mine; therefore (from gratitude, I presume) they persist that my "admirable likeness" shall appear and be published by Whitsunday, a project from which I gallantly defend myself, refusing either to sit or stand for the purpose, having a particular objection to such pretensions.

You must be well aware that your presence at the festival would not only be no *gêne* to me, but, on the contrary, would cause me first to feel true joy and delight in my success. Allow me to take this opportunity to say to you that the approbation and enjoyment of the public, to which I am certainly very sensible, only causes me real satisfaction when I can write to tell you of it, because I know it rejoices you, and one word of praise from you is more truly precious to me, and makes me happier, than all the publics in the world applauding me in concert; and thus to see you among the audience, would be the dearest of all rewards to me for my labours.

My oratorio* is to be performed in Frankfort in

---

* "St. Paul."

November, so Schelble writes to me; and much as I
should like you to hear it soon, still I should prefer
your hearing it first next year, at the Musical Festival.
Before decidedly accepting the proposal, I have stipu-
lated to wait till after the performance at Frankfort,
that I may judge whether it be suitable for the festival;
but should this prove to be the case, as I hope and
wish it may, it will have a much finer effect there;
and, besides, it is the festival that you like, and Whitsunday instead of November; and, above all, I shall
then know whether it pleases you or not, on which
point I feel by no means sure.

I cannot close this letter without speaking of the heavenly weather that delights us here. Light balmy air
and sunshine, and a profusion of green, and larks! To-
day I rode through the forest, and stopped for at least
a quarter of an hour to listen to the birds, who in the
deep solitude were fluttering about incessantly and
warbling.—Your

FELIX.

To HERR CONRAD SCHLEINITZ, LEIPZIG.

Düsseldorf, April 16th, 1835.

Sir,

I thank you cordially for your last letter, and for
the friendly interest which you take in me, and in my
coming to Leipzig. As I perceive by the Herr Stadt-
rath Porsche's letter, as well as by that of the Superintendent of the concerts, that my going there does not
interfere with any other person, one great difficulty is

thus obviated. But another has now arisen, as the
letter of the Superintendent contains different views
with regard to the situation from yours. The direction
of twenty concerts and extra concerts is named as
among the duties, but a benefit concert (about which
you wrote to me) is not mentioned. I have consequently said in my reply what I formerly wrote to
you, that, in order to induce me to consent to the exchange, I wish to see the same pecuniary advantages
secured to me that I enjoy here. If a benefit concert,
as you say, would bring from two hundred to three
hundred dollars, this sum would certainly be a considerable increase to my salary ; but I must say that I
never made such a proposal, and indeed would not
have accepted it had it been made to me. It would be
a different thing if the association chose to give an additional concert, and to devote a share of the profits
towards the increase of my established salary. During
my musical career, I have always resolved never to
give a concert for myself (for my own benefit). You
probably are aware that, personally, pecuniary considerations would be of less importance to me, were it
not that my parents (and I think rightly) exact from
me that I should follow my art as a profession and gain
my livelihood by means of it. I, however, reserved
the power of declining certain things which, in reference
to my favoured position in this respect, I will never
do; for example, giving concerts or lessons. But I
quite acknowledge the propriety of what my parents
insist on so strongly, that in all other relations I shall
gladly consider myself as a musician who lives by his
profession. Thus, before giving up my present situation,

I must ascertain that one equally advantageous is secured to me. I do not consider that what I require is at all presumptuous, as it has been offered to me here, and on this account I trust that a similar course may be pursued in Leipzig. An association was at that time formed here, who intrusted to me the duty of conducting the Vocal Association, concerts, etc., and made up my salary partly in common with the Vocal Association and partly by the profits of the concerts. Whether anything of this kind be possible with you, or whether it could be equalized by an additional concert, or whether the execution of particular duties is to be imposed on me, I cannot, of course, pretend to decide. I only wish that, in one way or another, a definite position should be assured to me, like the one I enjoy here; and if your idea about the benefit concert could be modified and carried out, there would then be a good hope for me that the affair might turn out according to my wish.

If you can induce the directors to fulfil the wishes I have expressed, you will exceedingly oblige me, for you know how welcome a residence and active employment in your city would be to me. In any event, continue your friendly feelings towards me, and accept my thanks for them.

To the Herr Regierungs-Secretair Hixte, Cologne.

Düsseldorf, May 18th, 1835.

Sir,

I thank you much for the kind letter you have grati-
fied me by addressing to me. The idea which you
communicate in it is very flattering for me, and yet I
confess that I feel a certain degree of dislike to what
you propose, and for a long time past I have entertained this feeling. It is now so very much the fashion
for obscure or commonplace people to have their likeness given to the public, in order to become more
known, and for young beginners to do so at first start-
ing in life, that I have always had a dread of doing so
too soon. I do not wish that my likeness should be
taken until I have accomplished something to render
me more worthy, according to my idea, of such an
honour. This, however, not being yet the case, I beg
to defer such a compliment till I am more deserving of
it; but receive my best thanks for the friendly good-
nature with which you made me this offer.*—I am, etc.,

Felix Mendelssohn Bartholdy.

To his Family.

Leipzig. October 6th, 1835.

For a week past I have been seeking for a leisure
hour to answer, and to thank you for, the charming let-

---

* Compare the passage on this subject in the letter of April 3d, 1835.

ters I have received from you; but the London days, with their distractions, were not worse than the time has been since Fanny left this till now. At length, after the successful result of the first concert, I have at last a certain degree of rest.

The day after I accompanied the Hensels to Delitsch, Chopin came; he intended only to remain one day, so we spent this entirely together in music. I cannot deny, dear Fanny, that I have lately found that you by no means do him justice in your judgment of his talents; perhaps he was not in a humour for playing when you heard him, which may not unfrequently be the case with him. But his playing has enchanted me afresh, and I am persuaded that if you, and my Father also, had heard some of his better pieces, as he played them to me, you would say the same. There is something thoroughly original in his pianoforte playing, and at the same time so masterly, that he may be called a most perfect virtuoso; and as every style of perfection is welcome and acceptable, that day was most agreeable to me, although so entirely different from the previous ones with you,—the Hensels.

It was so pleasant for me to be once more with a thorough musician, and not with those half virtuosos and half classics, who would gladly combine *les honneurs de la vertu et les plaisirs du vice*, but with one who has his perfect and well-defined phase; and however far asunder we may be in our different spheres, still I can get on famously with such a person; but not with those half-and-half people. Sunday evening was really very remarkable when Chopin made me play over my oratorio to him, while curious Leipzigers stole

into the room to see him, and when between the first
and second part he dashed into his new Études and a
new concerto, to the amazement of the Leipzigers, and
then I resumed my "St. Paul;" it was just as if a
Cherokee and a Kaffir had met to converse. He has
also such a lovely new *notturno*, a considerable part of
which I learnt by ear for the purpose of playing it for
Paul's amusement. So we got on most pleasantly
together; and he promised faithfully to return in the
course of the winter, when I intend to compose a new
symphony, and to perform it in honour of him. We
vowed these things in the presence of three witnesses,
and we shall see whether we both adhere to our word.
My collection of Handel's works arrived before Chopin's
departure, and were a source of quite childish delight
to him; they really are so beautiful that I am charmed
with them; thirty-two great folios, bound in thick green
leather, in the regular nice English fashion, and on the
back, in big gold letters, the title and contents of each
volume; and in the first volume, besides, there are the
following words, "To Director F. M. B., from the
Committee of the Cologne Musical Festival, 1835."
The books were accompanied by a very civil letter,
with the signatures of all the Committee, and on taking
up one of the volumes at random it happened to be
"Samson," and just at the very beginning I found a
grand aria for Samson which is quite unknown, because
Herr von Mosel struck it out, and which yields in
beauty to none of Handel's; so you see what pleasure
is in store for me in all the thirty-two volumes. You
may imagine my delight. Before setting off on his
journey, Moscheles came to see me, and during the first

half-hour he played over my second book of "songs without words" to my extreme pleasure. He is not the least changed, only somewhat older in appearance, but otherwise as fresh and in as good spirits as ever, and playing quite splendidly,—another kind of perfect virtuoso and master combined. The rehearsals of the first subscription gradually drew near, and the day before yesterday my Leipzig music-directorship commenced. I cannot tell you how much I am satisfied with this beginning, and with the whole aspect of my position here. It is a quiet, regular, official business. That the Institute has been established for fifty-six years is very perceptible, and moreover the people seem most friendly and well-disposed towards me and my music. The orchestra is very good, and thoroughly musical; and I think that six months hence it will be much improved, for the sympathy and attention with which these people receive my suggestions, and instantly adopt them, were really touching in both the rehearsals we have hitherto had; there was as great a difference as if another orchestra had been playing. There are still some deficiencies in the orchestra, but these will be supplied by degrees; and I look forward to a succession of pleasant evenings and good performances. I wish you had heard the introduction to my "Meeresstille" (for the concert began with that); there was such profound silence in the hall and in the orchestra, that the most delicate notes could be distinctly heard, and they played the adagio from first to last in the most masterly manner; the allegro not quite so well, for, being accustomed to a slower *tempo*, they rather dragged; but at the end, where the slow time $\frac{4}{4}$ $f\!f$ begins, they went

capitally, the violins attacking it with a degree of
vehemence that quite startled me and delighted the
publicus. The following pieces, an air in E major of
Weber, a violin concerto by Spohr, and the introduction
to "Ali Baba," did not go so well; the one rehearsal
was not sufficient, and they were often unsteady; but,
on the other hand, Beethoven's B flat symphony, which
formed the second part, was splendidly given, so that
the Leipzigers shouted with delight at the close of each
movement. I never in any orchestra saw such zeal and
excitement; they listened like—popinjays, Zelter would
say.

After the concert I received, and offered in turn, a
mass of congratulations: first the orchestra, then the
Thomas School collegians (who are capital fellows, and
always join in, so punctually and vigorously, that I
have promised them a medal); then came Moscheles,
with a Court suite of *dilettanti*, then two editors of musical papers, and so on. Moscheles' concert is on Friday,
and I am to play his piece for two pianos* with him,
and he is to play my new pianoforte-concerto. My
"Hebrides" have also contrived to creep into the concert. This afternoon Moscheles, Clara Wieck, and I,
play Sebastian Bach's triple concerto in D minor. How
amiable Moscheles is towards myself, how cordially he
is interested in my situation here, how it delights me
that he is so satisfied with it, how he plays my rondo
in E flat to my great admiration, and far better than I
originally conceived it, and how we dine together
every forenoon in his hotel, and every evening drink

* " Hommage à Handel."

tea and have music in mine,—all this you can imagine for yourself, for you know him,—especially you, dear Father. These are pleasant days; and if I have not much leisure to work, I mean to make up for it hereafter, and shall derive as much benefit from it then as now.

My first concert caused me no perturbation, dear Mother, but to my shame I confess that I never felt so embarrassed at the moment of appearing as on that occasion; I believe it arose from our long correspondence and treaty on the subject, and I had never before seen a concert of the kind. The locality and the lights confused me. Now farewell all. May you be well and happy, and pray write to me very often.—Your

FELIX.

To PASTOR JULIUS SCHUBRING, DESSAU.

Leipzig, December 6th 1835.

Dear Schubring,

You have no doubt heard of the heavy stroke that has fallen on my happy life and those dear to me.* It is the greatest misfortune that could have befallen me, and a trial that I must either strive to bear up against, or must utterly sink under. I say this to myself after the lapse of three weeks, without the acute anguish of the first days, but I now feel it even more deeply; a new life must now begin for me, or all must be at an end: the old life is now severed. For our consolation and example, our mother bears her loss with the most wonder-

---

* The death of his father.

ful composure and firmness; she comforts herself with
her children and grandchildren, and thus strives to hide
the chasm that never can be filled up.   My brother and
sisters do what they can to fulfil their duties better than
ever, the more difficult they have become.   I was ten
days in Berlin, that by my presence my mother should
at least be surrounded by her whole family; but I need
scarcely tell you what these days were; you know it
well, and no doubt you thought of me in that dark hour.
God granted to my father the prayer that he had often
uttered; his end was as peaceful and quiet and as sudden
and unexpected as he desired.   On Wednesday, the 18th,
he was surrounded by all his family, went to bed late
the same evening, complained a little early on Thursday,
and at half-past eleven his life was ended.   The physi-
cians can give his malady no name.   It seems that my
grandfather Moses died in a similar manner,—so my uncle told us,—at the same age, without sickness, and in a
calm and cheerful frame of mind.   I do not know whether
you are aware that more especially for some years past
my father was so good to me, so thoroughly my friend,
that I was devoted to him with my whole soul, and during my long absence I scarcely ever passed an hour
without thinking of him; but as you knew him in his
own home with us, in all his kindliness, you can well
realize my state of mind.   The only thing that now
remains is to do one's duty, and this I strive to accomplish with all my strength, for he would wish it to
be so if he were still present, and I shall never cease to
endeavour to gain his approval as I formerly did, though
I can no longer enjoy it.   When I delayed answering
your letter, I little thought I should have to answer it

8

thus; let me thank you for it now, and for all your kindness. One passage for "St. Paul" was excellent, "der Du der rechte Vater bist." I have a chorus in my head for it which I intend shortly to write down. I shall now work with double zeal at the completion of "St. Paul," for my father urged me to it in the very last letter he wrote to me, and he looked forward very impatiently to the completion of my work. I feel as if I must exert all my energies to finish it, and make it as good as possible, and then think that he takes an interest in it. If any good passages occur to you, pray send them to me, for you know the intention of the whole. To-day, for the first time, I have begun once more to work at it, and intend now to do so daily. When it is concluded, what is to come next, God will direct. Farewell, dear Schubring : bear me in your thoughts. —Your

FELIX MENDELSSOHN BARTHOLDY.

TO PASTOR BAUER, BESZIG.

Leipzig, December 9th, 1835.

I received your kind letter here, on the very day when the christening in your family was to take place, on my return from Berlin, where I had gone in the hope of alleviating my mother's grief, immediately after the loss of my father. So I received the intelligence of your happiness, on again crossing the threshold of my empty room, when I felt for the first time in my inmost being what it is to suffer the most painful and bitter anguish. Indeed, the wish which of all others every night recurred to my mind, was that I might not survive my loss, because I so entirely clung to my father, or rather still cling to him, that I do not know how I can now pass my life, for not only have I to deplore the loss of a father (a sorrow which of all others from my childhood I always thought the most acute), but also that of my best and most perfect friend during the last few years, and my instructor in art and in life.

It seemed to me so strange, reading your letter, which breathed only joy and satisfaction, calling on me to rejoice with you on your future prospects, at the moment when I felt that my past was lost and gone for ever; but I thank you for wishing me, though so distant, to become your guest at the christening; and though my name may make a graver impression now than you probably thought, I trust that impression will only be a grave, and not a painful, one, to you and your wife; and when, in later years, you tell your child of those whom you invited to his baptism, do not omit my name from your guests, but say to him that one of them on that day recommenced his life afresh,—though in another sense, with new purposes and wishes, and with new prayers to God.

My mother is well, and bears her sorrow with such composure and dignity that we can all only wonder and admire, and ascribe it to her love for her children and her wish for their happiness. As for myself, when I tell you that I strive to do my duty and thus to win my father's approval now as I always formerly did, and devote to the completion of "St. Paul," in which he took such pleasure, all the energies of my mind, to make it as good as I possibly can,—when I say that I force myself to the performance of my duties here, not to pass quite unprofitably these first days of sorrow, when to be perfectly idle is most consonant to one's feelings,—that, lastly, the people here are most kind and sympathizing, and endeavor to make life as little painful to me as they can,—you know the aspect of my inner and outer life at this moment.   Farewell.

To Ferdinand Hiller.

Leipzig, January 24th, 1836.

My dear Ferdinand,

I now send you my promised report of the performance of your D minor overture, which took place last Thursday evening.   It was well executed by the orchestra; we had studied it repeatedly and carefully, and a great many of the passages sounded so well as to exceed my expectations.   The most beautiful of all was the first passage in A minor, *piano*, given by wind instruments, followed by the melody,—which had an admirable effect; and also at the beginning of the free fantasia, the *forte* in G minor, and then the *piano* (your favourite passage), likewise the trombones and wind instruments, *piano*, at the end in D major.   The Finale, too, exceeded my expectations in the orchestra.   But, trusting to our good understanding, I could not resist striking out, after the first rehearsal, the *staccato* double-basses in the melody in A major, and each time the passage recurred in F and D major, replacing them by sustained notes; you can't think how confused the effect was, and therefore I hope you will not take this liberty amiss. I am convinced you would have done the same; it did not sound as you would have liked.

I have something else, too, on my conscience that I must tell you. The Overture neither excited myself nor the musicians during its performance as I could have wished; it left us rather cold. This would have been of little consequence, but it was remarkable that all the musicians to whom I spoke said the same. The first theme and all the beginning, the melodies in A minor and A major, particularly delighted them; and up to that point they had all felt enthusiastic; but then their sympathy gradually subsided, till, when the close came, they had quite forgotten the striking impression of the theme, and no longer felt any interest in the music. This seems to me important, for I think it is connected with the difference which we have so repeatedly discussed together, and the want of interest with which you at all times regard your art, being now at length become perceptible to others. I would not say this to you, were it not that I am perfectly convinced of this being a point which must be left to each *individual*, as neither nature nor talents, even of the highest order, can remedy it; a man's own will alone can do so. Nothing is more repugnant to me than casting blame on the nature or genius of any one; it only renders him irritable and bewildered, and does no good. No man can add one inch to his stature: in such a case all striving and toiling is vain, therefore it is best to be silent. Providence is answerable for this defect in his nature. But if it be the case, as it is with this work of yours, that precisely those very themes, and all that requires talent or genius (call it as you will), is excellent and beautiful and touching, but the development not so good,—then, I think, silence should not be observed; then, I think, blame can never be unwise, for this is the point where great progress can be made by the composer himself in his works; and as I believe that a man with fine capabilities has the absolute duty imposed on him of becoming something really superior, so I think that blame must be attributed to him if he does not develop himself according to the means with which he is endowed. And I maintain that it is the same with a musical composition. Do not tell me that it is so, and therefore it must remain so. I know well that no musician can alter the thoughts and talents which Heaven has bestowed on him; but I also know that when Providence grants him superior ones, he *must also develop* them properly. Do not declare, either, that we were all mistaken, and that the execution was as much in fault as the composition. I do not believe it. I do believe that your talents are such that you are inferior to *no* musician, but I scarcely know one piece of yours that is systematically carried out. The two overtures are certainly your best pieces, but the more distinctly you express your thoughts, the more perceptible are the defects, and, in my opinion, you must rectify them.

Do not ask me how, for that you know best yourself. After all, it is only the affair of a walk, or a moment,— in short, of a thought. If you laugh at me for this long lecture, perhaps you may be quite right; but certainly not so if you are displeased, or bear me a grudge for it; though indeed it is very stupid in me even to suggest such a possibility. But how many musicians are there who would permit another to address them thus? And though you must see in every expression of mine how much I love and revere your genius, still I have told you that you are not absolute perfection, and this musicians usually take amiss. But you will not; you know my sincere interest in you too well.

To FANNY HENSEL, BERLIN.

Leipzig, January 30th, 1836.

Dear Fanny,

To-day at length I can reply to your charming letters, and lecture you severely for saying in your first letter that it was long since you had been able to please me by your music, and asking me how this was. I totally deny this to be the fact, and assure you that all you compose pleases me. If two or three things in succession did not satisfy me as entirely as others of yours, I think the ground lay no deeper than this, that you have written less than in former days, when one or two songs that did not exactly suit my taste were so rapidly composed, and replaced so quickly by others, that neither of us considered much why it was that they were less attractive; we only laughed together about them, and there was an end of it.

I may quote here " Die Schönheit nicht, O Mädchen," and many others in the "*prima maniera* of our master," which we heartily abused. Then came beautiful songs in their turn, and so it is at present, only they cannot follow each other in such quick succession, because you must often now have other things to occupy your thoughts besides composing pretty songs, and that is a great blessing. But if you suppose that your more recent compositions seem to me inferior to your earlier ones, you are most entirely and totally mistaken, for I know no song of yours better than the English one in G minor, or the close of the "Liederkreis," and many others of later date : besides, you are aware that formerly there were entire *books* of your composition that were less acceptable to me than others, because my nature always was to be a screech-owl, and to belong to the savage tribe of brothers. But you know well how much I love *all* your productions, and some are especially dear to my heart; so I trust that you will write to me forthwith that you have done me injustice, by considering me a man devoid of taste, and that you will never again do so.

And, then, neither in this letter nor in your former one do you say one word about "St. Paul" or "Melusina," as one colleague should write to another,—that is, remarks on fifths, rhythm, and motion of the parts, on conceptions, counterpoint, *et cætera animalia.* You ought to have done so, however, and should do so still, for you know the value I attach to this; and as "St. Paul" is shortly to be sent to the publisher, a few strictures from you would come just at the right moment. I write to you to-day solely in the hope of soon receiving an answer from you, for I am very weary and exhausted from yesterday's concert, where, in addition to conducting three times, I was obliged to play Mozart's

D minor concerto. In the first movement I made a
cadenza, which succeeded famously, and caused a tremendous sensation among the Leipzigers. I must write
down the end of it for you. You remember the theme,
of course? Towards the close of the cadence, arpeggios
come in *pianissimo* in D minor, thus—

Then again G minor arpeggios ; then

Then   arpeggios, and

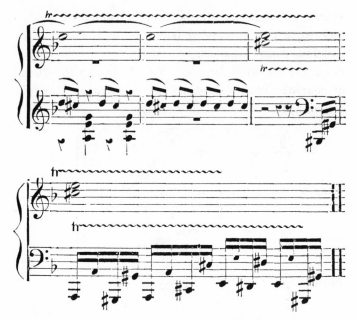

etc., to the close in D minor. Our second violin player, an old musician, said to me afterwards, when he met me in the passage, that he had heard it played in the same Hall by Mozart himself, but since that day he had heard no one introduce such good *cadenzas* as I did yesterday,—which gave me very great pleasure.

Do you know Handel's "Coronation Anthem?" It is most singular. The beginning is one of the finest which not only Handel, but any man, ever composed; and all the remainder, after the first short movement, horridly dry and commonplace. The performers could not master it, but are certainly far too busy to grieve much about that.

Many persons here consider "Melusina" to be my best overture; at all events, it is the most deeply felt;

but as to the fabulous nonsense of the musical papers, about red coral and green sea-monsters, and magic palaces, and deep seas, this is stupid stuff, and fills me with amazement. But now I take my leave of water for some time to come, and must see how things are going on elsewhere.* I received to-day a letter from Düsseldorf, with the news of the musical doings there, and a request to send " St. Paul' soon for the Musical Festival. I cannot deny that when I read the description of their concerts, and some concert bills which were enclosed, and realized the state of the musical world there, I had a most agreeable sensation at my change of position. They cannot well be compared; for while there they are engaged in perpetual quarrelling and strife and petty criticisms, here, on the contrary, during the course of this whole winter, my situation has not caused me to pass one disagreeable day, or to hear hardly one annoying expression, while I have enjoyed much pleasure and gratification. The whole orchestra, and there are some able men among them, strive to guess my wishes at a glance; they have made the most extraordinary progress in finish and refinement, and are so devoted to me, that I often feel quite affected by it.

Would that I were less sad and sorrowful; for sometimes I do not know what to do, and can only hope that the approaching spring and the warm weather may cheer me.

---

* This refers to the circumstance of Mendelssohn's father having advised him to " hang up on a nail" the elfin and spirit life with which, for a certain period, Mendelssohn had chiefly occupied himself in his compositions, and to proceed to graver works.

I trust you and yours may all continue well and happy, and sometimes think of me.—Your

FELIX.

To Dr. FREDERICK ROSEN, LONDON,

(PROFESSOR OF ORIENTAL LANGUAGES.)

Leipzig, February 6th, 1836.

My dear Friend,

I had intended writing to you long ago, but have always delayed it till now, when I am compelled to do so by Klingemann's announcement that your " Vedas" is finished. I wish therefore to send you my congratulations at once; and though I understand very little of it, and consequently can appreciate its merits as little, still I wish you joy of being able to give to the world a work so long cherished, and so interesting to you, and which cannot fail to bring you new fame and new delight. And when I feel how little I, who never learnt the language, can do justice to the vast circumference of such a work, I may indeed congratulate you on the fact that no spurious connoisseurs or *dilettanti* can grope their way into your most favourite thoughts, while you must feel the more secure and tranquil in your own vocation, because arrogant ignorance cannot presume to attack you behind your bulwarks of quaint letters and hieroglyphics. They must at least first be able to criticize; so you are better off in this respect than we are, against whom they always appeal to their own paltry conceptions.

I feel like a person waking drowsily. I cannot succeed in realizing the present, and there is a constant alternation of my old habitual cheerfulness and the most heartfelt deep grief, so that I cannot attain to anything like steady composure of mind. In the mean time, however, I occupy myself as much as possible, and that is the only thing that does me good. My position here is of the most agreeable nature,—cordial people, a good orchestra, the most susceptible and grateful musical public; only just as much work to do as I like, and an opportunity of hearing my new compositions at once. I have plenty of pleasant society besides, so that this would indeed seem to be all that was required to constitute happiness, were it not deeper seated!

Farewell, dear friend, and do not forget your

FELIX MENDELSSOHN BARTHOLDY.

To HIS MOTHER.

Leipzig, February 18th, 1836.

Dear Mother,

I cannot write home without enclosing a few lines for you, and thanking you a thousand times for your dear letter, and begging you to write to me as often as you wish to make me very happy. I have scarcely thanked you, and Fanny, and Rebecca, for the beautiful presents you sent me on the 3d, and which made the day so pleasant to me. The leader of the orchestra, when I went to rehearsal on the morning of that day,

9

addressed me in a complimentary speech, which was very gratifying, and when we sat down to dinner at S——'s, I found a silver cup, which four of my friends here had ordered for me with an inscription and their names, under my napkin. All this was welcome and cheering. In the evening, when I had carefully put away your store of linen, and placed Rebecca's travelling case beside my map of Germany and the keys of my trunk, and had read "Fiesco" in Fanny's book, which I was formerly so pleased with (but now less so), then I felt considerably older, and thought of Aunt Lette, who wrote me a note on my twentieth birthday, which began, "My poor Felix! actually ten years hence no longer a boy!"

I am curious to learn whether Gusikow pleased you as much as he did me. He is quite a phenomenon; a famous fellow, inferior to no virtuoso in the world, both in execution and facility; he therefore delights me more with his instrument of wood and straw, than many with their pianofortes, just because it is such a thankless kind of instrument. A capital scene took place at his concert here. I went out to join him in the room where he was, in order to speak to him and compliment him. Schleinitz and David wished to come with me; a whole group of Polish Jews followed in our wake, anxious to hear our eulogiums; but when we came to the side room, they pressed forward so quickly that David and Schleinitz were left in the rear, and the door shut right in their faces; then the Jews all stood quite still, waiting to hear the compliments Gusikow was about to receive. At first I could not speak for laughing, seeing the small room crammed full of these bearded fellows, and my two friends shut out. It is long since I so much enjoyed any concert as this, for the man is a true genius.

The direction of the St. Cecilia Association at Frankfort-on-the-Maine has been confidentially offered to me. I can with truth say that it caused me more pain than pleasure, because it is evident from this that Schelble's return is considered out of the question. If it really be so (which I shall take care to ascertain), I will on no account accept the offer. But if there were a possibility of improvement, and I could in any degree be of service to Schelble, by giving an impetus to his Institute next summer (for I hear that all the winter it has been almost dead), and if he could resume the duties himself next winter, I should feel real pleasure in doing this for him, even if all my travelling projects were to be overthrown. For once it would be doing a real service, both to a friend, and to the cause itself.

And now I must dress, for I am going to direct a concert. Merk is here; he gives a concert next Sunday, where I am to play with him again: it is the seventh time this winter, but I could not possibly refuse; for when I see my old companion again, the whole autumn of 1830 is brought before my eyes, and our music at Eskele's, our playing billiards at the Kärnthner Thor, and driving to Baden in a *fiacre*, etc. Besides, he is beyond all question the very first of all living violoncello-players. Farewell, dear Mother.—Your

FELIX.

To his Mother.

Düsseldorf, June 1st, 1836.

Dear Mother,

I hope you have forgiven my long silence. There was so much to do, both before and during my journey here, that I was scarcely able to attend even to the duties of the passing hour; and what has gone on here since my arrival* you know better than if I had myself written, for I trust Paul and Fanny are now happily returned, and of course described everything verbally to you.

On Saturday, the 4th, I am to go to Frankfort, a week hence to direct, for the first time, the St. Cecilia Association. To be sure, my charming Swiss projects, and the sea-baths in Genoa, have thus melted into air; but still my being able to do a real service to Schelble and his undertaking is of no small value in my eyes. There seemed to be an idea that the St. Cecilia Association would be dispersed, and Schelble appeared very much to dread the lukewarmness of the members during his absence. As they all hoped and believed that I could prevent this by my presence, I did not for a moment hesitate, though the Frankfort musicians will be desperately astonished, and will now see what can be done within eight weeks. Hiller, whom I like so much, is by chance to be in Frankfort the whole time, which will be a great advantage for me.

It gives me peculiar pleasure to be able to write to

---

* He alludes to the Musical Festival, where " St. Paul " was performed for the first time.

38282

you that I am now fairly established in Germany, and shall not require to make a pilgrimage into foreign countries to secure my existence. This, indeed, has only been evident during the last year, and since my being placed at Leipzig; but now I have no longer any doubts on the subject, and think there is no want of modesty in rejoicing at the fact and mentioning it to you.

The manner in which I was received on my journey, in Frankfort, and afterwards here, was all that a musician could desire; and although this may mean in reality little or nothing, still it is a token of friendship which is always gratifying; and I value all such tokens, because I am well aware that I have taken no steps to call them forth. I therefore almost rejoice when you call me "the reverse of a charlatan," and when many things fall to my share unasked for, about which others give themselves a great deal of trouble; for I may then venture to believe that I deserve them. I wish only I could have written these words to my father, for he would have read them with satisfaction. But his dearest wish was progress; he always directed me to press forwards, and so I think I am doing his will when I continue to labour in this sense, and endeavour to make progress without any ulterior views beyond my own improvement. Farewell, dear Mother.—Your

FELIX.

9*

Lincoln Christian College

To Herr Advocat Conrad Schleinitz, Leipzig

Cologne, July 5th, 1836.

Dear Schleinitz,

I have in vain sought a moment of leisure, after the Musical Festival, to send you my first greeting and letter since my journey. In Düsseldorf the bustle was great, and no end to all kinds of music, *fêtes*, and recreations, which never left me quiet a moment. I have been staying a day here to revive and rest, with my old President;* and as evening is now approaching, about the time when you used to peep into my room, I feel an impulse, if only for a moment, to shake hands and say good-evening.

You would certainly have been for some time well amused and delighted with the Musical Festival; and, from your taking so friendly an interest in me and my " St. Paul," I thought, a hundred times at least, during the rehearsals, what a pity it was that you were not there. You would assuredly have been delighted by the love and good will with which the whole affair was carried on, and the marvellous fire with which the chorus and orchestra burst forth,—though there were individual passages, especially in the solos, which might have annoyed you. I think I see your face, could you have heard the St. Paul's aria sung in an indifferent, mechanical manner, and I think I hear you breaking loose on the Apostle of the Gentiles in a dressing-gown; but then I know also how charmed you would have been with the " Mache dich auf," which went

---

* Verkenius.

really splendidly. My feelings were singular; during the whole of the rehearsals and the performance I thought little enough about directing, but listened eagerly to the general effect, and whether it went right according to my idea, without thinking of anything else. When the people gave me a flourish of trumpets or applauded, it was very welcome for the moment, but then my father came back to my mind, and I strove once more to recall my thoughts to my work. Thus, during the entire performance I was almost in the position of a listener, and tried to retain an impression of the whole. Many parts caused me much pleasure, others not so; but I learnt a lesson from it all, and hope to succeed better the next time I write an oratorio.

FELIX MENDELSSOHN BARTHOLDY.

Frankfort, July 14th, 1836.

Dear Mother and dear Rebecca,

I have just received your affectionate letters, and must answer them instantly, for indeed I had been eagerly expecting them for several days past, during which I have done nothing but lie on the sofa and read Eckermann's "Conversations with Goethe," and long for letters from home which I could answer. I am as much delighted with Eckermann as you are, my dear Mother and Sister. I feel just as if I heard the old gentleman speaking again, for there are many things introduced into the work which are the very same words I have heard him use, and I know his tone and gestures by heart. I must say that Eckermann is not sufficiently independent. He is always rejoicing over " this important phrase, which pray mark well." But it must be admitted that it was a difficult position for the old man, and we ought to be grateful to him for his faithful notices, and also for his delicacy,—a contrast to Riemer.

Here I am, seated in the well-known corner room with the beautiful view, in Schelble's house, he and his wife being gone to visit his property in Swabia, and they do not return to Frankfort so long as I am here; but the accounts his wife has sent here are very consolatory, and inspire us all with much hope. There is no one living in this house but Schelble's mother-in-law, and a maid-servant, on one side,—and myself, with two travelling-bags and a hat-box, on the other. At first I was unwilling to come here, owing to many remembrances, but now I am glad that I came. A very kind reception, an excellent grand pianoforte, plenty of music, entire rest, and undisturbed tranquillity, are all things which are nowhere to be found in an inn; and I might well be envied the view from my corner window. In this splendid summer weather I see all down the Maine, with its numerous boats, rafts, and ships, the gay shore opposite, and, above all, my old favourite, the Wartthurm, facing the south, and on the other side the blue hills. I came here with plans for great industry, but for nearly a week I have done little else every forenoon but admire the prospect and sun myself. I must go on in the same way for a couple of days still,—idleness is so pleasant, and agrees with

me so well. My last days in Düsseldorf, and my first
here, were crammed so full that I could only recover
my balance by degrees. The very day of my arrival
here, I had to direct the St. Cecilia Association ; then
came my numerous acquaintances, old and new, and
the arrangements for the next few weeks. I was
obliged to take a rest after all this, or at least I said so
to myself, to palliate, and furnish a pretext for, my
love of idleness. The St. Cecilia Association went on
well, and they·were very friendly ; I however made a
speech that deserved to have been written down. We
sang some things from " Samson," and some from the
B minor Mass of Bach. There was much worth remembering in the former. The Bach went almost
faultlessly, though it is fully twice as difficult; and so
I had a fresh opportunity of admiring how Schelble, by
dint of his admirable tenacity, has succeeded in making
his will obeyed. I shall not be able to do much for
the association. Six weeks are not sufficient; and,
even under the most favourable circumstances, Schelble's physician wishes him to rest the whole of the ensuing winter. How the matter will proceed then we
know not. All the musicians here think too much
about themselves, and too little about their work; but
we shall see how this may be, and what we have now
to do is to provide for the intervening time ; and I rejoice to be able in this respect to oblige Schelble. I
must say, my life assumes a most agreeable form here.
Never could I have thought that through my overtures
and songs I could have become such a lion with the
musical world. The "Melusina" and the "Hebrides"
are as familiar to them as to us at home (I mean No. 3,

Leipziger Strasse), and the *dilettanti* dispute warmly about my intentions.

Then Hiller is here, at all times a delightful sight to me, and we have always much that is interesting to discuss together. To my mind, he is not sufficiently —what shall I call it?—one-sided. By nature he loves Bach and Beethoven beyond all others, and would therefore prefer adopting wholly the graver style of music; but then he is much delighted also with Rossini, Auber, Bellini, etc., and with this variety of tastes no man makes real progress. So this forms the subject of all our conversations as soon as we see each other, and it is most agreeable to me to be with him for some time, and, if possible, to lead him to my mode of thinking. . . . Early yesterday I went to see him, and whom should I find sitting there but Rossini, as large as life, in his best and most amiable mood? I really know few men who can be so amusing and witty as he, when he chooses; he kept us laughing incessantly the whole time. I promised that the St. Cecilia Association should sing for him the B minor Mass, and some other things of Sebastian Bach's. It will be quite too charming to see Rossini obliged to admire Sebastian Bach; he thinks, however, "different countries, different customs," and is resolved to howl with the wolves. He says he is enchanted with Germany, and when he once gets the list of wines at the Rhine Hotel in the evening, the waiter is obliged to show him his room, or he could never manage to find it. He relates the most laughable and amusing things about Paris and all the musicians there, as well as of himself and his compositions, and entertains the most profound respect for all the men of the present day,—so that you might really believe him, if you had not eyes to see his sarcastic face. Intellect, and animation, and wit, sparkle in all his features and in every word, and those who do not consider him a genius ought to hear him expatiating in this way, and they would change their opinion.

I was lately with S——, also, but it was miserable to hear him grumbling and abusing everybody. At last he vowed that all men were nothing but a tiresome pack; I answered that I considered this very modest on his part, as I concluded he did not look upon himself as an angel or a demigod, when, quite contrary to my expectations, we instantly became the best of friends, and he ended by declaring that, after all, the world pleased him very well. This is not surprising, as he was sitting in his garden in the country, with a beautiful landscape and a lovely view; and in a region like this, in such weather and under such a sky, very little fault can be found with the world. The scenery round Frankfort pleases me this time beyond everything,—such fruitfulness, richness of verdure, gardens and fields, and the beautiful blue hills as a background! and then a forest beyond; to ramble there in the evenings under the splendid beech-trees, among the innumerable herbs and flowers and blackberries and strawberries, makes the heart swell with gratitude.

Yesterday afternoon I visited André at Offenbach; he sends you his kind regards, and is the same fiery, eager person he ever was. His reception of me was, however, more cordial and more gratifying than that of all the other musicians; he really does somewhat resemble my father. Is it not singular that several

persons here have lately said to me that I am like
what André was in his younger days? and you may
remember that *he* was formerly often mistaken for *my
father*. He scanned me closely from head to foot, and
said I had now my third face since he had first known
me; the second he had not at all approved of, but now
he liked me much better. The conversation then
tnrned on counterpoint and Vogler, and he attacked
him in spite of Zelter, and dragged forth a couple of
folios as proof on his side. I could not prevail on myself to go to the Rothschilds, in spite of their very
flattering invitation. I am not in the vein or humour
at present for balls or any other festivities, and "like
should draw to like." At the same time, these people
really cause me much pleasure, and their splendour
and luxury, and the universal respect with which the
citizens here are forced to regard them all (though they
would gladly assault them if they dared), is a real
source of exultation, for it is all owing entirely to their
own industry, good fortune, and abilities. The 15th
has actually dawned; this is a regular chattering, gos-
siping letter.—Your   FELIX.

To REBECCA DIRICHLET, BERLIN.

Frankfort, July 2d, 1836.

    . . . Such is my mood now the whole day; I can
neither compose nor write letters, nor play the piano;
the utmost I can do is to sketch a little,* but I must

---

* This letter was written a short time before his betrothal.

thank you for your kind expressions about "St. Paul;"
such words from you are the best and dearest that I
can ever hear, and what you and Fanny say on the
subject the public say also; . . . no other exists for me.
I only wish you would write to me a few times more
about it, and very minutely as to my other music. The
whole time that I have been here I have worked at
"St. Paul," because I wish to publish it in as complete
a form as possible; and, moreover, I am quite convinced
that the beginning of the first and the end of the second part are now nearly three times as good as they
were, and such was my duty; for in many points, especially as to subordinate matters in so large a work, I
only succeed by degrees in realizing my thoughts and
expressing them clearly; in the principal movements
and melodies I can no longer indeed make any alteration, because they occur at once to my mind just as
they are; but I am not sufficiently advanced to say
this of *every* part. I have now, however, been working
for rather more than two years at one oratorio; this is
certainly a very long time, and I rejoice at the approach
of the moment when I shall correct the proofs, and be
done with it, and begin something else.

I must tell you of the real delight with which I
have read here the first books of Goethe's " Wahrheit
und Dichtung." I had never taken up the book since
my boyhood, because I did not like it then ; but I cannot express how much it now pleases me, and how
much additional pleasure I take in it, from knowing all
the localities. One of its pages makes me forget all
the *misères* in literature and art of the present day.

10

To Rebecca Dirichlet, Berlin.

Leipzig, January 8th, 1837.

. . . Last Wednesday there was a *fête* at the Keils', where it rained Christmas gifts and poems; among others I got one, celebrating my betrothal in a romantic vein " at Frankfort-on-the-Zeil," and which was much admired. As they began to sing songs at table, and I was looking rather dismal, Schleinitz suddenly called out to me that I ought to compose music for my romance on the spot, that they might have something new to sing, and the young ladies bringing me a pencil and music-paper, the request amused me very much, and I composed the song under shelter of my napkin; while the rest were eating cakes, I wrote out the four parts, and before the pine-apples were finished, the singers got their A note, and sang it to such perfection and so *con amore* that it caused universal delight and animated the whole society.

To Ferdinand Hiller.

Leipzig, January 10th, 1837.

. . . You once extolled my position here because I had made friends of all the German composers: quite the reverse; I am in bad odour with them all this winter. Six new symphonies are lying before me; what they may be God knows (I would rather not know); not one of them pleases me, and no one is to blame for this but myself, who allow no other composer to come before the public,—I mean in the way of symphonies. Good heavens! should not these " Capellmeisters" be ashamed of themselves and search their own breasts? But that detestable artistic pedantry, which they all possess, and that baneful spark divine of which they so often read,—these ruin everything. I sent my six preludes and fugues to the printer's to-day : I fear they will not be much played; still I should like you to look over them once in a way, and to say if any of them pleased you, or the reverse. Next month three organ fugues are to be published,—*me voilà perruque!* Heaven grant that some spirited pianoforte piece may occur to me, to efface this unpleasant impression.

To FANNY HENSEL, BERLIN.

Frankfort-a.-M., May 29th, 1837.

This is but a sorry time for musicians. Look at the St. Cecilia Association,—experienced singers, good respectable people, obliging chiefs,—nothing requisite but a little pianoforte playing, and a little good will towards music. and a little knowledge; neither genius, nor energy, nor politics, nor anything else very particular. I should have thought that fifty people at least would have offered themselves, so that we might have had a choice; but scarcely two have come forward whom it is possible to appoint, and not one who is capable of carrying on the association in the right, true, and noble spirit in which it was commenced,— that is, in plain German, not one who can perceive that

Handel and Bach, and such people, are superior to what they themselves can do or say. Neukomm, in whom I would have placed most confidence in this respect, was in treaty for the situation, and had decidedly accepted it, and now all of a sudden he as decidedly declines it. So there will be no one to undertake the affair but Ries, who will probably do so, but unfortunately he is deficient in that necessary respect for the great works of art which is, and always will be, to me, the chief consideration. It is grievous to think of all the trouble and hard work which it cost Schelble to lay a good foundation, and now the end is that it will be finally broken up. People here are highly satisfied with Hiller's mode of directing, although they were so troublesome to him at first; but two months hence he goes to Italy, being resolved not to stay here; and who knows that this may not be the very reason why they all now regret him so much ! This is an odious thing in the world.

It has just occurred to me that if you wish to sing anything during the next few months, send for " Theodora," by Handel, and look it over; at all events it will please you, as there are some splendid choruses and airs in it, and perhaps you might manage to have it translated into German (which, indeed, ought to be very much better done, for the text is perfectly absurd) and perform it in your own house, with a small choir. Unluckily, it is not adapted for a performance on a large scale; but some parts of it, the final chorus for instance, are as fine as anything you ever heard of Handel's.

To his Mother.

Frankfort, June 2d, 1837.

. . . You write to me about Fanny's new composi‑ tions, and say that I ought to persuade her to publish them. Your praise is, however, quite unnecessary to make me heartily rejoice in them, or think them charm‑ ing and admirable; for I know by whom they are written. I hope, too, I need not say that, if she does resolve to publish anything, I will do all in my power to obtain every facility for her, and to relieve her, so far as I can, from all trouble which can possibly be spared her. But to *persuade* her to publish anything I cannot, because this is contrary to my views and to my convic‑ tions. We have often formerly discussed the subject, and I still remain exactly of the same opinion. I consider the publication of a work as a serious matter (at least it ought to be so), for I maintain that no one should publish unless they are resolved to appear as an author for the rest of their life. For this purpose, however, a *succession* of works is indispensable, one after another. Nothing but annoyance is to be looked for from publishing, where one or two works alone are in question; or it becomes what is called a " manuscript for private circulation," which I also dislike; and from my knowledge of Fanny I should say she has neither ‑nclination nor vocation for authorship. She is too much all that a woman ought to be for this. She regu‑ lates her house, and neither thinks of the public nor of the musical world, nor even of music at all, until her first duties are fulfilled. Publishing would only disturb her in these, and I cannot say that I approve of it. I

10*

will not, therefore, persuade her to this step : forgive me for saying so. If she resolves to publish, either from her own impulse or to please Hensel, I am, as I said before, quite ready to assist her so far as I can ; but to encourage her in what I do not consider right, is what I cannot do.

To his Mother.

Bingen, July 13th, 1837.

Dear Mother,

We have been here for the last eight days, having suddenly left Frankfort; and, as it is nearly decided that we are to reside here for some weeks, I now write to thank you for your affectionate letters.

I feel rather provoked that Fanny should say the new pianoforte school outgrows her: this is far from being the case; she could cut down all these petty fellows with ease. They can execute a few variations and *tours de force* cleverly enough, but all this facility, and coquetting with facility, no longer succeeds in dazzling even the public. There must be soul, in order to carry others along with you; thus, though I might perhaps prefer listening to D—— for an hour than to Fanny for an hour, still at the end of a week I am so tired of him that I can no longer listen to him, whereas then I first begin to enjoy hearing the other style of playing, and that is the right style. All this is not *more* than Kalkbrenner could do in his day, and it will pass away even during our day, if there be nothing better

than mere execution; but this Fanny also has: so she
has no cause to fear any one of them all.

The view from these windows is of itself well worth
a journey here, for our hotel is situated close to the
Rhine, opposite Niederwald,—the Mäusethurm to the
left, and to the right Johannisberg. To-day I have at
last succeeded in borrowing a piano and a Bible; both
were very difficult to hunt out, first because the people
at Bingen are not musical, and secondly because they
are Catholics, and therefore ignore both a piano and
Luther's translation; however, I have at length procured both, and so I begin to feel very comfortable here.
I must now be very busy, for as yet I have not written
out a single note of my concerto, and yesterday I heard
from Birmingham that the Musical Festival is all
arranged, and they are in hopes that Queen Victoria
will be present. That would be capital!

Old Schadow and W. Schadow were here lately,
along with their families, and we stumbled upon each
other quite unexpectedly in the entrance hall. I wish
you could have heard the description the old man gave
of Fanny's accompaniment on the piano; he was full
of *enthousiasme*, and most excited on the subject. A
sketch also of the *séances* of the musical section of the
Academy where he is obliged to preside, was not bad
by way of contrast; except Spontini, no one either
speaks or shows any signs of life in it, for which there
are good reasons.

It is indeed very sad to see the way in which the
latter contrives to irritate all Berlin against him,
destroying and ruining everything and yet causing
himself only vexation and anxiety and worry,—like an

ill-assorted marriage, where both parties are in the wrong when they come to blows.

Ask Fanny, dear Mother, what she says to my intention of playing Bach's organ prelude in E flat major in Birmingham—

and the fugue at the end of the same book. I suspect it will puzzle me; and yet I think I am right. I have an idea that *this* very prelude will be peculiarly acceptable to the English, and you can play both prelude and fugue *piano* and *pianissimo*, and also bring out the full power of the organ. Faith! I can tell you it is no stupid composition.

I have lately determined to have a new oratorio ready for the next Düsseldorf Musical Festival; two years are yet to come before then, but I must stick to my work. I will write about the text as soon as I have decided on the subject. I hear nothing of Holtei and his opera libretto, and so I must begin a second oratorio, much as I should have liked to write an opera just at this moment. I sadly want a true thorough-going man for many fine projects; whether he will appear, or whether I am mistaken, I know not, but hitherto I have never been able to discover him.

I occupy myself continually here in drawing figures, but I don't succeed very well. From want of practice this winter, I have forgotten what I knew much better last summer, when Schadow gave me every day a short drawing-lesson at Scheveling, and taught me to sketch peasants, soldiers, old apple-women, and street boys. Yesterday, however, I made a drawing of Bishop Hatto, at the moment of being eaten up by the mice,—a splendid subject for all beginners. In this letter, music, the Rheingau, and gossip go hand-in-hand. Forgive this, dear Mother. It is the same in real life.

To Pastor Julius Schubring, Dessau.

Bingen-a.-R., July 14th, 1837.

Dear Schubring,

I wish to ask your advice in a matter which is of importance to me, and I feel it will therefore not be indifferent to you either, having received so many proofs to the contrary from you. It concerns the selection of a subject of an oratorio, which I intend to begin next winter. I am most anxious to have your counsels, as the best suggestions and contributions for the text of my " St. Paul" came from you.

Many very apparent reasons are in favour of choosing St. Peter as the subject,—I mean its being intended for the Düsseldorf Musical Festival at Whitsuntide, and the prominent position the feast of Whitsunday would occupy in this subject. In addition to these grounds, I may add my wish (in connection with a greater plan for a later oratorio) to bring the two chief apostles and pillars of the Christian Church side by side in oratorios, —in short, that I should have a " St. Peter" as well as a " St. Paul." I need not tell you that there are sufficient internal grounds to make me prize the subject,

and far above all else stands the outpouring of the
Holy Ghost, which must form the central point, or
chief object. The question therefore is (and this you
can decide far better than I can, because you possess
the knowledge in which I am deficient, to guide you)
whether the place that Peter assumes *in the Bible*,
divested of the dignity which he enjoys in the Catholic
or Protestant Churches, as a martyr, or the first Pope,
etc. etc.,—whether *what is said of him in the Bible* is
alone and in itself sufficiently important to form the
basis of a *symbolical* oratorio. For, according to my
feeling, the subject must not be treated historically,
however indispensable this was in the case of "St.
Paul." In historic handling, Christ must appear in the
earlier part of St. Peter's career, and, where He appears,
St. Peter could not lay claim to the chief interest. I
think, therefore, it must be symbolical; though all the
historical points might probably be introduced,—the
betrayal and repentance, the keys of heaven given him
by Christ, his preaching at Pentecost—not in an historical, but prophetic light, if I may so express myself, in
close connection.

My question then is, whether you think this possible,
or at least so far possible, that it may become an important and personal object for every member of the
community?—also, whether it is your opinion, that, even
if actually feasible, it should be carried out entirely by
means of Scriptural passages, and what particular parts
of the Bible you would especially recommend for the
purpose? Lastly, if in this event you will hereafter, as
you previously did, make a selection of certain passages
out of the Bible, and send them to me?

The chief thing, however, is the first point, for I am still in the dark about it; in fact, about the possibility of the whole undertaking: write to me as soon as you can on the subject. In thinking it over, my first idea was that the subject must be divided into two parts: the first, from the moment of forsaking the fishermen's nets down to the "Tu es Petrus," with which it must close: the second to consist of the Feast of Pentecost only; from the misery after the death of Christ and repentance of Peter, to the outpouring of the Holy Ghost.*

Forgive me for assailing you so suddenly with all this. During the few months since we have met, I cannot tell you what a great and happy change has taken place in me.† I hope you will come and stay with us next winter, and pass some days here; then you will in a short time see for yourself, what even at any length I really could not describe. I intend to be in Leipzig again, the end of September, and till then shall remain principally here on the Rhine, or at Frankfort. Pray answer me soon, if only by a few lines.—
Your   F. M. B.

---

* This project was never fulfilled, but the letter is inserted, as it proves the deep earnestness with which Mendelssohn treated such subjects.

† Mendelssohn's marriage.

To his Mother.

Leipzig, October 4th, 1837.

Dearest Mother,

It ought to have been my first occupation to write to you as soon after the busy time of the last few weeks as I had some leisure, to thank you for so many loving letters. I wished also to let you know of our safe arrival here, and yet two days have elapsed without the possibility of doing so. I seize the early morning for this purpose, or people will again come, one succeeding another till the post hour is passed, which happened yesterday and the day before. I cannot at this time attempt to describe the Birmingham Musical Festival; it would require many sheets to do so, and whole evenings when we are once more together even cursorily to mention all the remarkable things crowded into those days.* One thing, however, I must tell you, because I know it will give you pleasure, which is, that I never had such brilliant success, and can never have any more unequivocal than at this festival. The applause and shouts at the least glimpse of me were incessant, and sometimes really made me laugh; for instance, they prevented my being able for long to sit down to the instrument to play a pianoforte concerto; and what is better than all this applause, and a sure proof of my success, were the offers made to me on all sides, and of a very different tenor this time from what they ever were before.

---

* "St. Paul" was performed for the first time in England at this Festival.

I may well say that I now see, beyond doubt, that all this is only bestowed on me because in the course of my work I do not in the least concern myself as to what people wish and praise and pay for, but solely as to what I consider good, so I shall now less than ever allow myself to be turned aside from my own path. I therefore peculiarly rejoice in my success, and I feel more confident than ever, that not the smallest effort shall be made by me to insure success, nor indeed ever has been made. I had besides a very striking proof of the value of all such things, in the manner in which Neukomm was on this occasion received in Birmingham. You know how highly they honoured and really overvalued him formerly, and how much all his works were prized and sought after here, so that the musicians used to call him the king of *Brummagem ;** whereas on this occasion they neglected him shamefully, giving only one short composition of his the first morning (the worst of all), and the public receiving him without the slightest attention; this is really disgraceful in those men who, three years ago, knew nothing better or higher than Neukomm's music. The only thing he can be reproached with is, that three years since he wrote an oratorio for the Musical Festival, where effect was chiefly studied. The huge organ, the choruses, the solo instruments, all were introduced on purpose to please the audience, and people soon find this out, and it never answers; but that they should treat him with such ingratitude in return, is a fresh proof of how little their favour is to be

* A provincial mode of pronouncing " Birmingham."

11

relied on, and what the fruits of it are when sought after.

I found him, as usual, most amiable, and as kind as ever, and may well take example from him in a hundred things. I never met with any one who combined greater integrity, with calmness and refinement, and he is indeed a steady, true friend.

I send you a complete *programme* of the Musical Festival. Imagine such a mass of music! and, besides this prodigious pile, the various acquaintances who came flocking thither at that time; a man must be as cold-blooded as a fish to stand all this. Immediately after I had played the last chord on the splendid organ, I hurried off to the Liverpool mail, and travelled six days and five nights in succession, till I arrived in Frankfort to rejoin my family. The mail goes to London in ten hours and a half, exactly the same distance as between this and Berlin; I calculated that on my journey, and envied the English on this account. I arrived in London towards midnight, where I was received by Klingemann, and we went together to the Committee of the Sacred Harmonic Society, who formally presented to me a large solid silver box, with an inscription. At half-past twelve o'clock I was again in the mail, and at Dover next morning at nine, when there was no time even for breakfast, as I was obliged to go off directly to the small boat which conveyed us to the steamboat, for being low water it could not remain in the harbour, so I was already sea-sick when I reached the ship, had a miserable passage, and, instead of arriving at Calais in three hours, we were five hours before landing at Boulogne, and just so much further from Frankfort. I went to the Hôtel Meurice, where I made myself as comfortable as I could, and set off at nine at night in the diligence to Lille. This is the moment (however furious Dirichlet may be) to impress on you that French and Belgian diligences, with their glass windows, on a paved *chaussée*, with their three clumsy horses in front, whose tails are tied up, and who do not go forwards but slowly creep, are the most utterly detestable means of being expedited in the whole world, and that a German *Schnell-post* is a hundred times pleasanter, quicker, and better than these utterly detestable, etc., *vide supra*. The September days were being celebrated all over Belgium, and trees of liberty erected in the squares in front of the town-halls. I arrived at Cologne at ten o'clock in the morning ; a steamboat was to sail at eleven, and to go on through the night, so I took my place in it, rejoicing to be able to lie down full length on this the fifth night, and free from the rattle of the pavement. I fell asleep about nine, and did not wake till two in the morning, when I perceived that the steamboat was not moving, and in answer to my questions I was told that the fog was so thick (as on the previous day) that it would be impossible to set off again at all events before six o'clock the same evening, and we should not arrive in Mayence till six at night. The steamer was lying-to quite close to Horchheim, so I hired two sailors to go with me to carry my things ; I showed them the old familiar footpath by the side of the Rhine, got to Co-blenz at three o'clock in the morning, took post-horses, and was at Frankfort on Wednesday afternoon at half past three o'clock. I found them all well, and we have since made out our journey famously, from Thursday afternoon till Sunday at two o'clock, when we arrived here.

The first subscription concert began at six o'clock the same evening. I directed the "Jubilee" overture and the C minor symphony, but the trombones and drums were so noisy that at the end of the concert I own I felt rather *caput*. These were fourteen of the most crowded days any one could imagine; but, as I lived so entirely for enjoyment and pleasure the whole of last summer, I am glad, just before my return here, to have had such a busy time, and one so important for my vocation. It is quite too lovely here, and every hour of my new domestic life is like a festival; whereas in England, notwithstanding all its honours and pleasures, I had not one single moment of real heartfelt enjoyment; but now every day brings only a succession of joy and happiness, and I once more know what it is to prize life. Have I not entered into as many minute details about myself as if I were some sickly potentate, dear Mother?—Your

FELIX.

To PAUL MENDELSSOHN BARTHOLDY.

Leipzig, October 29th, 1837.

Dear Brother,

First of all, my most cordial congratulations on the day when this letter will reach you; may you pass it happily, and may it prove a good harbinger of the coming year. You mention in your letter of yesterday,

that your quiet, settled, and untroubled position sometimes makes you almost anxious and uneasy; but I
cannot think you right in this feeling; as little as if
you were to complain of the very opposite extreme.
Why should it not be sufficient for a man to know how
to secure and to enjoy his happiness? I cannot believe that it is at all indispensable first to earn it by
trials or misfortunes; in my opinion, heartfelt grateful
acknowledgment is the best Polycrates' ring; and
truly in these days it is a difficult problem to acknowledge and to enjoy good fortune, and other blessings,
in such a manner as to share them with others, thus
rendering them cheerful and glad also, and showing,
too, that the difference is equally great between this
and idle arrogance. It is singular that in my position
I might complain of the very reverse of what troubles
you; the more I find what are termed encouragement
and recognition in my vocation, the more restless and
unsettled does it become in my hands, and I cannot
deny that I often long for that rest of which you complain. So few traces remain of performances and musical festivals, and all that is personal; the people indeed shout and applaud, but that quickly passes away,
without leaving a vestige behind, and yet it absorbs as
much of one's life and strength as *better* things, or perhaps even more; and the evil of this is, that it is impracticable to come half out, when you are once in;
you must either go on the whole way, or not at all. I
dare not even attempt to withdraw, or the cause which
I have undertaken will suffer, and yet I would gladly
see that it was not merely *my* cause, but considered a
good and universal one. But this is the very point

11*

where people are wanting to pursue the same path,—
not an approving public (for that is a matter of indifference), but fellow-workers (and they are indispensable).
So in *this* sense I long for a less busy life, in order to
be able to devote myself to my peculiar province, composition of music, and to leave the execution of it to
others. It seems, however, that this is not to be ; and
I should be ungrateful were I dissatisfied with my life
as it is.

Fanny will probably give you to-morrow the parts
of my new quartett from me. Whether it will please
you or not is uncertain ; but think of me when you
play it and come to any passage which is peculiarly in
my style. How gladly would I have given you something better and prettier in honour of your birthday !
but I did not know what to send.

Yesterday evening my C minor quartett was played
in public by David, and had great success. They were
made to play the scherzo twice, and the adagio pleased
the audience best of all, which caused me very great
astonishment. In a few days I mean to begin a new
quartett, which may please me better. I also intend
soon to compose a sonata for violoncello and piano for
you,—by my beard, I will !

And now farewell : till our happy, happy meeting in
February.—Your

FELIX.

To Ferdinand Hiller, Milan.

Leipzig, December 10th, 1837.

My dear Ferdinand,

You have written to me in spite of my want of punctuality last month, for which I am heartily grateful, though I really could scarcely have hoped it. The arrangement of a new house, taking possession of it, the numerous concerts and affairs, in short, all the various hindrances, of whatever nature, that a steady-going civilian like myself can venture to enumerate to a joyous, lively Italian like you,—my installation as master and tenant of the mansion, music director of the subscription concerts,—all these things prevented my being a punctual correspondent last month. But for that very reason I wished to entreat of you, and now do so right heartily, even amid the vast difference in our position, and the objects that surround us, let us steadily adhere to our promise to write monthly letters. I think it would be a source of great interest and benefit to both, to hear from each other now, when we must mutually appear so desperately outlandish,— though for this very reason nearer than ever. I at least, when I think of Milan, and Liszt, and Rossini, have a singular feeling in knowing that you are in the midst of them all; and probably you feel the same, when, in the plains of Lombardy, you think of Leipzig and of me. But next time you must really write me a long minute letter, full of details; you do not know how much they interest me; you must tell me where you are living, and what you are writing, and all about Liszt, and Pixis, and Rossini; about the white Duomo and the Corso. I do dearly love that bright land, and when you write to me from thence I love it more than ever. You are not to halve your sheet of paper. Above all, tell me if you amuse yourself there as thoroughly and divinely as I did. Do so, I beg, and inhale the air with the same delight, and idle away your days as deliberately as I did. But why say all this? you are sure to do so at all events. But pray do write me about it at full length. Do you wish to know whether I like this as much as ever? When I am living as a married man in a pretty, new, comfortable house, with a fine view over gardens and fields, and the towers of the city, and feel so comfortable and happy, so glad and so peaceful, as I have never done since I quitted the parental roof; when, in addition to this, I have good means, and good will on every side, I ask you how I can be otherwise than happy? If I am to hold any situation, this is the best; but there are many days when I think that to have no fixed situation would be best, after all. Directing so perpetually during two such months, takes more out of me than the two years when I was composing all day long. I can scarcely ever compose here in winter, and when I ask myself, after the greatest excitement, what has really occurred, it is in fact scarcely worth naming; at least it does not interest me much whether the acknowledged good works are given a degree oftener, or a degree better, or not. The only things that interest me are new compositions, and of these there is a great lack; often therefore I feel as if I should like to retire altogether, and not conduct any longer, but only write; and yet such a regular musical life, and the duty of directing it, has a certain charm too. What care you for this in Milan? and still I must write it if you wish to know how I like my position here. I felt just the same in Birmingham; I never made such a decided effect with my music as there, and never saw the public so much or so exclusively occupied with myself individually, and yet there is even in this something—what shall I call it?—fleeting and evanescent, which I find irksome and depressing, rather than cheering. Would that there had not been an instance of the exact reverse of all these enthusiastic praises, with regard to Neukomm, whom they on this occasion criticized so disdainfully, and received with as much coldness and neglect, in fact set aside as completely, as three years ago they extolled him to the skies, when they placed him above all other composers and applauded him at every step. Of what value, then, is their favour? You will, no doubt, say that Neukomm's music is not worth much,— there we quite agree; but those who were formerly enchanted with it, and now give themselves such airs, don't know this. The whole thing made me feel most indignant, while Neukomm's calm and perfectly indifferent demeanour appeared to me the more admirable and dignified, when contrasted with the others, and I like him better than ever since this manly conduct.

To Edouard Franck, Breslau.

(Now Director of the Berne Conservatorium.)

Leipzig, January 8th, 1838.

I did not receive your letter of the 25th of October till two days ago, and at the same time a splendid copy of your " Études." I was afraid you had given up the completion of the work, as it was so long since I had heard anything of it; I was therefore the more agreeably surprised by its arrival. You wish me to give you an opinion about the compositions themselves; but you are well aware how superfluous I consider all such criticisms, whether of my own or of others; to go on working I consider the best and only thing to do, and when friends urge this after every fresh work, their doing so in itself contains a kind of verdict. I believe that no man ever yet succeeded in controlling and commanding the minds of others by *one* work; a succession of works all aiming at one point can alone do it. Such then is your function, and the duty which God has imposed on you by the talents he has given you. Fulfil it, then; I believe that the happiness of life lies entirely on this, and cannot be attained without it, and the omission would be a very great sin.

Thus the wish that you may go forward on your path, and pursue your labours, is the sole criticism I have at present to send you of your work.

We have already discussed most of the details; there are no faults, and you are master of your tools; but continue to use them more and more, as I have already said.

No doubt, you can almost imagine you hear me say-ing all this, and at last I shall appear to you in the light of a *basso ostinato*, who is perpetually growling, and ends by being tiresome beyond measure; for in-stead of expressing my thanks, I begin the old song all over again, but still I am not deficient in gratitude either, and I wish to tell you so again and again in my very best manner. Write to me soon and at length (or rather by music, which says all things); you know what sincere pleasure every letter of yours causes me. Farewell, and once more accept my thanks for the gratification you have bestowed on me, and doubtless on many others, by your first work.—I am, with esteem, yours,

FELIX MENDELSSOHN BARTHOLDY.

TO THE HON. COMMITTEE OF THIS YEAR'S LOWER RHINE
MUSICAL FESTIVAL.

Leipzig, January 18th, 1838.

I am deeply grateful for the invitation contained in your letter of the 8th of January. Your kind remem-brance is not less prized by me than the prospect of again attending such a pleasant festival, and deriving from it as much enjoyment as that for which I have al-ready to thank the Rhenish Musical Festivals. I there-fore accept your invitation with sincere delight, if God grants health to me and mine, and if we can mutually agree on the selection of the music to the full satisfac-tion of both parties. The more successful the previous

Cologne festival was with regard to the arrangement of
the pieces performed, especially in Handel's work with
the organ, the more important it seems to me to have
at least *one* piece in the programme by which this
year's festival may be distinguished from others, and
by means of which progress may, as far as possible, be
manifested. For this purpose I consider it absolutely
necessary to have the name of Sebastian Bach in the
programme, if only for one short piece; for it is certainly high time that at these festivals, on which the
name of Handel has shed such lustre, another immortal
master, who is in no one point inferior to any master,
and in many points superior to all, should no longer be
forgotten. The same scruples which exist in opposition to this must also have existed in former years with
regard to the works of Handel, and you are all grateful
to those who, disregarding these obstacles, revealed to
you such treasures of sublimity and elevation. Earn
for yourself, then, similar thanks from the Rhenish
friends of music by making a beginning which is indeed difficult (for this I do not deny) and must be pro-
ceeded with cautiously, but which will certainly be
attended with the best results and universally imitated
by others. When anything of Bach's has been once
performed, it will be easy to discover that it is beautiful, and to perform it again; but the difficulty is the
beginning. The proposal that I wish to make to you
on this subject is, to introduce into this Musical Festival a short Psalm of Bach's (about twenty minutes or
half an hour in length), and if you are afraid of doing
this on the second day, from the dread of scaring away
the public, whom this learned name might alarm, then

do so on the first day, and give in · addition a rather shorter oratorio of Handel's. It is pretty certain that no fewer people will come to hear Handel, for those who do not fear the one will be equally disposed to like the other, and there are still three or four totally unknown and truly admirable oratorios of his, which would not occupy more than an hour and a half, or scarcely two hours at most, and would be a welcome novelty to all lovers of music. I became first acquainted with these works by the splendid gift of the previous committee,* and I shall be very glad if you can derive any benefit from these volumes for this year's festival. With regard to the second day, I may first inquire whether you intend to apply to Cherubini for his grand " Requiem;" it must be translated, and is entirely for men's voices, but as it will only last an hour, or even less, that would not much matter, and according to the universal verdict it is a splendid work. At present, however, the chief object seems to me to be the first point in this letter, and I therefore beg you will arrange about it as soon as possible.

To Rebecca Dirichlet.

Leipzig, February, 1838.

. . . In our concerts we are playing a great deal of what is called historical music, so in the last but one we had the whole of Bach's *suite* in D major, some of

---

* See Letter of October 6th, 1835.

Hande. and Gluck, etc. etc., and a violin concerto of Viotti's; in the last of all, Haydn, Righini, Naumann, etc.; and in conclusion Haydn's "Farewell Symphony," in which, to the great delight of the public, the musicians literally blew out their lights, and went away in succession till the violinists at the first desk alone remained, and finished in F sharp major. It is a curious, melancholy little piece. We previously played Haydn's trio in C major, when all the people were filled with amazement that anything so beautiful should exist; and yet it was very long ago published by Breitkopf and Härtel. The next time we have Mozart, whose C minor concerto I am to play, and we are also to have a quartett of his for the first time from his unfinished opera, "Zaïde." Then comes Beethoven, and two concerts remain for every possible kind of modern composition, to make up the full number of twenty.

Yesterday evening we thought much of you. At a late hour, when I had finished writing, I read aloud "Nausikaa" to Cécile, in Voss's translation, repeating to her at the end of every ten verses the profound philological remarks which you made when we used to read it together during our Greek lesson, and which now recurred to me in hundreds. Moreover, this poem is really irresistible when it becomes sentimental. I always felt an inclination to set it to music, of course not for the theatre, only as an epic, and this whole day I feel renewed pleasure in the idea; but is anything at this moment to be done with German poets? Last week four opera *libretti* were sent to me, each one more ridiculous than the other; the only result is to make enemies for myself. I therefore write instrumental music, and long for the unknown poet, who perhaps lives close to me or at Timbuctoo,—who knows? . . .

To his Family.

Leipzig, April 2d, 1838.

. . . This evening Madame Botgorscheck's concert takes place,—an excellent contralto singer, who persecuted me so much to play, that I agreed to do so, and it did not occur to me till afterwards that I had nothing either short or suitable to play, so I resolved to compose a rondo, not one single note of which was written the day before yesterday, but which I am to perform this evening with the whole orchestra, and rehearsed this morning.* It sounds very gay ; but how I shall play it the gods alone know,—indeed hardly they, for in one passage I have marked a pause of fifteen bars in the accompaniment, and have not as yet the most remote idea what I am to introduce during this time. Any one, however, who plays thus *en gros* as I do, can get through a good deal. . . .

To A. Simrock, Bonn.

Berlin. July 10th, 1838.

In recommencing our correspondence, I must first of all thank you for the great friendliness you showed

---

* It appeared afterwards under the title of "Serenade and Allegro Giojoso," Op. 43.

towards me in Cologne. It is the first time that any
publisher ever assured me of his satisfaction at the
success of my compositions; this occurrence would in
itself have been a source of lively gratification to me,
but it is much enhanced by the kind and flattering
manner in which you manifest your satisfaction, and
for which I shall ever feel indebted to you. From the
time of your first letter about "St. Paul," in which you
expressed a wish to have it for your house, when I had
not yet thought of publication at all, much less of success,—also during the period of its being printed, with
its manifold alterations and interpolations, up to the present moment,—you have been cordial and complaisant
towards me to a degree which, as I already said, I never
before met with, and for which I cordially thank you.

Would it not be well worth while for any publisher
in Germany to publish just now some of Handel's
principal oratorios from the *original* scores ? This ought
to be done by subscription, which would, I think, be
successful, as not one of these scores exists with us. I
thought of composing the organ parts for this purpose;
they must, however, appear in small notes in the score,
or in notes of another colour, so that, first, those who
wished it could have Handel pure; second, my organ
parts in addition if required, and where there was an
organ; and third, in a *supplement*, the organ part
arranged for clarionets, bassoons, and other wind instruments of the modern orchestra, when no organ can be
had. Such a score would be useful to all institutes for
oratorio music, and we should at last have the true
Handel in Germany, not one first dipped in the waters
of the Moselle and thoroughly diluted. I was assured in

England that a very considerable number of subscribers
to such a score might be procured there. What do you
think of this? You have published the pianoforte edi-
tions of these oratorios,—perhaps a selection might be
made from some of them. Of course I am anxious to
have your really candid and sincere opinion of this proposal, which I only mention to you because it has often
suggested itself to me, and recurs to me at this moment.
—I am, with sincere esteem, your obedient

FELIX MENDELSSOHN BARTHOLDY.

To FERDINAND HILLER.

Berlin, July 18th, 1838.

. . The whole condition of music here is connected
with the sand, with the situation, and with official life,
so that, however much the events taking place in the
musical world may please you, you can never really
love them. Gluck's operas are indeed most charming.
Is it not remarkable that they always attract a full
house, and that the public applaud, and are amused, and
shout? And that this should be the only place in the
world where such a thing seems possible? And that
on the next evening the "Postillon" should draw an
equally crowded house? And that in Bavaria it is
forbidden to have music in any church, either Catholic
or Protestant, because it is supposed to desecrate them?
And that chorales seem to have become indispensable
in the theatre? The chief thing, however, is to have
novelty, and plenty of good and fine compositions in the

12*

world; thence it is that I am so eagerly expecting your overture and your opera.

You probably heard that I was at Cologne during the Musical Festival: all went off well. The organ had a fine effect with Handel, and still more so with Sebastian Bach (in a newly-discovered composition of his, which you have not yet seen, with a stately double chorus); but even there, to my mind at least, new and untried works were wanting to excite interest; I should like so much to have something doubtful, to furnish both the public and myself with an opportunity of giving an opinion. We all know beforehand what we are to think of Beethoven, Bach, and Handel. This ought to be so, but let us have other things besides. You are quite right in saying that it is better in Italy, where the people insist every year on having new music, and every year a fresh criticism,—if only the music, and likewise the criticisms, were a shade better! I hear you growl and say, what is better? Well, then, more according to my taste, if you will. To be sure, my taste is peculiar, such a possibility sometimes suggests itself to me; but I must make use of it as it is, in which case I can contrive to swallow as little as the stork out of the flat dish. . . .

To CONCERTMEISTER FERDINAND DAVID, LEIPZIG.

Berlin, July 30th, 1838.

Dear David,

Many thanks for your letter, which gave me great pleasure. Since I came here I have been constantly thinking how really delightful it is that we are to meet and live together, instead of your being in one place and I in another, following our avocations without hearing much of each other, which is, no doubt, the case with many good fellows in our dear yet rather aggravating Fatherland; but, on reflecting further, I discovered that there are not many musicians who, like yourself, pursue steadily the broad straight road in art, or in whose active course I could feel the same intense delight that I do in yours. Such things are seldom said in conversation: therefore let me write, to-day, how much your rapid and welcome development during the last few years has surprised and rejoiced me : ·it is often grievous to me to see so many with the noblest aspirations but inferior talents, and others with great talents yet low tendencies; so that to see true genius combined with right good will is doubly cheering. People of the former class swarm here; almost all of the young musicians who visit me may, with few exceptions, be included in that number. They praise and prize Gluck and Handel, and all that is good, and talk about them perpetually, and yet what they do is an utter failure, and so very tedious. Of the second class there are examples everywhere. As I said, therefore, the very thought of your character rejoices me, and may Heaven permit us to succeed more and more in candidly expressing our wishes and our inmost thoughts, and in holding fast all that is dear and sacred in art, so that it shall not perish ! . . .

No doubt you are preparing many new things for next winter, and I rejoice heartily in the idea of hearing them. I have just finished my third quartett in D major, and like it much. May it only please you as well !—I almost think it will, for it is more spirited, and seems to me likely to be more grateful to the players than the others. I intend in a few days to begin to write out my symphony, and to complete it in a short time, probably while I am still here. I should also like to write a violin concerto for you next winter. One in E minor runs in my head, the beginning of which gives me no peace. My symphony shall certainly be as good as I can make it, but whether it will be popular and played on the barrel-organs, I cannot tell. I feel that in every fresh piece I succeed better in learning to write exactly what is in my heart, and, after all, that is the only right rule I know. If I am not adapted for popularity, I will not try to acquire it, nor seek after it; and if you think this wrong, then I ought rather to say I *cannot* seek after it, for really I *cannot*, but would not if I could. What proceeds from within, makes me glad in its outward workings also, and therefore it would be very gratifying to me were I able to fulfil the wish you and my friends express; but I can do nothing towards it or about it. So much in my path has fallen to my share without my having even once thought of it, and without any effort on my part, that perhaps it may be the case with this also; if not, I shall not grumble on the subject, but console myself by knowing that I did what I could, according to my best powers and my best judgment. I have *your* sympathy, and *your* delight in my works, and also that of some valued friends. More could scarcely be desired. A thousand thanks, then, for your kind expressions and for all your friendship towards me.—Your

FELIX M. B.

TO HERR ADVOCAT CONRAD SCHLEINITZ, LEIPZIG.

Berlin, August 1st, 1838.

Dear Schleinitz,

. . . What you write me about your increased business rejoices me much. You know how often we have talked over the subject, but I cannot share your sentiment, that any one profession is preferable to another. I always think that whatever an intelligent man gives his heart to, and really understands, must become a noble vocation; and I only personally dislike those in whom there is nothing personal, and in whom all individuality disappears; as, for example, the military profession in peace, of which we have instances here. But with regard to the others it is more or less untrue. When one profession is compared with another, the one is usually taken in its naked reality, and the other in the most beautiful ideality, and then the decision is quickly made. How easy it is for an artist to feel such reality in his sphere, and yet esteem *practical* men happy who have studied and known the different relations of men towards each other, and who help others to

live by their own life and progress, and at once see the
fruits of all that is tangible, useful, and benevolent in-
stituted by them! In one respect, too, an upright man
has the hardest stand to make, in knowing that the
public are more attracted by outward show than by
truth. But individual failures and strife must not be
allowed to have their growth in the heart: there must
be something to occupy and to elevate it far above
these isolated external things. This speaks strongly in
favour of my opinion, for it is the best part of every
calling, and common to all,—to yours, to mine, and to
every other. Where is it that you find beauty when I
am working at a quartett or a symphony? Merely in
that portion of myself that I transfer to it, or can succeed in expressing; and you can do this in as full a
measure as any man, in your defence of a culprit, or in
a case of libel, or in any one thing that entirely en-
grosses you, and that is the great point. If you can
only give utterance to your most inmost thoughts, and
if these inmost thoughts become more and more worthy of being expressed, . . . all the rest is indifferent.
I thank you, therefore, for the report you give me of
your occupations, and hope you will often send me
equally good tidings.—Your

FELIX MENDELSSOHN BARTHOLDY.

To I. Moscheles, London.

Leipzig, October 28th, 1838.

My dear Friend,

A thousand thanks for your continued friendship towards me, and also for occasionally assuring me of it; a letter from you cheers me for a long time to come, and what you write of yourself and others is always so fertile, and as much yourself as if I heard you speaking, and were agreeing with you and rejoicing in doing so. If I were a little more mild, and a little more just, and a little more judicious, and a good many other things a little more, perhaps I too might then have a judgment equal to yours; but I am so soon irritated, and become unreasonable, whereas you love what is good, and yet what is bad appears to you worth amendment.

On the occasion of Clara Novello's concert, a vast amount of rivalry and bad artistic feeling was brought to the light of day, which I neither wish to exist by day, nor by night, nor indeed in the world at all. In fact, when really *good* musicians condescend to depreciate each other, and to be malicious, and to sting in secret, I would sooner renounce music altogether, or rather, I should say, musicians; it is such petty, tinkering work, and yet it seems to be the fashion! formerly I thought it was so only with bunglers, but I see it is the same with all. A straightforward character alone is a protection against such an example, and a straightforward fellow, who despises it. Yet this serves to endear goodness to us still more, and we rejoice doubly in the contrast, and in good art, and in good artists, and in letters from you; and thus the world is by no means so bad, after all.

———————

To Pastor Julius Schubring, Dessau.

Leipzig, November 2d, 1838.

Dear Schubring,

Many, many thanks for your letter, which I received the day before yesterday, and for the parcel, which came to-day. You have again rendered me an essential service, and I feel most grateful to you; how can you ask whether I wish you to proceed in the same way? When all is so well put together, I have almost nothing to do but to write music for the words. I ought to have previously told you that the sheets you took away with you are by no means to be regarded as containing a mature design, but as a mere combination of the materials I had before me for the purpose of eventually forming a plan. So the passage of the widow, and also of the raven, being left out, is decidedly most advisable, and also the whole commencement being abridged, in order that the main points may be dwelt on to one's heart's content. I would urgently entreat you to proceed with your work, so far as your time and leisure will permit, and soon to send me the continuation of the first part, from where you left off, and which must now be of considerable length. Rest assured that, as I already told you, you will earn my most sincere gratitude.

You say that at first you could not make anything

of the subject, but that a sudden light dawned on you. I figured to myself Elijah as a grand, mighty prophet, such as we might again require in our own day,— energetic and zealous, but also stern, wrathful, and gloomy; a striking contrast to the Court myrmidons and popular rabble,—in fact, in opposition to the whole world, and yet borne on angels' wings. Is this the inference you drew from the subject, and this the sense in which you conceived an affection for it? I am anxious to do justice to the *dramatic* element, and, as you say, no epic narrative must be introduced. I am glad to learn that you are searching out the real sense of the Scriptural words, which cannot fail to touch every heart; but, if I might make one observation, it is that I would fain see the Dramatic Element more prominent, as well as more exuberant and defined,—appeal and rejoinder, question and answer, sudden interruptions, etc. etc. Not that it disturbs me, for example, Elijah first speaking of the assembling of the people, and then forthwith addressing them. All such liberties are the natural privileges of such a representation in an oratorio; but I should like the representation itself to be as spirited as possible; for instance, it annoys me that Elijah does not reply to Ahab's words, No. 16 till No. 18,— various other speeches and a chorus intervening. I should like to have had an instant and eager rejoinder, etc. etc.

But we shall no doubt presently agree on such points, and I would only entreat you, when you resume your work, to think of this wish of mine. Above all, accept my thanks for your kindness, and write to me soon on the same subject.—Ever your

FELIX M. B.

13

To his Family.

Leipzig, November 5th, 1838.

I have felt unequal to resume the train of my musical compositions since the measles. You cannot conceive the chaos that accumulates round me, when I am obliged neither to write, nor to go out, for three weeks. At last here I am, correcting the parts of my three violin quartetts which are to appear this winter; but I never can contrive to complete them, owing to so many letters, and affairs, and other *odiosa*. The Shaws are here, who don't know one word of German, and not many words of French, and yet they live with thorough, downright Leipzigers, who only speak their Leipzig vernacular; and Bennett, with two young English musicians, and six new symphonies, and letters, and passing strangers, and rehearsals, and Heaven knows what all the other things are, which swallow up the day, leaving no more trace than if it had never existed. Truly the most delightful of all things is to be enabled to store up precious and enduring memorials of past days, to tell that these days were; and the most hateful of all things is, when time passes on, and we pass with it, and yet grasp nothing.

I am reading Lessing just now frequently, with true enjoyment and gratitude. At the end of the most fatiguing day, this famous fellow makes me feel quite fresh again; though Germany fares rather badly when you read his letters to his grandfather, or to Nicolai, Gleim, and Eckert; and yet Lessing wrote in German, and in such German, too, that it cannot be well translated!

To Professor Schirmer, Düsseldorf.

(Now Director of the Carlsruhe Academy.)

Berlin, November 21st, 1838.

So I am said to be a saint! If this is intended to convey what I conceive to be the meaning of the word, and what your expressions lead me to think you also understand by it, then I can only say that, alas! I am not so, though every day of my life I strive with greater earnestness, according to my ability, more and more to resemble this character. I know indeed that I can never hope to be altogether a saint, but if I ever approach to one, it will be well. If people, however, understand by the word "saint" a Pietist, one of those who lay their hands on their laps and expect that Providence will do their work for them, and who, instead of striving in their vocation to press on towards perfection, talk of a heavenly calling being incompatible with an earthly one, and are incapable of loving with their whole hearts any human being, or anything on earth,—then God be praised! such a one I am not, and hope never to become, so long as I live; and though I am sincerely desirous to live piously, and really to be so, I hope this does not necessarily entail the other character. It is singular that people should select precisely *this* time to say such a thing, when I am in the enjoyment of so much happiness, both through my inner and outer life, and my new domestic ties, as well as busy work, that I really never know how sufficiently to show my thankfulness. And, as you wish me to follow the path which leads to rest and peace, believe

me, I never expected to live in the rest and peace
which have now fallen to my lot. I offer you a thousand
thanks for your good wishes, and beg you not to be
uneasy on either of these points.

It is pleasant to learn what you write to me of yourself and your works, and that you also are persuaded
that what people usually call honour and fame are but
doubtful advantages, while another species of honour,
of a more elevated and spiritual nature, is as essential
as it is rare. The truth of this is best seen in the case
of those who possess all possible worldly distinctions,
without deriving from them one moment of real
pleasure, but only causing them the more greedily to
crave after them; and this fact was first made quite
evident to me in Paris. I rejoice that you are not one
of those who speak in a contemptuous strain of French
painters, for I have always received great pleasure
from the good ones of the present day, and I cannot
believe in the sincerity of those persons who, at sight
of one of your pictures, fall into ecstasies, and yet presume from the height of their throne to look down on
one of Horace Vernet's. What I mean is, that if one
beautiful object pleases the eye, another cannot fail also
to inspire sympathy; at least, so is it with myself.

To Pastor Julius Schubring, Dessau.

Leipzig, December 6th, 1838.

Dear Schubring,

Along with this you will receive the organ pieces
and "Bonifacius," which I also enclose. Thank you

much for the latter, and for the manuscripts you have from time to time sent me for "Elijah;" they are of the greatest possible use to me, and though I may here and there make some alterations, still the whole affair, by your aid, is now placed on a much firmer footing. With regard to the dramatic element, there still seems to be a diversity of opinion between us. In such a character as that of Elijah, like every one in the Old Testament, except perhaps Moses, it appears to me that the dramatic should predominate,—the personages should be introduced as acting and speaking with fervour; not, however, for Heaven's sake, to become mere musical pictures, but inhabitants of a positive, practical world, such as we see in every chapter of the Old Testament; and the contemplative and pathetic element which you desire must be entirely conveyed to our apprehension by the words and the mood of the acting personages.

In your "Bonifacius," for instance, this was a point to which I was by no means reconciled; in my opinion he ought to have been treated dramatically throughout, like a theatrical representation (in its best sense) only without *visible* action. The Scriptural allusions, too, should, according to my idea, be more sparingly introduced, and placed in his mouth alone. The contrast between this style of language (which pervades the whole) and that at the coronation is not sufficiently equalized. Pepin, and all the pagans, and pagan priests, flit before me like shadows or misty forms, whereas, to satisfy me, they must be solid, robust men. Do not be displeased that I send you a bit of criticism along with my thanks, for such is my insufferable custom. Be-

13*

sides, a cold and cough make me unusually rabid to-day. I am now about to set to work on the "Elijah," and to plough away at the soil as best I can; if I do not get on with it, you must come to my aid, and, I hope, as kindly as ever, and preserve the same regard for your

FELIX MENDELSSOHN BARTHOLDY.

TO A. SIMROCK, BONN.

Leipzig, March 4th, 1839.

The manuscripts which I ought to have sent you last year are not yet finished; I wished to make them as perfect as I could; but for this both leisure and good humour were requisite, and during the period of constant concerts these too often failed. Now I hope shortly to complete the pieces, and thus free myself from debt.

But they are not "songs without words," for I have no intention of writing any more of that sort, let the Hamburgers say what they will! If there were too many such *animalcula* between heaven and earth, at last no one would care about them; and there really is quite a mass of piano music composed now in a similar style; another chord should be struck, I say.—I am, with entire esteem, your obedient

FELIX MENDELSSOHN BARTHOLDY.

To his Mother.

Leipzig, March 18th, 1830.

You wished to know how the overture to " Ruy Blas" went off. Famously. Six or eight weeks since an application was made to me in favour of a representation to be given for the Theatrical Pension Fund (an excellent benevolent institution here, for the benefit of which " Ruy Blas" was to be given). I was requested to compose an overture for it, and the music of the romance in the piece, for it was thought the receipts would be better if my name appeared in the bills. I read the piece, which is detestable, and more utterly beneath contempt than you could believe, and said that I had no leisure to write the overture, but I composed the romance for them. The performance was to take place last Monday week; on the previous Tuesday the people came to thank me politely for the romance, and said it was such a pity I had not also written an overture, but they were perfectly aware that time was indispensable for such a work, and the ensuing year, if I would permit them, they would give me longer previous notice. This put me on my mettle. I reflected on the matter the same evening, and began my score. On Wednesday there was a concert rehearsal, which occupied the whole forenoon. Thursday the concert itself, yet the overture was in the hands of the copyist early on Friday; played three times on Monday in the concert room, tried over once in the theatre, and given in the evening as an introduction to the odious play. Few of my works have caused me more amusing excitement. It is to be repeated, by

desire, at the next concert, but I mean to call it, not
the overture to "Ruy Blas," but to the Theatrical Pension Fund.

To FANNY HENSEL, BERLIN.

Frankfort, June 18th, 1839.

Dear Fanny,

Give me your best advice! The eccentric Capellmeister Guhr is become my particular friend, and we
are quite inseparable. Lately we were in a pleasant
cordial mood, and I was eagerly questioning him about
his extensive and rare collection of Bach's works,
among which are two autographs, the choral preludes
for the organ, and the "Passecaille," with a grand
fugue at the end of it,—

when he suddenly said, "I'll tell you what, you shall
have one of these autographs; I will make you a present of it, for you take as great delight in them as I
do; choose which you prefer,—the preludes or the
'Passecaille.'" This was really no trifling gift, for I
know that he has been offered a considerable sum of
money for these pieces, but he refused to part with
them, and I would myself have paid a good price for
them had they been for sale, and now he freely gives
me one; but the question is, which shall I take? I
have by far the strongest inclination for the preludes,

because they begin with the "Altes Jahr, because they include other great favourites of mine, and because the " Passecaille " and the fugue are already published. But you must also have a voice in the matter, for you will feel no common interest in it. So send me your vote, *Cantor !*

Is not Guhr a most singular being? and yet I can get on better with him than with any other of the Frankfort musicians. He enjoys life, and lives and lets live, but is sharp enough as a director, and beats common time so distinctly that they cannot fail to play to it, as if they were in arm-chairs; and my other colleagues here are so desperately melancholy, and always talking of musical critiques, and recognition, and flattering testimonials, and constantly thinking about themselves, and constantly fishing for compliments (but these compliments must be genuine; they even aspire to outpourings of the heart!). This is both provoking and sad; and yet (behind people's backs) they can play as mad pranks as any one. Much as I like Frankfort for a summer visit, I do not wish to be settled here as a musician, owing to all the above reasons, and many others besides.

At the concert of the St. Cecilia Association, where I had an opportunity of fairly estimating their musical organization, I felt quite melancholy at the difference between our sense of music in Leipzig and what was given here; for though it goes on very fairly, and sometimes sounds well, still, as a rule; it seems as if they were playing from sheer weariness, or from compulsion, and vastly little of that zeal and love are apparent in the orchestra which so often prevails among us. In fact, when I compare the whole elements of the orchestra here with ours at Leipzig, I feel just as I did when I returned from Düsseldorf and thought myself in Paradise. The St. Cecilia Association, too, has deteriorated, which is not the fault of one person or another, but of all combined, for the soil here is far from being favourable to music, though all the better for apples and cherries and wine, and other good things. I wish you could see the Sachsenhäusen hill at this moment, with all its ripe cherries and blooming vines! Moreover, there are many delightful people here, and some among them genuinely musical. For painting much is done, and it seems to be making real progress. This is a very different life from what it was three or four years ago when I was here, and found everything disorganized by discord and strife.

A tolerably good, though not very extensive, exhibition of paintings is just closed, which contained some admirable and many very pretty things. This change of tune and subject brings us back to Hensel. When does he go to England? when does he return? does he take any pictures with him? and what may they be? are you going to Italy? do I know anything of anything? I am writing a trio (the first part is finished), a sonata for the violin (ditto), a symphony (not ditto), and a letter to you (which is now quite finished). But when will you write to me?—Your

FELIX.

To CARL KLINGEMANN, LONDON.

Hochheim, near Coblenz, August 1st, 1839.

My dearest Friend,

I earnestly hope that you may fulfil your intention of visiting us late in the autumn. The time seems tc me endless till you become acquainted with my wife; besides, it is indeed very long since you and I have conversed in the unreserved confidence of home. When I was in England, two years ago, my wife kept a small diary, which she began after our marriage, and every day during my stay in England she left a blank space in its pages, that I might write the record of my days opposite to hers. For some time past I have accustomed myself to do this, and entered every detail minutely into the little green book,(you ought to know it, for you gave it to me in 1832),—the date of Rosen's death, that of my visit to Birmingham, etc. Now I have arrived exactly at the anniversary, and my diary clearly shows me how much I was then out of sorts, and very different from what I ought to have been. The constant publicity, the grand scale of things on every side, in fact, everything around me, attracted me less than formerly, and made me feel bewildered and irritable. May we therefore soon meet in Germany! You certainly would not enjoy yourself less here after England, and I do delight in this beautiful country. The summer months I recently passed in Frankfort have thoroughly refreshed me; in the morning I worked, then bathed or sketched; in the afternoon I played the organ or the piano, and afterwards rambled in the forest, then into society, or home, where I always

found the most charming of all society : this was the
mode in which my life was agreeably spent, and you
must add to all this the glorious summer days which
followed each other in uninterrupted succession.

We have now been here nearly a fortnight, and three
or four days hence we intend to go up the Rhine, back
to Frankfort, and return to Leipzig about the middle of
the month. Your wish to have X—— in London
(though very natural, I admit) is one in which we do
not at all agree, and yet my reasons are by no means
egotistical,—quite the reverse. I am convinced that it
would not be for his benefit were he to assume a position in the world which would oblige him to take an
interest in so many things, not only foreign to art, but
actually adverse to it. A certain number of guineas
might accrue to him, but no real gain, either for his
happiness or his progress in art. Formerly I used positively to hate all speculators in art, but now I feel
chiefly compassion for them, because I see so few who
are at rest ; it is a never-ending strife for money and
fame, and the most superior talents, as well as inferior
ones, join in it. Highly as I esteem X——, I am by
no means sure that he would not make shipwreck on
this rock, and, even if he did not lose the brightest
part of his genius, he would certainly have to deplore
the best part of his life and happiness ; and, after all,
for what ? The reformation and improvement of individual cities, even were they as important as London,
is in fact either impossible or indifferent ; but if a man
only strives thoroughly to perfect his own being, and
to purify himself by degrees from all dross, in acting
thus he is working for all cities alike ; and if he does

so even in a village, his labours are certain to make their way into the world, and there to exercise their due influence. I would rather, therefore, that X—— remained in Germany wherever music is most appreciated; but you must not ask me where that is,— whether at Frankfort or Vienna; but it lies in the air, no doubt: therefore I shall always advise his not leaving Germany.

Planché's work gets on very slowly, and possibly I may have a new oratorio ready before his text is completed. The number of friends that "St. Paul" has gained me is really quite remarkable. I could never have anticipated it. It was performed twice at Vienna in the spring, and they want to have a festival there in November, with one thousand performers ("St. Paul" is to be given), which I shall probably go to conduct. This has surprised me the more, because no other work of mine has ever made its way into Vienna. I must be in Brunswick for the Musical Festival the end of this month, in order to conduct "St. Paul;" and it is always a source of twofold pleasure to me when I have no personal acquaintances in a place, which will be the case there.

My new pieces are a trio, completed for piano, violin, and violoncello, in D minor; a book of four-part songs, to be sung in the open air; some songs for one voice, organ fugues, half a Psalm, etc. I mean to continue the four-part songs, and have thought a good deal about the capabilities of this style; and it does seem the most natural of all music when four people are rambling together in the woods, or sailing in a boat, and have the melody all ready with them and within them.

14

In quartetts for male voices alone, both for musical and other reasons, there is something prosaic in the four male voices, which has always been perceptible; whereas in those I allude to, the combination of male and female voices will sound more poetical, and this will, I hope, also be perceptible.

Do send me a song or two, to sing in autumn, or, better still, in summer, or in spring, or on the water, on the grass, or on a bridge, or in the woods, or in the garden; to the stork, or to a kind Providence, or to the people of the cities and plains, or for a dance, or a wedding, or as a *souvenir*. It might be a popular romance!

I should like much to hear your sentiments about the events in your Fatherland;* they interest me more than you perhaps imagine. Be sure you come to us the end of autumn! Cecilia says your room is ready, and sends you her remembrances.—I am always yours,

FELIX M. B.

To HIS MOTHER.

Frankfort, July 3d, 1839.

We are leading the most agreeable, happy life imaginable here. I am therefore resolved not to go away till obliged to do so, and to give myself up entirely for the present to a sense of comfort and pleasure. The most delightful thing I ever saw in society was a *fête* in the forest here; I really must tell you all about it,

---

* Hanover.

because it was unique of its kind. Within a quarter
of an hour's drive from the road, deep in the forest
where lofty spreading beech-trees stand in solitary
grandeur, forming an impenetrable canopy above, and
where all around nothing was to be seen but green
foliage glistening through innumerable trunks of trees,
—this was the locality. We made our way through
the thick underwood, by a narrow footpath, to the spot,
where, on arriving, a number of white figures were
visible in the distance, under a group of trees, encircled
with massive garlands of flowers, which formed the
concert-room. How lovely the voices sounded, and
how brilliantly the soprano tones vibrated in the air!
what charm and melting sweetness pervaded every
strain! All was so still and retired, and yet so bright!
I had formed no conception of such an effect. The
choir consisted of about twenty good voices; during
the previous rehearsal in a room, there had been some
deficiencies, and want of steadiness. Towards evening,
however, when they stood under the trees, and uplifting
their voices gave my first song, " Ihr Vöglein in den
Zweigen schwank," it was so enchanting in the silence
of the woods, that it almost brought tears to my eyes.

It sounded like genuine poetry. The scene, too, was
so beautiful; all the pretty female figures in white, and
Herr B—— standing in the centre, beating time in his
shirt-sleeves, and the audience seated on camp-stools,
or hampers, or lying on the moss. They sang through
the whole book, and then three new songs which I had
composed for the occasion. The third (" Lerchengesang") was rather exultingly shouted than sung, and
repeated three times, while in the interim strawberries,

cherries, and oranges were served on the most delicate china, and quantities of ice and wine and raspberry syrup carried round. People were emerging in every direction out of the thicket, attracted from a distance by the sound of the music, and they stretched themselves on the ground and listened.

As it grew dark, great lanterns and torches were set up in the middle of the choir, and they sang songs by Schelble and Hiller, and Schnyder, and Weber. Presently a large table, profusely decorated with flowers and brilliantly lighted, was brought forward, on which was an excellent supper with all sorts of good dishes and wines; and it was most quiet, withal, and lonely in the wood, the nearest house being at the distance of at least an hour, and the gigantic trunks of the trees looking every moment more dark and stern, and the people under their branches more noisy and jovial. After supper they began again with the first song, and sang through the whole six, and then the three new ones, and the " Lerchengesang" once more' three times over. At length it was time to go; in the thicket we met the wagon in which all the china and plate was to be taken back to the town; it could not stir from the spot, nor could we either, but we contrived to get on at last, and arrived about midnight at our homes in Frankfort. The donors of the *fête* were detained in the forest till two o'clock, packing up everything, and lost their way along with the large wagon, finding themselves unexpectedly at Isenburg; so they did not get home till long afterwards. There were three families who had the merit of this idea, and whom we have to thank for this memorable *fête*. Two of these we were not at all acquainted with, and the third only slightly. I know now how songs ought to sound in the open air, and hope shortly to compose a gay book of them.

It must be tiresome enough for you to read descriptions of *fêtes* long past, and indeed such descriptions are of no great interest even to those who were present, but far more trying to those who were not; and yet I cannot resist telling you also of an entertainment given by Herr E——, which took place last week, because I know you rejoice in any marks of honour bestowed on me, and this was indeed a very great one. We were invited, along with many whom we knew and some whom we did not know, chiefly members of the St Cecilia Association. First, we had some music, and played and sang; then the door of a dark room was thrown open, and from an opposite direction resounded my overture to the "Midsummer Night's Dream." While it was being played, a curtain drew up, and displayed a most charming tableau, Titania sleeping in a flower; hovering over her was Cobweb spreading out the curtain, Peaseblossom fanning her, Moth, and the others,—all represented by lovely young girls; and a whole succession of tableaux followed, accompanied by my music. The second was a German girl of the olden time in her chamber, while her lover, in rain and snow, was singing under her window, "Leucht't heller als die Sonne," which seemed to please her uncommonly. This was succeeded by an "Ave" for eight voices, with the Angel, bearing a lily in his hand, appearing to the kneeling Mary. Then came a beautiful Zuleika, in a Persian apartment, who, without changing her attitude, sang my song in E minor

14*

very sweetly and prettily. This was followed by a masterpiece—Spanish peasants' nuptials,—three handsome couples of lovers dancing, admirably costumed and placed, and behind them a pathetic Don Quixote, when the little chorus in C, "Nun zündet an," was appropriately sung. Next came a youth with a small neckcloth and a large shirt-collar, in a vineyard with a sketch-book, and he sang "Ist es wahr?" and mo t charmingly he sang it. Seventhly (for I am now falling into the catalogue style), a chapel, with a handsome Gothic (mock) organ, at which was seated a nun, with two others standing by her, who sang from the printed music "Beati omnes," the choir responding behind the scenes. Eighthly, two girls at a well, singing by heart, in the most enchanting manner, my duett, "Ich wollt', meine Liebe," having contrived, under some pretext, to get the music transcribed. Ninthly, St. Paul on the ground, his escort in alarm, and a chorus of women singing behind the scenes. Tenth and last, before the curtain was drawn up, "As the hart panteth after the waterbrooks" was sung, while I was wondering how they would manage to represent the panting of the hart, and who was to attempt it. But now comes something more especially for you, Mother. They had dressed S——, who is thought to resemble me, to personate myself; and there he was, sitting in an inspired attitude, writing music, and chewing away at his handkerchief,* and by his side a lovely St. Cecilia with a wreath. Now, Mother, I hope you will no longer call me the "reverse of a charlatan;" for my describing all

---

* A habit of Mendelssohn's.

this myself, without the ink turning red for shame, is really a strong measure!

As I am in a boasting mood, I may as well tell you at once that I have proposals from two musical festivals for 1840. And now enough of myself and my braggadocio. I have, however, been very busy here, and have completed a pianoforte trio, five four-part songs for the open air, and three fugues for the organ, as well as commenced many others. I have practised the organ so steadily, that on my return to Leipzig I purpose giving an organ concert there, and I think that my pedal playing is now very tolerable.

Dear Fanny! I beg that among the six great organ preludes and fugues of Bach, published by Riedl, you will look at the fugue No. 3, in C major. Formerly I did not care much about them, they are in a very simple style; but observe particularly the four last bars; natural and simple as they are, I feel quite in love with them, and played them over at least fifty times yesterday. How the left hand glides and turns, and how gently it dies away towards the close! It pleased me beyond all measure.

To FANNY HENSEL, BERLIN.*

Leipzig, September 14th, 1839.
Dear Fanny,

Wishing to note down a great many things for your benefit, I examined my diaries, but found very little in

---

* Just before his sister's journey to Italy.

them, and say to myself, "Hensel will show her and tell all this a hundred times better than I can."

So only with a view to perform my promise:—

Isola Bella.—Place yourself on the very highest point, and look right and left, before and behind you,—the whole of the island and the whole of the lake are at your feet.

Venice.—Do not forget Casa Pisani, with its Paul Veronese, and the Manfrini Gallery, with its marvellous "Cithern Player" by Giorgione, and a ditto, "Entombment," by Titian (Hensel laughs at me). Compose something in honour of the "Cithern Player;" I did so. When you see the "Assumption of the Virgin," think of me. Observe how dark the head of Mary,—and indeed her whole figure stands out against the bright sky; the head looks quite brown, and there is an ineffable expression of enthusiasm and overflowing felicity, that no one could believe without having actually seen it. If you don't think of me, too, at sight of the golden glory of the sky behind Mary,—then there is an end of all things! Likewise to certain Cherubs' heads, from which an ox might learn what true beauty is; and if the "Presentation of Mary," and the woman selling eggs underneath, do not please you, —then call me a blockhead! Think of Goethe when you see the Lions in front of the Arsenal: "Stehen zwei altgriechische Löwen," etc. Sail in a gondola at night, meeting other black gondolas hurrying along. If you don't then think of all sorts of love-stories, and other things which might occur within them while they glide by so quickly,—then am I a dolt!

Florence.—The following are among my notes on the

portrait-gallery (see if you find them true, and write to me on the subject) :—

"Comparison between the head and its production, between the man's work and his exterior,—the artist and his portrait. Titian, vigorous and royal; Domenichino, precise, bright, very astute, and buoyant; Guido, pale, dignified, masterly, keen; Lanfranco, a grotesque mask; Leonello Spada, a good-natured *fanfaron* and a reveller; Annibale Carracci, peeping and prying; the two Caraccis, like the members of a guild; Caravaggio, rather commonplace and cat-like; Guercino, handsome and affected, melancholy and dark; Bellini the red-haired, the stern, old-fashioned teacher; Giorgione, chivalrous, fantastic, serene, and clear; Leonardo da Vinci, the lion; in the middle, the fragile, heavenly Raphael, and over him Michael Angelo, ugly, vigorous, malignant; Carlo Dolce, a coxcomb; Gerard Dow, a mere appendage among his kitchen utensils," etc. etc.

In the large gallery to the left of the tribune, look at a little picture by Fra Bartolommeo, scarcely larger than this sheet of paper, but with two doors, all so neatly and carefully painted and finished. When you enter the gallery, salute first the busts of the Medici, for they were its founders. In the tribune there are some good things. Do not fail to see all the painted churches, which are quite beyond belief,—Maria Novella, St. Annunziata (you must see Andrea del Sarto there; remark also Fra Bartolommeo falling backwards down-stairs from terror, because the angel has already been painting on his canvas). Examine also this said angel's painting in the "Annunciation" of Fra Bartolommeo; it is very fine (Hensel laughs).

To St. Marco, the Academy, etc. etc.

If the site of Brunelli's statue, near the Duomo, does not please you, I can't help you. The Duomo itself is not bad. Walk about a great deal.

Milan.—Don't fail to go to the top of the cathedral, on account of the millions of pinnacles, and the splendid view.

Genoa.—It is pleasant to be in the Villetta Negri at nightfall.

Betwixt Genoa and Florence, see everything. Do not miss visiting the church of St. Francesco in Assisi, on any account whatever. The same with regard to all Perugia.

Drink a flask of *aleatico* in Florence, and add another of *vino santo.*

Rome.—Holy week; be as weary as you please during the whole chanting of the Psalms, it's no matter, but listen carefully when they intone the *last* "Benedictus Dominus Israel,"—all four voices *unisono fortissimo* in D minor: it sounds very grand. Observe the strange modulations produced by chance, when one unmusical priest after another takes the book and sings; the one finishing in D major, and the other commencing in B flat minor. Above all, see and hear everything in the Sistine Chapel, and write some melodies, or something, from thence to your F. M. B. Greet old Santini. Feast your eyes on the brilliant aspect of the chapel on Palm Sunday, when all the Cardinals are robed and carry palms, and when the procession with the singers arrives. The "Improperia," on Good Friday, in B flat major, are very fine. Notice when the old Cardinal sings the "Credo" the first day of Easter, and all the bells ring out, and the ceremony becomes all alive once more, with cannon-shots, etc. etc. Drive to the *Grotta ferrata*, it is really quite too lovely, and all painted by Domenichino. Don't forget the echo near Cecilia Metella. The tower stands to the left of the road. In the same direction, about fifty yards further, among some old ruined walls and stones, there is the most perfect echo I ever chanced to meet with in my life; it seems as if it never would cease muttering and murmuring. It begins in a slight degree, close behind the tower, but the further you proceed, the more mystical it becomes. You must try to find the right spot. Learn to distinguish between the different orders of monks.

Naples.—When there is a storm at Chiatamone, and the gray sea is foaming, think of me. Don't fail to live close to the sea. I lived at Santi Combi, Santa Lucia (I think No. 13), it was most lovely there. Be sure you go from Castellamare to Amalfi, *over* Mount St. Angelo. It is the chief highway of all Italy. Proceed from Amalfi to Atrani, and see the church there, and then view the whole glorious landscape from above. Never get overheated. And never fly into a passion. And never be so delighted as to agitate yourself. Be wonderfully haughty and stately ; all the beauty is there for you only.

Eat, as a salad, brocoli with ham, and write to me if it is not capital. So far my good advice. Enough for to-day. Farewell, dearest Fanny, and dear Hensel family all. We think of you daily and hourly, and rejoice in your good fortune and in your enjoyment.

FELIX.

To Professor Naumann, Bonn.

Leipzig, September 19th, 1839.

Sir,

Pray accept my thanks for the great proof of confidence you show me, by the purport of your esteemed letter of the 12th of this month. Believe me, I thoroughly appreciate it, and can indeed feel how important to you must be the development and future destiny of a child so beloved and so talented. My sole wish is, like your own, that *those* steps should be taken, best calculated to reward his assiduity and to cultivate his talents. As an artist, I consider this to be my duty, but in this case it would cause me peculiar pleasure, from its recalling an early and happy period of my life.

But I should unworthily respond to your confidence, did I not communicate frankly to you the many and great scruples which prevent my *immediately* accepting your proposal. In the first place, I am convinced, from repeated experience, that I am totally deficient in the talent requisite for a practical teacher, and for giving regular progressive instruction; whether it be that I take too little pleasure in tuition, or have not sufficient patience for it, I cannot tell, but, in short, I do not succeed in it. Occasionally, indeed, young people have stayed with me, but any improvement they have derived was solely from our studying music together, from unreserved intercourse, or casual conversation on various subjects, and also from discussions; and none of these things are compatible with actual teaching. Now the question is, whether in such early youth a consecutive, unremitting, strict course of discipline be not of more value than all the rest? It also appears to me that the estrangement of your son from the paternal roof just at his age forms a second, and not less important, objection. Where the rudiments of education are not wholly wanting (and the talents of your wife alone are a security against this), then I consider that the vicinity of his parents, and the prosecution of the usual elements of study, the acquirement of languages, and the various branches of scholarship and science, are of more value to the boy than a one-sided, even though more perfect, cultivation of his genius. In any event such genius is sure to force its way to the light, and to shape its course accordingly, and in riper years will submit to no other permanent vocation, so that the early acquired treasures of interest, and the hours enjoyed in early youth under the roof of a parent, become doubly dear.

I speak in this strain from my own experience, for I can well remember that in my fifteenth year there was a question as to my studying with Cherubini in Paris, and I know how grateful I was to my father at the time, and often since, that he at last gave up the idea, and kept me with himself. It would of course be very different if there were no means in Bonn, of obtaining good and solid intstruction in thorough-bass and the piano ; but this I cannot believe, and whether that instruction be rather better or more intellectual (provided it be not positively objectionable) is of less moment when compared with the advantages of a longer stay in his own home. Further, my life hitherto has been so unsettled, that no summer has passed without my taking considerable journeys, and next year I shall

15

probably be absent from here for five or six months; this change of associations would only be prejudicial to youthful talent. The young man, therefore, must either remain here alone all summer or travel with me; and neither of these is advisable for him.

I state all these disadvantages, because I am myself so well aware of them, and fully estimate the import-ance of the subject. If you do not participate in my views on mature consideration, and are still of opinion that *I* alone can assist your boy in the attainment of his wish, then I repeat that in any case (irrespective of this) I should esteem it my duty to be useful and serviceable, so far as my ability goes, to a youthful genius, and to contribute to his development by the exercise of my own powers; but, even in this event, a personal interview is indispensable, if only for a few hours, in order to arrange everything clearly, and until then I cannot give an unqualified consent.

Were you to bring the lad to me at Easter, I fear I should have already set off on my summer excursion. Indeed, the only period when I am certain to be in Leipzig is from autumn till Easter. I quite agree with Madame Naumann, that it is most essential to cultivate pianoforte-playing at present as much as possible, and not to fail in studying Cramer's exercises assiduously and steadily; but along with this daily training on the piano, two hours a week devoted to thorough-bass might be useful, as such a variety would be a pleasant change, rather than an interruption. The latter study indeed ought to be pursued in an easy and almost playful manner, and chiefly the practical part, that of deciphering and playing figured bass; these are the main points, and can be entirely mastered in a short time; but the sooner it is begun, the sooner is it got quit of, and this is always a relief with such dry things. And now once more accept my thanks for the trust you have reposed in me, which I thought I could only adequately respond to by entire sincerity.—I am, your faithful

FELIX MENDELSSOHN BARTHOLDY.

To I. MOSCHELES, LONDON.

Leipzig, November 30th, 1839.

My dear Friend,

Your letter from Paris delighted me exceedingly, although the proceedings you describe are not very gratifying. The state of matters there must be very curious. I own that I always felt a kind of repugnance towards it, and this impression has not been diminished by all we have recently heard from thence. Nowhere do variety and outward consideration play so prominent a part as there, and what makes the case still worse is, that they not only coquet with orders and decorations, but with artistic inspiration and soul. The very great inward poverty which this betrays, along with the outward glitter of grandeur and worldly importance which such *misères* assume, is truly revolting to me, even when I merely read of them in a letter. I infinitely prefer our German homeliness and torpor and tobacco-pipes, though, indeed, I can't say much in their favour since the recent events in Hanover, in

which I am deeply interested, though I grieve to say
they do not exhibit our Fatherland in a pleasing aspect;
so that neither here nor there is life at present very
enjoyable: therefore we ought the more heartily to
thank God that within the domain of art there lies a
world far removed from all besides; solitary, yet re-
plete with life, where refuge is to be found, and where
we can feel that it is well with us.

Chorley seems to have taken great pleasure in our
concerts. On what a splendid scale we could have
them if a very little money were only forthcoming!
but this hateful money is a hindrance and a stumbling-
block all over the world, and we do not get forward as
we ought. On one side we have the worthy civilians,
who think that Leipzig is Paris, and that everything is
admirable, and that if the members of the orchestra
were not starving it would no longer be Leipzig; and
on the other side we have the musicians, or rather they
leave us as soon as they possibly can, and I give them
letters to you in the hope that they may be thus rescued
from their misery.

I have not assisted Pott's undertaking by any musical contribution. If you could only see the detestable
proceedings in Germany at present with regard to
monuments, you would have given nothing, either.
They speculate on great men, in order, through their
reputation, to make a name for themselves, and trumpet forth in the newspapers, while with their real trumpets they make very bad music, "as deadening as a
foggy breeze." If Halle for Handel, Salzburg for Mozart, and Bonn for Beethoven, etc., are really desirous
to form good orchestras, capable of playing and com-

prehending thoroughly their works, then I shall be delighted to give them my aid, but not for mere stones, when the orchestra are themselves even more worthless stones, and not for their *conservatoriums*, where there is nothing worth conservation. My present hobby is our poor orchestra and its improvement. By dint of incessant running to and fro, writing, and tormenting others, I have at last contrived to scrape together about five hundred *thalers*, and before I leave this I expect to get twice that sum for them. If the town does this, it can then proceed to erect a monument to Sebastian Bach, in front of the Thomas School. But first of all, the money. You see I am a rabid Leipziger. It would touch your feelings, too, if you saw all this close at hand, and could hear how the people strain every nerve to accomplish what is really good.

Has Onslow written anything new? and old Cherubini? That is a matchless fellow! I have got his "Abencerrages," and cannot sufficiently admire the sparkling fire, the clever original phrases, the extraordinary delicacy and refinement with which the whole is written, or feel sufficiently grateful to the grand old man for it. Besides, it is all so free and bold and spirited.

15*

To FANNY HENSEL, ROME.

Leipzig. January 4th, 1840.

This little page shall go to Rome from here,
And wish you prettily a good new year.

You see my letter begins in the true ballad-monger
style; if you chance to be in the Coliseum at the moment you receive it, the contrast will be rather grotesque. Whereabouts do you live in Rome? Have
you eaten broccoli and ham? or *zuppa Inglese?* Is
the convent of San Giovanni and Paolo still standing?
and does the sun shine every morning on your buttered
roll? I have just played to Ferdinand Hiller your Caprices in B flat major, G major, E major, and F major,
which surprised us both; and though we tried hard to
detect the cloven foot in them, we could not do so,—
all was unmixed delight. Then I vowed at last to
break through my obstinate silence. Pray forgive it!
It happened thus. First came the christening, and
with it my mother and Paul. In the meantime the
subscription concerts had begun; then my mother left
us; then Paul, a fortnight later; then came Hiller to
stay with us, intending to remain a week, heard a
couple of rehearsals, and decided to remain the whole
winter, for the purpose of completing his oratorio of
" Jeremiah," and producing it here in March; then
came an abominable cold and catarrh, which for three
weeks confined me to bed, or to my room, but always
in very bad humour; then came Breitkopf and Härtel,
begging to have the manuscript of my second set of
four-part songs, which they have now got, and the

trio, which they have not yet got; then came the copyist, petitioning for the score of the new Psalm, which
was performed most gloriously the day before yesterday, as a commencement to the new year's concert;
then came 116 friends; then came Madame Pleyel, who
counts for 216 more, and she played the piano right
well; then came Christmas, to which I was forced to
contribute fourteen gifts, some musical, some pictorial,
some practical, and some juvenile; and now comes the
benefit concert of Madlle. Meerti: so here you have an
abrégé of my *histoire universelle* since my last letter.

But tell me, for Heaven's sake, what are you doing
at Rome ? "The finest part of the *old hole* is its situation," said General Lepel once; but he is mistaken.
There are still greater charms within her walls. What
do you say, by the by, to the drone of the *Pifferari*,
whom the painters paint so admirably, and which produce such indescribable sensations in every nose, while
sounding through it ?—and to the church music in St.
Luigi dei Francesi and others ? I should like to hear
you on that subject. Can you tell me the names of all
the Cardinals from a mere glimpse of their hoods or
trains ? I could do this. When you are with a certain
Madame by Titian in the Sciarra Palace, and with two
other certain *Mesdames* also by him (the one in a state
of nature, the other unfortunately not) in the Borghese
Palace,* or with the "Galatea," or any other Raphael,
if you do not then think of me and wish I were in
Rome, I shall assuredly in that case wish you were the
Marchesa Muti Papazurri, whose breadth is greater

---

* "Earthly and Heavenly Love."

than her height, and that is five feet six inches. I will now give you some advice. Go to Monte Testaccio, and settle yourself comfortably in one of the little inns there; you will feel precisely the same as if you were in Rome. If you have already seen Guido's "Aurora," be sure you go to see it again. Mark well the horrible fifths of the Papal singers when they adorn each of their four parts at the same moment with flourishes. On a fine Sunday, go on walking the whole day, till the sun sets, and it becomes cool; then come down from Monte Pincio, or wherever you may be, and have your dinner. Compose a vast deal, for it gets on famously at Rome. Write me soon a long letter. Look out of the windows of any convent near the Lateran, towards the Albano mountains. Count the houses in Frascati in the sunshine; it is far more beautiful there than in all Prussia and Poland too.

Forgive this harebrained letter, for I could not make it better. Farewell, dearest Fanny. May God bless you, and your journey, and your whole year; and continue to love your   FELIX

To I. Fürst, Berlin.

(On the subject of a Libretto that he was writing for an Opera.)

Leipzig, January 4th, 1840

Dear Fürst,

You upbraid me extravagantly in the beginning of your welcome letter, but at its close you draw so admirable a moral, that I have only to thank you anew for the whole. You do me injustice in suggesting that my sole reason for wishing to see the *scenarium* is that I may raise difficulties from the starting-point, and bring the child into the world forthwith in its sickly condition.

It is precisely on opposite grounds that I wish this, in order to obviate subsequent difficulties and organic maladies. If these are, as you declare, born with him, it is best to abstract them from the child, while it is still possible, without injuring every part; if the injury admits of a remedy at all, it can now be cured, without attacking the whole organization.

No longer to speak figuratively, what deters me, and has always hitherto deterred me, from the composition of a *libretto*, is neither the verse, nor the individual words, nor the mode of handling (or whatever you call it), but the course of the action, the dramatic essence, the march of events,—in short, the *scenarium*. If I do not consider this to be good and solid in itself, then my firm conviction is that the music will not be so either, nor the whole satisfy the pretensions that I must make in executing such a work, though they may indeed entirely differ from those which are usually made, and from those of the public. But I have long since given up all idea of conforming to their tastes, simply for this reason, that it is impossible ; so I must follow the dictates of my own conscience, now as ever.

Planché's text can never, even with the best will on both sides, become such a work as I want; I am almost disposed to give up my purpose as utterly hopeless. I would rather never compose an opera at all, than one which from the very commencement I considered only indifferent; moreover, I could not possibly compose for

such a one, were you to give me the whole kingdom of
Prussia to do so. All this, and the many annoyances,
certain to occur at the completion of a text, if I should
not feel disposed to undertake it, render it my duty to
proceed step by step, and rather to move too slowly
than too hastily; on this account I have resolved, unless
we first agree about the *scenarium*, never to beguile
any poet into undertaking so laborious a work, which
may after all prove vain. This *scenarium* may be prolix
or brief, detailed or merely sketched,—on these points
I do not presume to dictate, and quite as little, whether
the opera should be in three, four, or five acts; if it be
really good, just as it is written, then eight acts would
not be too many for me, nor one too few; and I say
the same as to a ballet or no ballet. The only criterion
is, whether it harmonizes or not with the musical and
other existing feelings of my nature; and I believe
that I am able to discern this quite as well from the
scenarium as from the finished text, and that is, moreover, a point which no one can decide save myself
personally.

I have thus placed the whole truth before you, and
Heaven grant that all these things may not deter you
from writing an opera, that you may also intrust it to
me for composition, and that I may at length through
you see a long-cherished wish fulfilled. I need not tell
you how eagerly I shall await your decision.—Yours,

FELIX MENDELSSOHN BARTHOLDY.

To PAUL MENDELSSOHN BARTHOLDY.

Leipzig, February 7th, 1840.

Dear Brother,

Every word, alas! that you write about Berlin and the course of things there, corresponds but too well with my own views on the subject. The proceedings there are far from gratifying, and what strikes me as the most hopeless part is, that all its inhabitants are of one accord on the subject, and yet, in spite of this universal feeling, no change to what is good and healthy is ever effected. But where cannot the individual man live and thrive? especially in Germany, where we are all compelled to isolation, and must, from the very first, renounce all idea of working together in unison. Still it has its bright side and its original aspect. When are you coming here again to play billiards with us? I have been living a stirring life all through this winter. Fancy my being obliged to play in public four times last week, and two pieces on each occasion. Last Saturday week, the first Quartett Soirée took place, where pianoforte music was introduced; so I played Mozart's sonata in A major, with David, and the B flat major trio of Beethoven. On Sunday evening Ernst played four quartetts at Hiller's; one of them was the E minor of Beethoven, and mine in E flat major. Early on Monday the rehearsal took place, and in the evening the concert, where I accompanied him in his "Elegie," and in three songs besides; on the following Thursday, Hiller and I played Mozart's concerto, written for two pianos, into which we introduced two grand *cadenzos*, and at the close of the second part of

the concert, we played Moscheles' duett in G major.*
The Saturday after, I again played with David at the
Quartett Soirée, a new rondo of Spohr's, and wound
up with my trio.   In addition, we are to have a musical soirée at D——'s, a meeting of the Liedertafel, a
ball, etc. etc.; and yet with all this, every one com-
plains that I persist in living so retired.   Latterly I
have become quite tired of music, and think I must
take to painting once more; but my Swiss sketches
are coming to an end, and fain would I return thither
to make new ones, but I already see that there is no
hope of such a thing this summer.   Hiller lately said
that I was like those ancient barbarians, who took such
delight in the luscious fruits and the warm sun of the
South, that they were always longing for them once
more; and there really is some truth in this.   Would
that our orchestra had not so many attractions.   Yesterday they played the B flat major symphony of Beethoven famously.   In the course of a few days the
choruses (now completed) in Hiller's oratorio are to be
rehearsed.   I feel as much anxiety on the subject as if
they were my own, or even greater.

Last week I had an agreeable occupation, which was
that of distributing the five hundred dollars, granted to
the orchestra, amongst its various members; the sum
is small and the aid trifling, still I felt great satisfaction
in having even accomplished this much.   Next year I
mean to begin it all over again, and then I hope to do
a real service to the musicians; whether they thank
me or not, is, after all, quite a matter of indifference.

Pray send for a little work which contains the most

---

* " Hommage à Handel."

beautiful and interesting descriptions I have read for a long time. They are Eastern translations by Rückert, and the title is ' Erbauliches und Beschauliches aus dem Morgenlande.' If this book does not delight you beyond measure, I will never recommend one to you again. Do look into it often, for it is most extraordinary.—Your

FELIX.

To HIS MOTHER.

Leipzig, March 30th, 1840.

The turmoil of the last few weeks was overpowering. Liszt was here for a fortnight, and caused quite a paroxysm of excitement among us, both in a good and evil sense. I consider him to be in reality an amiable warm-hearted man, and an admirable artist. That he plays with more execution than all the others, does not admit of a doubt; yet Thalberg, with his composure, and within his more restricted sphere, is more perfect, taken as a virtuoso; and this is the standard which must also be applied to Liszt, for his compositions are inferior to his playing, and, in fact, are only calculated for virtuosos. A fantasia by Thalberg (especially that on the " Donna del Lago ") is an accumulation of the most exquisite and delicate effects, and a continued succession of difficulties and embellishments that excite our astonishment; all is so well devised and so finished, carried out with such security and skill, and pervaded by the most refined taste.

On the other hand, Liszt possesses a degree of velocity

16

and complete independence of finger, and a thoroughly musical feeling, which can scarcely be equalled. In a word, I have heard no performer whose musical perceptions, like those of Liszt, extended to the very tips of his fingers, emanating directly from them. With this power, and his enormous technicality and practice, he must have far surpassed all others, if a man's own ideas were not, after all, the chief point, and these, hitherto at least, seem denied to him; so that in this phase of art most of the great virtuosos equal, and indeed excel him. But that he, along with Thalberg, *alone* represents the highest class of pianists of the present day, is, I think, undeniable. Unhappily, the manner in which Liszt has acted towards the public here has not pleased them. The whole misunderstanding is, in fact, as if you were listening to two persons disputing, who are both in the wrong, and whom you would fain interrupt at every word. As for the citizens in general, who are angry at the high prices, and do not wish to see a clever fellow prosper too much, and grumble accordingly, I don't in the least care about them; and then the newspaper discussions, explanations, and counter-explanations, criticisms and complaints, and all kinds of things are poured down on us, totally unconnected with music; so that his stay here has caused us almost as much annoyance as pleasure, though the latter was, indeed, often great beyond measure.

It occurred to me that this unpleasant state of feeling might be most effectually allayed, by people seeing and hearing him in private; so I suddenly determined to give him a *soirée* in the Gewandhaus, of three hundred and fifty persons, with orchestra, choir, mulled

wine, cakes, my "Meeresstille," a Psalm, a triple concerto by Bach (Liszt, Hiller, and I), choruses from "St.
Paul," fantasia on "Lucia di Lammermoor," the "Erl
King," the "*devil and his grandmother*," and goodness knows what else; and all the people were delighted, and played and sang with the utmost enthusiasm,
and vowed they had never passed a more capital evening; so my object was thus happily effected in a
most agreeable manner.

I have to-day formed a resolution, in which I heartily
rejoice, and that is, never again to take any part as
judge of the prizes at a musical competition. Several
proposals of this kind were made to me, and I did not
know why I should be so annoyed by these, till I clearly
saw that it was in fact a display of arrogance on my
part, to which I would not myself submit from others,
and should therefore carefully avoid,—thus setting oneself up as a proficient, and my taste as incontrover-
tible, and in idle hour passing in review all the assembled competitors, and criticizing them, and, God knows,
possibly being guilty of the most glaring injustice
towards them. So I resolved once for all to renounce
the office, and feel quite relieved by having done so.

———————

To the Kreis-Director von Falkenstein, Dresden.

Leipzig, April 8th, 1840.

Sir,

Emboldened by the assurance of your kind feelings
in our recent conversation, and by the conviction that

you have sincerely at heart the condition of art here, and its further cultivation (of which you have already given so many proofs), permit me to lay before you a question which seems to me of the highest importance to the interest of music.

Would it not be possible to entreat his Majesty the King to dispose of the sum bequeathed by the late Herr Blümner for the purpose of establishing an institution for art and science (the investment of which is left to the discretion of his Majesty), in favour of the erection and maintenance of a fundamental music academy in Leipzig?

Permit me to make a few observations on the importance of such an institution, and to state why I consider that Leipzig is peculiarly entitled to aspire to such a one, and also what I consider to be the fitting basis for its organization.

For a long period music has been indigenous in this country, and the sense of what is true and genuine, the very phase which must be nearest the heart of every ardent and thoughtful friend to art, has at all times struck its roots deep into this soil. Such universal sympathy does not certainly come by chance, nor is it without influential results on general cultivation; music having thus become an important power, not as a mere passing enjoyment, but as a more elevated and intellectual requirement. Those who feel sincere solicitude about this art must eagerly wish that its future prospects in this land should rest on the most solid foundation.

The positive, technical, and material tendencies so prevalent at the present day render the preservation of a genuine sense of art, and its further advancement, of twofold importance, but also of twofold difficulty. A solid basis alone can accomplish this purpose ; and as the extension of sound instruction is the best mode of promoting every species of moral improvement, so it is with music also. If we had a good music academy,—embracing all the various branches of this art, and teaching them from one sole point of view, as only the means to a higher end,—then the practical and material tenets, which, alas ! can number even among our artists many influential adherents, might, no doubt, yet be effectually checked.

Mere private instruction, which once bore much good fruit for the world at large, on many accounts now no longer suffices. Formerly, students of various instruments were to be found in every class of society, whereas now this amateurship is gradually passing away, or is chiefly confined to one instrument,—the piano.

Scholars desirous of enjoying further instructions almost invariably consist of those who propose devoting themselves to this branch of art, and who rarely possess the means of paying for private lessons. The most admirable talent is indeed often to be found amongst this class ; but, on the other hand, teachers are seldom placed in such fortunate circumstances as to be able to devote their time, without remuneration, to the training of even the finest genius ; thus both sides endure privation,—the former being unable to obtain the wished for instruction, and the latter losing the opportunity of implanting, and practically enforcing, their own knowledge. A public institution would, at this moment, be of the most vital importance to teachers as well as to

16*

pupils; and the latter would thus acquire the means of improving capabilities which otherwise must often remain undeveloped and wasted; while, for the teachers of music, such a standard of combined action from *one* point of view, and for the attainment of *one* purpose, would also be advantageous, as the best remedy against lukewarmness and isolation, the unfruitfulness of which, in these days, is but too apt to exercise a ruinous influence on the mind.

In Leipzig the need of a school for music, in which Art may be pursued with conscientious study and an earnest mind, is deeply felt; and for various reasons Leipzig seems peculiarly suited for it. The university already a central locality for intellectual aspiring young men, and the school of knowledge, would, in many relations, connect itself with that of music. In most of the other large towns of Germany public amusements dissipate the mind, and exercise an injurious influence over the young; here, however, most of these amusements are more or less connected with music, or consist wholly of it; thus there are very few public recreations except those allied to music; so this institution would benefit both the cause and the individual; moreover, for that especial branch of art which must always remain the chief basis of musical studies—the more elevated class of instrumental and sacred compositions —Leipzig, by its very numerous concerts and oratorios, possesses the means of cultivating the taste of young artists to an extent that few other German cities can offer.

Through the lively sympathy with which the principal works of the great .masters for the last fifty years

have been received and acknowledged here (often for
the first time in Germany), and by the careful attention with which these works have been invariably
executed, Leipzig has assumed a high position among
the musical cities of our Fatherland.   Lastly, in support
of this petition I may add that Herr Hofkriegsrath
Blümner, who cherished so great a love for poetry
and the poetical in every art, always devoted special
attention to the state of music here, and indeed took
an active charge in the direction of the concerts, in
which he was warmly interested; so that such an
apportionment of his bequest would undoubtedly be
quite in accordance with the artistic feelings of the
testator.

While other establishments of public utility are constantly encouraged, and some even richly endowed, the
music here has never received the smallest aid from any
quarter.   The musical institution in the capital being
supported by Government, is it not then peculiarly
desirable that this city should receive the sum bequeathed by one of its inhabitants, where such a boon
would be received with peculiar gratitude on every
side?   On all these grounds, may his Majesty then be
graciously disposed not to refuse the fulfilment of a
wish so warmly cherished, and thus impart a new
stimulus and a fresh impulse to art.   It would give an
impetus to musical life here, the effects of which would
speedily and enduringly be disseminated, with the best
influence.

Allow me to enclose in this envelope some general
outlines for the arrangement of such a musical academy,
and receive the assurance of the distinguished esteem

with which I have the honour to remain your devoted
servant,

FELIX MENDELSSOHN BARTHOLDY.

To his Mother.

Leipzig, August 10th, 1840.

On Thursday I gave an organ concert here in the
Thomas Church, from the proceeds of which old Sebastian Bach is to have a monument erected to his memory,
in front of the Thomas School. I gave it *solissimo*, and
played nine pieces, winding up with an extempore fantasia. This was the whole programme. Although my
expenses were considerable, I had a clear gain of three
hundred dollars. I mean to try this again in the autumn or spring, and then a very handsome memorial
may be put up.* I practised hard for eight days previously, till I could really scarcely stand upright, and
executed nothing but organ passages along the street
in my gait when I walked out.

To Fanny Hensel, Berlin.

Leipzig, October 24th, 1840.

Dear Fanny,

I make use of my first morning's leisure since my
return from England, to thank you for your most admi-

---

* This has been done. The monument is on the promenade, under
the windows of Sebastian Bach's rooms, in the Thomas School.

rable and charming letter, which welcomed me on my return here. When I first saw it lying, and broke the seal, I had somehow a kind of presentiment that it might contain some bad news (I mean, something momentous). I don't know how this was, but the very first lines made me see it in a very different light, and I read on and on with the greatest delight. What a pleasure it is to receive such a letter, with such a flavour of life and joy, and all that is good! The only tone in a minor key, is that you do not expect to like Berlin much after Rome; but this I consider a very transitory feeling; after a long sojourn in Italy where could any one be contented? There, all is so glowing! and our dear German home life, which I do so heartily love, has this in common with all that is German and dear, that it is neither splendid nor brilliant, but its stillness and repose only the more surely fascinate the heart. After every absence I felt just the same when the joy of the first days of reunion was past; I missed the variety and the excitement of travelling so much, that home seemed sadly monotonous, and I discovered all sorts of deficiencies, whereas during my journey all was perfect and all was good. The same feelings have often recurred to me recently at the Leipzig Liedertafel, and at the innumerable demands and intrusions, etc. etc.; but this did not last, and was certainly only a fallacy. All that is good, and that we like in our travels, is, in fact, our wonted property at home, only we there exact a still larger portion. If we could only preserve through life the fresh, contented, and lofty tone of feeling which, for the first few days on returning from a journey, leads us to look at every object with such satisfaction, and

on the journey makes us rise superior to all annoyances,—if we could only remain inwardly in this buoyant travelling spirit, while continuing to live in the
quiet of home,—we should indeed be vastly perfect!
Instead of this, last night, at the twenty-fifth anniversary of the Liedertafel, I was as angry as if I had been
a young boy. They sang so false, and talked even more
falsely; and when it became peculiarly tiresome, it was
in the name of "our German Fatherland," or "in the
good old German fashion." Yet when I came back
from England I had formed such a strong resolution
never to discompose myself about anything, and to
remain entirely neutral!* I was eight days in London,
and the same in Birmingham, and to me the period
passed like a troubled dream; but nothing could be
more gratifying than meeting with so many friends
quite unchanged. Although I could only see them for
so short a time, yet the glimpse into so friendly an
existence, of which we hear nothing for years, but
which remains still linked with our own, and will ever
continue to be so, causes most pleasurable sensations.

Of course I was constantly with Klingemann and
Moscheles, and with the Alexanders also, where, in the

---

* It is characteristic of both, that Mendelssohn's sister set the following poem of Goethe's to music:—

> "Here are we then, my friend, at home once more!
> And tranquilly reclines the artist's eye
> On scenes of peace and love from door to door,
> Where life to life in kindliness draws nigh.

> "Back with our household gods, here are we then!
> For though through distant regions we may roam,
> From all these ravishments we turn again
> Back to the magic sphere we call our home."

most elegant *rococo* drawing-rooms, among all the new-
est and most fashionable objects, I found my father's
portrait, painted by Hensel, in its old favourite place,
and standing on its own little table; and I was with
the Horsleys also, and in many other houses where I
felt happy and at home; when I recall my excessive
uneasiness at the prospect of the journey, and how we
paced up and down here together and discussed it,
making each other, in fact, only mutually more nervous,
and yet all is now so happily over and I so happily returned to my family, I ought scarcely to do anything
all day long but rejoice and be thankful,—instead of
which I fly into a passion with the Liedertafel, and you
do the same with the Art Exhibition?

You ask me whether we are to have peace or war?
How have I got such a fine reputation as a news-
monger? Not that I do not deserve it, for I maintain
through thick and thin that we shall have peace, but
combined with much warlike agitation; though when
a *politicus* by profession like Paul is in the family, he
must be applied to. He may say what he likes, but no
war shall we have.

Though, when I think of yesterday's Liedertafel, I
almost wish we had!

Pray write again soon, my very dear sister, and a
long letter.—Your

FELIX.

To his Mother.

Dear Mother,

Leipzig, October 27th, 1840.

A thousand thanks for your kind letter, received yesterday, which was truly charming, in spite of the well-merited little hit at the beginning. I ought indeed to have written to you long since; but during the last three months you can have no idea how entirely I have been obliged to play the part of "Hans of all work." There are trifling minute occupations, too, such as notes, etc., of daily recurrence, which seem to me as tiresome and useless in our existence as dust on books, and which, like it, at last thickly accumulate, and do much harm, unless fairly cleared away every morning; and then I feel so keenly the impulse to make some progress with my daily labours as soon as I am in a happy vein. All these things cause the weeks and months to fly past like the wind.

You probably already know, through the newspapers, that we had recently a second performance of the "Hymn of Praise" for the King of Saxony, at an extra subscription concert, and it went off famously. All the music was given with such precision that it was a real pleasure to listen to it. The King sent for me between the parts, which obliged me to pass through a double row of ladies (you know the arrangement of our concert-room) in order to reach the place where the King and his Court were seated. He conversed with me for some time, in the most good-natured and friendly manner, and spoke very judiciously about music. The "Hymn of Praise" was given in the second part, and at the conclusion, just as I had quitted my music-desk, I suddenly heard people round me saying, "The King is coming to him this time;" and he was in fact passing through the rows of ladies, and came up to my desk (you may imagine what universal satisfaction this caused). He spoke to me in so animated a manner, and with such cordiality and warmth, that I did indeed feel it to be a great pleasure and honour. He mentioned the particular passages that had pleased him most, and, after thanking all the singers, he took his departure, while the whole orchestra, and the whole audience, made the very best bows and curtsies they could accomplish. Then came a hubbub and confusion like Noah's ark. Perhaps the King will now bestow the twenty thousand *thalers* which I long ago petitioned might be given towards the music here. In that case, I could with truth say that I had done good service to the music of Leipzig.*

Eckert has returned here in the character of a zealous Prussian patriot, and goes nearly as far as the Prussian Government paper, which declares that the rain which beat in the King's face only fanned his fire still more. But to my incredulous grimaces Eckert replied that *you* were quite of his way of thinking, and had charged him to let me know this. It is so provoking that a distance even of twenty miles should exercise so irresistible an influence, and that, notwithstanding all the minute descriptions and details in the newspapers, we cannot rightly understand the proceedings which take place in your presence, and *vice versâ*. A thousand minutiæ are involved in the affair, which appear insig-

---

* See the letter to Herr von Falkenstein, April 8th, 1840.

nificant, and are consequently omitted by the narrator;
and yet they are the links that connect the whole, and
the chief cause of many of these events.

So far as I can gather the real meaning of it all, just
so far does it displease me, and that is perhaps the reason why I cannot approve of all the other fine ad-
juncts, down to the "fiery rain" of the Government
paper. In the mean while, time pursues its steady jog-
trot pace. Thiers is no longer minister. A number of
arrests have been made in Frankfort, and Queen Chris-
tina is welcome to my little room. By Heavens! I
would at this moment far rather be a musician than a
sovereign!

I say nothing about the silver wedding day of the
Leipzig Liedertafel, for I have not yet recovered from
it. God help us! what a tiresome thing our German
Fatherland is, when viewed in this light! I can well
remember my Father's violent wrath against Lieder-
tafels, and indeed against everything at all connected
with *Vetter Michel;* and I feel something similar
stirring within me.

Farewell, dearest mother.—Ever your

FELIX.

To FANNY HENSEL, BERLIN.

Leipzig, November 14th, 1840.

Dear Fanny,

My brightest, best, and most heartfelt good wishes
for this day! Once upon a time, I used to send you a

new manuscript, bound in green, in honour of the occasion; now I must content myself with a mere scanty letter; and yet the old custom pleases me very much better.

No doubt, in the course of your birthday, you too think of us here; but that does not mend matters much for me. This evening, at the recommencement of the Quartett Soirées, I am to play to the Leipzigers Mozart's quartett in G minor, and the Beethoven trio in D major, and, as I already said, the kind of birthday celebration does not please me; it will be very differently commemorated where you are. Would that we could be with you! My best thanks also for your last letter. Do you know, I think your suggestion as to the "Nibelungen" most luminous! It has been constantly in my head ever since, and I mean to employ my first leisure day in reading over the poem, for I have forgotten the details, and can only recall the general colouring and outlines, which seem to me gloriously dramatic. Will you kindly communicate to me your specific ideas on this subject? The poem is evidently more present to your memory than to mine. I scarcely remember what your allusion means, as to the sinking into the Rhine. Can you point out to me the various passages which struck you as particularly dramatic, when the idea first occurred to you? and, above all, say something more definite on the subject, as the whole tone and colouring, and characteristics, take my fancy strongly; therefore I beg of you to do so, and soon, too; it will be an essential service to me. Refer entirely to the poem itself, for before your letter can arrive I shall certainly have read it, though I shall not

the less eagerly expect your opinion. Accept my
thanks for this happy thought, as for all else.

Yes! the arpeggios in the chromatic fantasia* are
certainly the chief effect. I take the liberty to play
them with all possible *crescendos*, and *pianos*, and *for-*
tissimos, pedal of course, and to double the notes in the
bass; further, to mark the small passing notes at the beginning of the arpeggios (the crotchets in the middle
parts), etc., and likewise the principal notes of the melody just as they come: rendered thus, the succession
of glorious harmonies produces an admirable effect on
our rich-toned new pianos. For example, the commencement, merely thus:—

N.B.—Each chord played in double arpeggios, afterwards only
once, as they come.

* By Sebastian Bach.

Then to the end thus:—

People vow that this is quite as fine as Thalberg, and even more so. Don't show this receipt, however, to

17*

any one; it is a mystery like all domestic receipts.
When you see Herr v. Zucalmaglio, thank him for his
packet and the letter I received from him; at the same
time (though this is quite between ourselves), I cannot
compose music for the songs he sent me; they are
patriotic, and at this moment I have no taste whatever
for this style of song,—they might cause a great deal
of bad feeling; and in the present state of things,
people seem to me to begin to sing against the French,
at the very moment when they must know that the
French will not fight against them : for such a purpose
I have no music. But adieu for the present. I do wish
that instead of being obliged to dress, and to go through
a vast amount of music, I were going across to you.
We could play at " Black Peter," or some other merry
game, and eat cakes.—Your

FELIX.

To CARL KLINGEMANN, LONDON.

Leipzig, November 18th, 1840.

My dearest Friend,

I am living here in as entire quiet and solitude as I
could possibly desire; my wife and children are well,
God be praised! and I have work in abundance ; what
can any man wish for beyond this? I only long for its
continuance, and pray that Heaven may grant it, while
I daily rejoice afresh in the peaceful monotony of my
life. At the beginning of the winter, however, I had
some difficulty in avoiding the social gatherings which

bloom and thrive here, and which would cause both a
sad loss of time and of pleasure if you were to accept
them, but now I have pretty well succeeded in getting
rid of them.   Moreover, this week there is a fast, so
we have no subscription concert, which gives us a
pleasant domestic season of rest.   My "Hymn of
Praise" is to be performed the end of this month for
the benefit of old invalided musicians. I am determined, however, that it shall not be produced in the imperfect form in which, owing to my illness, it was given in
Birmingham: so that makes me work hard.   Four new
pieces are to be added, and I have also much improved
the three sets of symphonies, which are now in the
hands of the copyist. As an introduction to the chorus
" Die Nacht ist vergangen," I have found far finer
words in the Bible, and admirably adapted to the
music.   By the by, you have much to answer for in
the admirable title you hit on so cleverly, for not only
have I sent forth the piece into the world as a *symphony
cantata*, but I have serious thoughts of resuming the
first " Walpurgis Nacht" (which has been so long lying
by me) under the same cognomen, and finishing and
getting rid of it at last.   It is singular enough that
at the very first suggestion of this idea I should have
written to Berlin that I was resolved to compose a
symphony with a chorus ; subsequently I had not
courage to begin, because the three movements were too
long for an introduction, and yet I never could divest
myself of the impression that something was wanting
in the shape of an introduction.   Now the symphony
is to be inserted, according to my original intention,
and the piece brought out at once.   Do you know it ?

I scarcely think that it is well adapted for performance, and yet I like it much.

The whole town here is ringing with a song, supposed to have a political tendency against the French, and the journals are striving with all their might to render it popular. In the present dearth of public topics, they succeed in this without any difficulty, and every one is speaking of the " Rheinlied," or the *Colognaise,* as they significantly call it. The thing is characteristic, for the first line begins, " Sie sollen ihn nicht haben, den freien Deutschen Rhein," and at the commencement of each verse is repeated, " Never shall they have it," as if there were the least sense in such words! If they were at least changed into " We mean to keep it,"— but " Never shall they have it," seems to me so sterile and futile. There is certainly something very boyish in this idea; for when I actually possess an object, and hold it sure and fast, it is quite superfluous to sing, or to say, that it shall belong to no one else. This song is now sung at Court in Berlin, and in the clubs and casinos here, and of course the musicians pounce upon it like mad, and are immortalizing themselves by setting it. The Leipzig composers have already brought out no less than three melodies for it, and every day the papers make some allusion to it. Yesterday, amongst other things, they said I had also set the song, where-as I never even dreamt of meddling with such a merely defensive inspiration.

So the people here lie like print, just as they do with you, and everywhere else.

To Paul Mendelssohn Bartholdy.

Leipzig, November 20th, 1840.

Dear Paul,

How much I wish that you would perform your promise, and come here for the " Hymn of Praise "! I shall be glad to know what you think of it, and to hear if it pleases you, for I own that it lies very near my heart. I think, too, that it will be well executed by our orchestra; but in spite of this, if by arriving in time for its performance your proposed visit must be in any degree shortened, then I would urge you to come on some other occasion, for our happy quiet intercourse must always form the chief object in our Leipzig life, and even one day more is pure gain. If indeed both could be combined, a visit of the usual length *and* the concert, that would of course be best of all. The " Hymn of Praise " is to form the second part; in the first, probably Weber's " Jubilee Overture " will be given, Kreuzer's " Rheinlied," and some other pieces. I could write you a long complaint about this said " Rheinlied." You can have no idea of the fuss they make about it here, and how utterly repugnant to me this newspaper enthusiasm is; to make such a piece of work about a song, the chief burden of which is, that others shall not deprive us of what we have already got,—truly this is worthy of such a commotion and such music! I never wish to hear a single note of it sung, when the *refrain* is always the resolve not to give up what you possess. Young lads and timid men may make this outcry, but true men make no such piece of work about what is their own; they have it, and that suffices. I felt provoked to see recently in a newspaper that, in addition to four compositions on these words, one by me had just appeared, and my name was printed full length; yet I cannot give a direct contradiction to this, for as regards the public I am dumb. At the same time Härtel sent me a message that if I would compose for it, he would undertake to dispose of six thousand copies in two months. No, Paul, I won't do it. May we soon have a happy meeting!—Your   FELIX.

To PAUL MENDELSSOHN BARTHOLDY.

Leipzig, December 7th, 1840.

Dear Brother,

Just as I was about to write to you yesterday, to thank you cordially again and again for the fresh proof of your true brotherly love which you have given me,*

---

*. His brother had gone to Leipzig, at the instigation of the Wirk-lich Geheimrath Herr von Massow, to negotiate with Mendelssohn the subject of a situation in Berlin. It was proposed to divide the Academy of Arts into four classes,—namely, painting, sculpture, archi-tecture, and music,—and to appoint a director for each class, to whom the superintendence of the Academy should be intrusted alternately, and in fixed succession. The music class, for which Mendelssohn had been selected as Director, was to consist essentially of a large Conserva-torium, in the expectation that, in connection with the resources of the Royal Theatre, public concerts, partly of a sacred and partly of a secular nature, should be given. However promising Mendelssohn considered this project, he at once expressed considerable doubts, not so much that the plan *could* not be carried out, but that it *would* not be so; and the result proved how correct his judgment was on the point.

your letter arrived, and I can only repeat the same thing. Even if the affair leads to nothing further than to show me (what is the fact) that you participate in my wish once more to pass a portion of our lives together, that you, too, feel there is something wanting when we are not all united in one spot, this is to me invaluable, and more gratifying than I can express. Whether it be attended with a happy result or not, I would not give up such a conviction for anything in the world.

Your letter, indeed, demands mature deliberation, but I prefer replying to it at once, for the coincidence of Herr Massow's journey is most fortunate, and you can thus hear my opinion before your interview with him.

I am prepared to acknowledge to the utmost extent the high honour conferred on me, and the excellence of the possession offered to me. On this very account, however, I wish to obviate any difficulties, and to make the matter as clear as possible. One thing occurs to me in the proposal, which you can perhaps remedy in your conversation with Massow. It would not be easy to explain it by letter, and at all events it would lose much time, and not further the affair.

You may remember the general overtures as to the Academy and school for music that you brought me, and you know that I named the concerts as a positive *stipulation;* on the other hand, I said to you that *without* a definite sphere of work (as an appointed composer, like Grimms, you can say) I should hesitate much to accept the proposal. Either of these situations would suit me, but not the two combined. I would at once most decidedly refuse this, much as I should regret being obliged to do so, and however advantageous it might seem to me in other points. Your condition No. 2 sets forth that I am to be director of the musical classes, without any definite sphere of work, etc.; and then No 4 declares that I am to give sundry concerts every year,—but that is a combination to which I never can consent. For instance, were I to undertake to give concerts in Berlin (and the acceptance of these proposals would render it my duty to so do, even towards you), then I must stand in a different relation to the orchestra from what I could possibly do as the mere director of the music classes. I must be quite as much their real chief there as I am here, and as every ordinary director must be, which is only possible by the establishment of a Musical Academy as a Royal Institution, and by its connection with the orchestra in Berlin. The number, too, of such concerts should not be very limited, as you say, otherwise they would not repay the trouble of such great preparations. In a word, you may easily perceive that I can only accept proposals that either define *every* point, or are confined to my personal and *not* to my official position; if the two are to be blended, I cannot consent to undertake them.

Finding (after you left us) on more mature deliberation that a situation as a composer is impossible, and, in fact, is nowhere to be met with, it occurred to me that the offer might be renewed of a public sphere of activity, and that I am quite prepared to accept; it must, however, be within special limits, despotic as regards the musicians, and consequently imposing even in outward position (not merely brilliant in a pecuniary point of view), otherwise, according to my ideas, it would be fatal to my authority after the very first rehearsal. I merely say all this, in order to indicate to you the point of the compass for which you must steer your course, in your conversation with Massow, and that the affair may pursue as clear a path as possible.— Ever your

FELIX.

To Paul Mendelssohn Bartholdy.

Leipzig, December 20th, 1840.

Dear Brother,

You wish to have some tidings from me as to *our* affair (for well may I call it so). The letter from Massow came eight days since, and I answered it on Wednesday, just as I would have written or spoken to yourself, without reservation or disguise, but still without that eager acceptance which was probably expected. I think you would have been satisfied with my letter, and I hope and trust Massow may be so also. He wrote far less explicitly about the details of the institution than you did in a former letter; he mentions the salary, the direction of the classes, and the concerts to be given by royal command, but without entering into any further particulars. I replied that I was so fully aware of the advantage and honour of his offer, that I feared he would be surprised by my not instantly closing with it. There was but one obstacle in the way, which

18

was, that I did not precisely know what was expected from me in return for such a proposal. I then brought under his notice the difficulties opposed to a *bond fide* direction of the present classes; and as he had mentioned that these would not now occupy much of my time, but that it was expected I should, under the new system, undertake additional work, I begged, therefore, at least to be told what were the limits of this system, and the duties I had to perform; that I was indeed quite willing to work, but did not choose to pledge myself to the performance of functions that were not precisely defined. With regard to the concerts, I told him my opinion as to the only mode of arranging them now in Berlin; that little good could accrue from merely occasional performances, even by royal command; for in that case all sorts of counter-influences (and those I specified to him) would have full scope; that an institute must be founded exclusively for similar concerts, and likewise days fixed for the rehearsals and concerts, and the instruction of the performers, etc.; that I would have nothing to do with the orchestra, except on *this* condition, that I was to be absolute director-in-chief of these concerts, etc.

In short, I showed that I was well disposed to accept the situation, but should require the most unqualified support throughout, otherwise I could not efficiently perform the duties of the office,—it being a public one. I hope you agree with me on this point, for though money and ready complaisance are indeed of no small value, still neither are sufficient, without that entire tranquillity and security about the future, which can now be given if they are in earnest in the matter. I

can assure you that there was no undue particularity
in my words, but I am certain you will not blame me
for going on sure grounds, before giving up such a
position as my present one.

I considered it also my duty, before writing to
Massow, to communicate the circumstance under the
seal of the strictest secrecy to my friends here,
Schleinitz and David, who are quite of my opinion,
that I ought to leave this, however much they regret
it, if my wishes are fulfilled with regard to a defined
position. At the same time, I purpose, in the course
of a few days, to make known to our Concert Director,
and Government President, that I have received such
an offer (without naming the place), and that it is
probable I may accept it. Perhaps you may not
approve of this, but I feel I cannot act otherwise. If
my negotiations with Massow were to terminate by our
agreeing, without my having given any hint of such a
transaction, it would show a want of good feeling on
my part, and, indeed, in my present circumstances, a
want of common gratitude. But this is in fact a mere
matter of form, for it is not probable that they will for
a moment think of entering into competition with the
recent overtures from Berlin, and yet I delay the
announcement from day to day, because such a step
must be final.—Your

FELIX.

To Paul Mendelssohn Bartholdy.

Leipzig, Jan. 2d, 1841.

Dear Paul,

Receive my heartfelt good wishes, and may God grant us all a happy new year! Now I have one earnest request to make. Do not allow any misunderstanding between Massow and me to impair that delightful and perfect harmony between us which always rejoices me and makes me so happy. I will not say, let us not become more mistrustful, but not even more reserved towards each other. Since the great sacrifice that you unhesitatingly made for my sake in coming here, I confess I am in great anxiety on this subject, and it makes me very uneasy when I think it possible that you may be dissatisfied with me for not being prepared to accept your opinion at once,— *angry* I do not think you will be, but, as I have already said, do not permit anything whatever to be changed between you and me: promise me this; you know how much I have at heart our being able to live together at some future day; but if we were only to pass a few untroubled years together, and I were then to go on my way in vexation, that would be worse than it is now, and I would gladly avoid this. I tell you so, because in your letter you urge me so strongly fairly to speak out, as if I had not in my answer to Massow already spoken out on many points, more, perhaps, than I ought to have done. You also wish to persuade me to go now to Berlin, but you will soon be convinced that, this winter, such a thing is impossible. I have five subscription concerts, and

three extra concerts to direct in January, and in the
beginning of March, Bach's "Passion," of which not a
single note is known here, and I certainly cannot get
away during the time of the concerts without injuring
them. But, independent of this, what should I do in
Berlin? The statutes of a new Academy are better
arranged by writing than verbally, and, from the tenor
of Massow's letters, the affair does not seem so far advanced as to permit of its being definitively settled in
the course of a couple of days; at least not in the
sense that we mutually wish; so, as I said, dear Paul,
promise me never, under any circumstances, to be displeased with me.

I told Massow in a letter to-day that I should be
happy to explain my views with regard to reorganizing
the Musical Academy, either to him, or to Eichhorn;
for this purpose he has only to send me the statutes
hitherto in force, and the composition of the classes, of
which I am entirely ignorant, and also say how far the
modifications are to be carried, whether to the extent
of a radical change, or merely a reform; this I must
learn, of course, or I should not know what to say; I
will gladly devote my time and efforts to the mere
possibility of our once more living together, but I must
confess that since Massow's last letter such a possibility
seems even more distant than I myself thought. It
sounds all so different from what they commissioned
you to say to me when you came here; and if it begins
in such a way, no doubt the sequel will be still worse.
The salary they offer is certainly handsome and liberal,
but if they in return expect me to accept an unlimit-
ed obligation to work, that also would be a change

18*

in their proposals, and no compensation to me. The salary is the only point on which Massow spoke in a decided manner to me, and my position is too fortunate for mere money to influence my views. All that you told me here about a *rota* between the different directors, and the duties of the Capellmeister of the Royal Chapel, and of the engagement of other foreign musicians,—not a word of this was brought forward; on the contrary, Massow writes to me that he is glad I have declared myself satisfied with the title and the salary, which is totally opposed to the sense of my previous letter, in which I expressed a wish to know my duties before I could explain my intentions. Indeed, even if the alteration in the musical class were to be entered into, and carried through exactly according to my wishes, I scarcely know (as the title is in question) whether I should quite like to go to Berlin as "Director of the Musical Class," which is by no means in good odour with musicians at present. I can say all this to you without incurring the suspicion of a fondness for titles, for what annoys me is their *drawing back* in all their proposals; perhaps I am mistaken; at all events, I hope in my letter to Massow you will find no trace of the dissatisfaction which I have frankly expressed to you. I shall assist in establishing the new regulations as well and as firmly as possible; in any event, good service will be done to the cause, so far as I can accomplish it, and if the result is to be satisfactory, the affair must first be made clear,—not merely in reference to my personal acceptance, but because it is right and desirable for the affair itself, and in order to enable *any* good musician (not merely myself) to interest themselves in it hereafter; for now the question again recurs, whether I or some other efficient musician shall be placed at the head, and all the other questions become mere secondary considerations.

For Heaven's sake, tell me, how came you to be reading that abominable thing of Diderot's? He was ashamed of it later in life, but the traces of his genius are to be discovered even in this muddy pool. I may possibly feel more mildly disposed towards him just now, because two pietistic works were sent to me yesterday from Berlin, so gloomy, such a perfect type of the worst time of the priesthood, that I am almost inclined to welcome the French with their audacity and Voltaire with his broom. Perhaps you know one of these? It is called "Die Passion, ein kirchliches Festspiel;" it is written in doggerel rhymes, and is the most wretched trash I have lately read,—Heine included. The other is a criticism written by a person on his own oratorio, in which he exhorts the people to piety and frequent communion, and says no one is entitled to pronounce any opinion on his music who does not listen to it in the spirit of true piety and in faith. Alas! alas!

Remember my first request in this new year, and love me as much as ever.—Your

FELIX.

To Paul Mendelssohn Bartholdy.

Leipzig, Jan. 9th, 1841.

Dear Paul,

Your letter of yesterday made me very happy; God knows why I could not get it out of my head that you were angry with me for delaying an affair which you wished to expedite, and have so kindly expedited. I however see from your letter that I was entirely and totally wrong, and I thank you much for it, and subscribe to all you say on the subject. But there is one idea you must dismiss from your thoughts as much as I have done the other, and that is the dread of foreign influences, as you call them, which you allude to in your letter. You must not suppose that I ever act in any affair but from my own conscientious impulses, far less in a matter in which I myself and my happiness are so very closely involved. Believe me that, in general, I invariably strive to do and say nothing but what I hold to be right in my conscience and instinct, and it is a proof that we have, alas! lived much asunder, and only met in days of enjoyment, and not of work, when you fear that I am easily swayed, not only in conversation, but in action. No! all goes on very slowly with me, but when at last I do a foolish thing I have at least *one* merit, which is, to have devised it entirely myself. With regard to this *special* case, I probably gave you cause for suspicion, by writing to you that I told my friends here, David and Schleinitz, of the offer, and in my last letter I did not allude to them again. I can assure you, however, that both have long ago given me such proofs of sincere friendship, that I could not possibly have been silent to them on this occasion, and both urged my acceptance, and saw the thing in the most favourable light.

That not the smallest step I have taken in the whole affair may be unknown to you, I must add that I felt myself obliged to communicate the circumstance candidly, some days ago, to the Kreis-Director, Herr von Falkenstein; for in this month the money becomes due which the King has the disposal of, and which, as you are aware, I last winter petitioned might be appropriated to found a school of music here. The King, who expressed himself in a very kind manner towards me when he came to one of our subscription concerts, seemed well disposed to give his consent; then came Falkenstein to ask me if I would pledge myself (which really was my idea at that time) to organize this music school for some years to come. I now no longer could or would do this: so I thought it best to tell him the whole affair. He gave me his faithful promise to preserve the strictest silence, and I in turn agreed to give him due notice if I settled to go to Berlin, because that, he said, might be prejudicial to the plan of the music school; and thus it now stands.

I await the arrival of the statutes; at all events, an opportunity may then occur to render an occasional service to the cause there, and to place many things on a better footing, and perhaps to introduce a better system into the whole class, and some good would be thus effected.

The examples of which you speak in regard to public opinion interested me very much, but, I own, were far from pleasing to me. I do not call that public opinion which is shown by sending anonymous and libellous verses, and by hissing an old masterpiece.* You will perhaps say this is only the beginning; but that is the very point: if a thing is not rightly begun it never comes to a good end, and I do not believe that public *tracasseries* can pave the way to public opinion; indeed, I believe that such things have always existed, and always will exist, independent of the *vox populi*, which is the *vox Dei*. It would be more important to me if you would tell me some particulars of the *curiosa* which are related of Minister Schön; pray do this, if you possibly can. He seems to be a determined fellow!—Your

FELIX.

To HERR X——.

Leipzig, January 22d, 1841.

Sir,

I beg to offer you my thanks for the confidence you have shown me by your polite letter, and the accompanying music. I have looked over your overture with much pleasure, and discovered many unmistakable traces of talent in it, so that I should rejoice to have an opportunity of seeing some more new works of yours, and thus to make your musical acquaintance in a more intimate and confidential manner. The greater part of the instrumentation, and especially the melodious passage which is in fact the principal subject,

---

* The performance of "Athalie," with Schultz's music, had caused considerable excitement in the Berlin Theatre.

pleased me much. If I were to find any fault, it would be one with which I have often reproached myself in my own works; in the very overtures you allude to, sometimes in a greater and sometimes in a lesser degree. It is often very difficult, in such fantastical airy subjects, to hit the right medium. If you grasp it too firmly, it is apt to become formal and prosaic; and if too delicately, it dissolves into air and melody, and does not become a defined form. This last rock you seem to have split upon; in many passages, especially at the very beginning, but also here and there in other parts, and towards the close again, I feel the want of a musical well-defined form, the outlines of which I can recognize, however misty, and grasp and enjoy. I should like, besides the *meno allegro*, to see some other more definite idea, and to have it worked out; only then, the other rock is too apt to show itself, and modulations be seen, where there should be nothing but moonlight. In order, however, to give free course to these poetical thoughts, the spirit of entire supremacy must hover over the whole (that fact should not become too dry, nor fancy too misty); and it is only where this complete mastery over thought and arrangement exists, that the reins may be given to imagination. This is the very point which we are all obliged, more or less, to study; I hope you will not be offended, therefore, that I do not find this problem entirely solved in your work either; in your future productions, with which I hope to become acquainted, the connection will, no doubt, be closer, and my critical remarks rendered unnecessary.—I am, with sincere esteem, yours,

FELIX MENDELSSOHN BARTHOLDY.

To his Mother.

Leipzig, January 25th, 1841.

. . . This is the thirty-fifth letter I have written since the day before yesterday; it makes me quite uneasy to see how the flood swells, if a few days elapse without my stemming it and guarding against it. Variations from Lausitz and Mayence; overtures from Hanover, Copenhagen, Brunswick, and Rudolstadt; German Fatherland songs from Weimar, Brunswick, and Berlin, the latter of which I am to set to music, and the former to look over and take to a publisher: and all these accompanied by such amiable, polite letters, that I should be ashamed if I were not to reply to them in as amiable and kind a manner as I possibly can. But who can give me back the precious days which pass away in these things? Add to this, persons who wish to be examined, eagerly awaiting my report for their anxious relatives, whether they are to become professional musicians or not; two Rhenish youths are here at this moment for that purpose, and the verdict is to be given in the course of a few hours. It is really a heavy responsibility, and I often think of La Fontaine's rat, who retired into a cheese and thence delivered oracles.

To Paul Mendelssohn Bartholdy.

Leipzig, February 13th, 1841.

My dear Brother,

It is curious how certain years elapse, when both time and people seem to stand quietly still; and then

again come weeks, when everything seems to run about
like billiard-balls, making cannons, and losing and win-
ning hazards, etc. etc. (*vide* the Temperance Hotel in
Gohlis). Such has been the case with me during the
last few months. Since you were here, everything is
so far advanced and altered, that it would take me a
week at least, and walks innumerable, without letting
you utter a word, before I could tell you all; and probably it has been the same with you.

The Berlin affair is much in my thoughts, and is a
subject for serious consideration. I doubt whether it
will ever lead to *that* result which we both (I believe)
would prefer; for I still have misgivings as to Berlin
being a soil where a person of my profession could feel
even tolerably at home, in spite of all honours and
money; but the mere offer in itself gives me an inward
impulse, a certain satisfaction, which is of infinite value
to me, even if I were never to speak of it to any one;
in a word, I feel that an honour has been done me, and
I rejoice in it. Massow writes in his last letter, which
I received before yours, that the King wishes to delay
the definitive arrangement of the Academy till I go to
Berlin in spring; whether I choose to make proposals
in writing as to the alteration of the statutes which he
sends me, he leaves entirely to my own decision. As
this point is left to myself, and I would far rather *not*
write at all on the subject, I shall delay doing so till I
know to a certainty whether I go to Berlin in spring
or not, and only in the latter case write. Remarkable,
very remarkable, these statutes are, especially those of
the school for composition. Imagine! out of eleven
different branches of instruction which they have insti-

tuted, seven are positively useless, and indeed preposterous. What do you think of the following, among others? No. 8. "The relation Music bears to the other arts, especially to the *plastic* and to the stage;" and also No. 11, "A guide to the spiritual and worldly Drama." I formerly read these things in the Government paper, and laughed at them; but when a grave minister or official actually sends such stuff, it is pitiable. Pray do go to some public place where newspapers are collected, and send me the one which advertises this course, and where the teachers of the different branches are named. I require these *data* thoroughly to understand the affair. It is all in the worst possible state. You will say this is the very reason why I should try to extricate it. In that case there would indeed be plenty to do, if I could only think myself the man to do it: to improve what is already good, or to create what is new and good, would be an undertaking that I should rejoice in, and which might be learned, even if there were no previous knowledge of the subject; but to change what is positively bad into better things, is both a hard and a thankless task.

A very momentous change has taken place here since what is called the King's concert. You cannot think what a good impulse the mere visit of the King, and his really cordial and kind approbation, has imparted to our concerts here. A person is almost to be envied who, by pure, kindly, natural feelings, and words of the same tenor, can give such an immediate impetus, were it not after all quite as difficult, in such a position, to preserve such feelings (which is the main point) as it is with us to maintain many less essential. By his

demeanour here, as well as by the way in which he has
sounded forth our praises in Dresden, he has facilitated
a number of things for us which were not thought of
formerly.   Since that time, we have strangers from
Dresden at every concert, and the female singers there
vie with each other in their efforts to appear in public
here.   The grant, too, of the legacy bequeathed two
years ago, will now probably be entirely devoted to
musical purposes, and perhaps be finally decided this
month.   All these are only mere outlines; but how
many details I might have added during the walks I
alluded to!   There has been one thing, however, and
that indeed the chief thing, which I have not been able
to accomplish during all these winter months, and that
is composition.   I sent my "Hymn of Praise" to be
published, and have written a couple of songs; this is,
however, all, and little enough too.

Now, as to literature, I am but in a poor state in
that respect.   Last week I had scarcely time to eat or
to sleep my *pensum*, without being fairly stranded, and
no possibility of reading.   I read Immermann's "Münch-
hausen" some time ago, but only the first volume; and
I must confess that the first half of it, which you too
do not praise, displeased me so much, that I was out
of sorts with the second also, although I do not deny
the great beauties in the second Westphalian portion,
and in all those works of his which I have seen.   I feel
the same with regard to X——'s critical article.   When
I see an old companion, endowed by a kind Providence
with every good capability, roaming about for many
long years, employing his really fine talents in writing
for newspapers, and criticizing a book which perhaps

had better never have been written (but for the money the bookseller gave for it), and with these exceptions bringing nothing of his own into the world, advancing nothing and contributing nothing, I cannot help thinking that it is the greatest blasphemy which can be committed against Providence, and so I don't wish to know anything of his clever criticisms, and feel a much higher esteem for every honest bookbinder and cobbler. This is, no doubt, one-sided, and too severe also; but I know nothing worse than the abuse or non-use of God's gifts, and have no sympathy for those who trifle with them.

Fie, for shame! what a cynical tone I have adopted! and I have not yet thanked you for all the good and loving and kind things you say to me of my music! But you must not estimate it so highly in contradistinction to that of others. To deserve all your praise, it ought to be very much better; and this I hope it will one day become. At all events, I think that the recitative, and the middle of my "Hymn of Praise," are more fervent and spirited than anything I have yet written. When shall we be able to sing it to you?

With this I close my letter. Write to me soon again. —Your   FELIX.

To FANNY HENSEL, BERLIN.

Leipzig, February 14th, 1841.

Salut et Fraternité!

Have you read the wrathful letter which the Emperor of China wrote to Lin, with a bright red pencil?

Were this the fashion with us, I would write to you to-day with a grass-green pencil, or with a sky-blue one, or with whatever colour a pleasant pencil ought to assume, in gratitude for your admirable epistle on my birthday. My especial thanks also for the kind and friendly interest you have shown in the faithful Eckert; he is a sound, practical musician, and further than this, in my opinion (to which I sometimes adhere for twenty-four hours), no man should concern himself about another. Whether a person be anything extraordinary, unique, etc., is entirely a private matter. But in this world, every one ought to be honest and useful, and he who is not so must and ought to be abused, from the Lord Chamberlain to the cobbler. Of all the young people whom I have had anything to do with here, he is the most good-natured, and by far the most inoffensive; and these are two precious qualities.

Don't, I beg, write me anything more about your Sunday music; it is really a sin and a shame that I have not heard it; but, though I feel so provoked at this, it is equally vexatious that you have heard none of our truly brilliant subscription concerts. I tell you we glitter brightly—in Bengal fire. The other day, in our last historical concert (Beethoven), Herr Schmidt was suddenly taken ill, and could not sing to his "Ferne Geliebte" in the "Liederkreis." In the middle of the first part David said, "I see Madame Devrient." She had arrived that morning by rail, and was to return next day. So during an interval I went up to her, was vastly polite, and she agreed to sing "Adelaide;" on which an old piano was carried into the orchestra from the anteroom. This was greeted with much applause,

19*

for people suspected that Devrient was coming. So come she did, in a shabby travelling costume, and Leipzig bellowed and shouted without end. She took off her bonnet before the *publicum*, and pointed to her black pelisse, as if to apologize for it. I believe they are still applauding! She sang beautifully, and there was a grand flourish of trumpets in her honour, and the audience clapped their hands, till not a single bow of the shabby pelisse was any longer visible. The next time we are to have a medley of Molique, Kalliwoda, and Lipinsky,—and thus, according to Franck's witticism, we descend from Adam to Holtei.

As to the *tempi* in my Psalm, all I have to say is, that the passage of the Jordan must be kept very watery; it would have a good effect if the chorus were to reel to and fro, that people might think they saw the waves; here we have achieved this effect. If you do not know how to take the other *tempi*, ask G——about them. He understands that capitally in my Psalms. With submission, allow me to suggest that the last movement be taken very slow indeed, as it is called "Sing to the Lord for ever and ever," and ought therefore to last for a very long time! Forgive this dreadful joke. Adieu, dear Fanny.—Your

FELIX.

To Pastor Julius Schubring, Dessau.

Leipzig, February 27th, 1841.

Dear Schubring,

Thank you a thousand times for your friendly letter, which caused me much pleasure, and was a most

welcome birthday gift. Our correspondence had certainly become rather threadbare, but pray don't give
up sending me your little notes of introduction; large
letters would indeed be better, but in default of these I
must be contented with little ones, and you well know
that they will always be received with joy, and those
who bring them welcomed to the best of my ability.

Now for my critical spectacles, and a reply about
your Becker " Rheinlied." I like it very much; it is
well written, and sounds joyous and exhilarating, but
(for a *but* must of course be uttered by every critic)
the whole poem is quite unsuitable for composition, and
essentially unmusical. I am well aware that in saying
this I rashly throw down the gauntlet both to you, and
many of my colleagues in Germany; but such is my
opinion, and the worst part of it is, that I am confirmed
in it by most of the compositions that I know. (For
Heaven's sake, let this remain a secret between us,
other wise,as journalists publish every trifle nowadays,
I may possibly be some day conveyed across the fron-
tiers as a Frenchman.) But, jesting apart, I can only
imagine music when I can realize the mood from which
it emanates; mere artistically correct tones to suit the
rhythm of the poetry, becoming *forte* when the words
are vehement, and *piano* when they are meek, sounding
very pretty, but expressing nothing,—I never yet could
comprehend; and still such is the only music I can
discover for this poem. Neither forcible, nor effective,
nor poetical, but only supplementary, collateral, musical
music. The latter, however, I do not choose to write.
In such cases, the fable of the two vases often recurs
to me, who set off together on a voyage, but in rolling

to and fro one smashed his companion, the one being made of clay and the other of iron. Besides, I consider the poem to be neither bold nor cautious, neither enthusiastic nor stoical, but only very positive, very practical, very suitable indeed for many at the present day; however, I cannot even momentarily interest myself in any object of which I can perceive the momentary nature, and from which I can expect no durability. I am becoming philosophical; pray forgive me, and forgive the whole diatribe, which is uncivil besides, because you composed the song yourself. But, as you have an immense majority of musicians on your side, you will not, I think, be offended by my dissentient protestation, but probably rather disposed to laugh at it. I could not help coming out with what I thought.

You wish to know how I am. As well as possible. Yet if we see each other in the course of a few weeks, you may perhaps hear the same complaints from me that you did last year. I often thought of them since, and laughed at them, because I was so well and so gay; but for a week past such languor seems to creep over me, that, as I told you, I might sing the very same old song of a year ago. I don't know whether this arises from the approach of spring, or the enormous quantity of music which I was engaged in during the winter, and which has fairly exhausted me; for several years past the two always come together. But I believe it is the latter; I have conducted fifteen public performances since January,—enough to knock up any man. Farewell, my dear friend.—Your

FELIX MENDELSSOHN BARTHOLDY.

To Paul Mendelssohn Bartholdy.

Leipzig, March 3d, 1841.

Dear Paul,

You gave me extreme pleasure by the *brochure** you sent me yesterday, and, after having exulted not a little in its contents, I must now thank you much for having forwarded it to me. I read of it in the " Allgemeine Zeitung," but had it not been for your kindness, this clever publication would not have found its way to my room for many a day. I have read it through twice with the deepest attention, and agree with you that it is a most remarkable sign of the present time in Prussia, that nothing more true, more candid, or more sober in form and style could be desired, and that a year ago a similar pamphlet could not have appeared. In the mean while, it is prohibited, and we shall soon see in how far it is merely an individual lofty spirit expressing his views, or a spirit that has really impressed and fired the whole community, for the great misfortune with us has always been want of unanimity, of *esprit de corps*. A sorrowful feeling oppresses me when I so surely see, or think I see, that the path lies open, level, and plain, on which the whole of Germany might receive a development which it probably never had, except in years of war, and not even then, because these years of war were years of violence also,—a path on which no one would lose, and all would gain in life, power, movement, and activity ; this path is likewise

* The " Vier Fragen " of Jacobi, a pamphlet of the day, the purport and contents of which would certainly no longer cause the smallest annoyance to either party.

that of truth, and honour, and fidelity to promises, and yet time after time it is never trodden, while new reasons are perpetually found for avoiding it. This is most melancholy! In the mean time, it is fortunate that there are people who know how to set forth what by far the greater number feel but cannot express. I should have to quote the whole of the pamphlet, to name all the particular passages written so entirely in consonance with the feelings of my heart; but I started up from joy at both the little paragraphs on the Dantzic letter and Hanover, for they came in so naturally, and quite as a matter of course; and then the glorious close! As I said before, the next fortnight will prove whether such a spirit has the right on his side in these days, not merely in theory but in practice. God grant it may be so!

If you hear anything further of your statesman* (I do not believe the *brochure* is his, though quite in accordance with his creed), or any more details that can be communicated to me, I beg you will not fail to do so. I begin to interest myself very much in this man. What a glorious contrast this work forms to all the French ones of last year that I have seen! Here is indeed real substance, not merely subtleties; vigorous truth and inborn dignity, not merely well-bred politeness or evasion of the laws.

But the work is prohibited! This is a humiliation, even amid all my delight. Farewell; thank you again cordially for your kindness always.—Your

FELIX.

---

* At the time of the appearance of the " Vier Fragen," Minister Schön was unquestionably supposed by the public to be the author.

To JULIUS RIETZ, MUSIC DIRECTOR AT DÜSSELDORF,

(*Now Capellmeister at Dresden.*)

Dear Rietz,

Leipzig, April 23d, 1841.

Yesterday evening we performed your overture to "Hero and Leander" and the "Battle Song," amid loud and universal applause, and with the unanimous approbation of the musicians and the public. Even during the rehearsal of the overture, towards the end in D major, I perceived in the orchestra those smiling faces and nodding heads which at a new piece of yours I am so glad to see among the players; it pleased them all uncommonly, and the audience, who yesterday sat as still as mice and never uttered a sound, broke out at the close into very warm applause, and fully confirmed the judgment of the others. I have had great delight in all these rehearsals, and in the performance also; there is something so genuinely artistic and so genuinely musical in your orchestral works, that I feel happy at the first bar, and they captivate and interest me till the very end. But, as you persist in wishing me to place my critical spectacles on my nose, I must tell you that there was one wish I formed in hearing both pieces: that you may now write many works in succession. The chief reason for this I do not require to tell you, for it lies on the surface. But I have yet another wish: I perceive a certain spirit, especially in the overture, which I myself know only too well, for in my opinion it caused my "Reformation Symphony"*

---

* An unpublished composition of Mendelssohn's.

to fail, but which can be surely and infallibly banished by assiduous work of different kinds. Just as the French, by conjuring tricks and overwrought sentiment, endeavour to make their style harrowing and exciting, so I believe it possible, through a natural repugnance to this style, to fall into the other extreme, and so greatly to dread all that is *piquant* or sensuous, that at last the musical idea does not remain sufficiently bold or interesting; that instead of a tumour there is a wasting away: it is the contrast between the Jesuit churches, and their thousand glittering objects, and the Calvinists, with their four white walls; true piety may exist in both, but still the right path lies between the two. I entreat you to pardon this preaching tone; but how is it possible to make oneself understood on such subjects? The fundamental thoughts in your overture and my " Reformation Symphony " (both having, in my opinion, similar qualities) are more interesting from what they indicate, than actually interesting in themselves; of course I do not plead for the latter quality alone (as that would lead us to the French), nor for the first alone either; both must be united and blended. The most important point is to make a thema, or anything of the kind which is in itself musical, really interesting: this you well understand in your instrumentation, with every second oboe or trumpet, and I should like to see you steer boldly in *that* direction in your next works,—without, however, injuring by the greater finish and sharpness of your musical thoughts, your excellent foundation, or your masterly and admirably carried-out details of instrumentation, etc. As ideas cannot be either more highly finished or sharpened, but must be taken and made use of as they come, and as a kind Providence sends them, so work is the only thing which either I or others can possibly desire for such an artist as yourself, and for works of art like yours, where the only question is of any trifling deviation in their tendency.

Report to his Majesty the King of Prussia,* from the Wirklich Geheimrath Herr von Massow.

Berlin, May 20th, 1841.

Your Majesty was pleased verbally to desire me to enter into communication with Herr Felix Mendelssohn Bartholdy, in Leipzig, with a view to summon him to Berlin, and to fix his residence there by appointment. I therefore on the 11th of December last wrote to Herr Mendelssohn, in accordance with your Majesty's commands, and made the following offer :—

That he should be appointed Director of the musical class of the Academy of Arts, with a salary of three thousand thalers.

I also mentioned that it was your Majesty's intention to reorganize the musical class of the Academy, and to connect it with some existing establishments for the development of musical cultivation, as well as with others yet to be formed; that Herr Mendelssohn's advice on the subject was requested ; that he was to be

---

* In this Report, the result of the negotiations with Mendelssohn, which finally caused him to go to Berlin, are fully detailed,—so it was considered necessary to give it a place here.

appointed the future head of this institute. Further, that it was your Majesty's pleasure a certain number of concerts (to be hereafter fixed) were to be given every year under his direction, with the aid of the Royal orchestra and the members of the opera, in which oratorios especially, but also other works, such as symphonies, etc., were to be performed. Herr Mendelssohn, in two letters addressed to me, on the 15th December and the 2d January, expressed his gratitude to your Majesty for so honourable an offer, as well as his entire satisfaction with regard to the title and the salary; he however reserved his full acceptance of the proposal until the duties involved in the situation offered to him in Berlin were more minutely detailed. The conscientiousness thus shown by Herr Mendelssohn cannot fail to be acknowledged and respected; at the same time, he promised to come to Berlin this spring.

The Academy of Arts being regulated by the *Ministerium* of the departments of science, instruction, and medicine, it was from this source alone that the wished-for copy of the rules could be obtained for Herr Mendelssohn; as this, however, could not be immediately effected, Minister Eichhorn resolved to discuss the whole affair himself with Herr Mendelssohn regarding the reorganization of the musical class, and your Majesty was pleased to permit the affair to rest for the time. Herr Mendelssohn, according to his promise, recently came here, and he adheres to his resolution not to accept any *fixed situation* in your Majesty's service till he is previously informed what duties he is expected to undertake.

The proposed reforms in the musical section, which
are probably to be effected, in connection with many
other changes in the Academy of Arts, necessitate the
dissolution of existing arrangements, and the formation
of entirely new relations.   The Royal *Ministerium*, if a
larger musical institute were established, would put in
their claim for the Royal Theatre, which, by previous
regulations of existing institutes, must be included,
along with most of the artists attached to it.   The sum
of money requisite for this purpose must be fixed and
granted.   These are all reasons which prevent the
Royal Ministerium, within so short a period, being able
to arrange such a comprehensive affair sufficiently to
lay these proposals before your Majesty, and also render
it impossible to define the situation for Herr Mendelssohn, or to prescribe the duties which, as Director of
the musical class, he must undertake to fulfil.

Herr Mendelssohn, on the other hand, must declare.
in the course of a few weeks, whether it is his intention
to give up his situation in Leipzig or not: he therefore
presses for a decision.

Under these circumstances, with the express stipulation, however, of your Majesty's approbation, I have
made the following proposal to Herr Mendelssohn :—

That for the present he should only for a certain
period fix his residence in Berlin,—say, a year,—*placing
himself at your Majesty's disposal,* in return for which,
your Majesty should confer on him the title of *Capellmeister,* but without imposing on him the performance
of the duties of this office in the Royal Opera; likewise the previously-named salary of three thousand
thalers pro anno to be bestowed on him ; during this

time, however, he is neither to hold *any* office, nor to undertake any *definite duties*, unless in the course of this period Herr Eichhorn should furnish him with the long-wished-for details, and he should declare himself satisfied with them, in which case the reserved consent as to a definitive nomination should ensue.

Herr Mendelssohn has already assured me that he is prepared to accept the proposal, and if your Majesty be pleased to give your consent, Herr Eichhorn would gain time to consult with Herr Mendelssohn on this affair, and to place distinct proposals before your Majesty. From the well-known honourable character of Herr Mendelssohn, it may be confidently anticipated that in this kind of interim relation he will be the more anxious to devote all his powers to your Majesty, from the very fact of his duties not being more closely defined. Such a relation, however, can only be advisable for a certain time ; one year has therefore been agreed on. If, contrary to expectation, the re-organization of the musical class of the Academy and the establishment of a musical institute be not so carried out as to cause Herr Mendelssohn the conviction of finding a field of activity for his bent and his vocation, or if the claims on him should prevent his acceptance, or, lastly,— which I subjoin at the express desire of Herr Mendelssohn,—should the expectations now entertained by your Majesty with regard to him not be fulfilled, then the relation now formed shall be dissolved at the end of the appointed period on the above conditions, and, therefore, in an honourable manner.

Herr Eichhorn, whom I have informed of the proposal made through me to Herr Mendelssohn, and also of his acceptance, has, on his side, stated no objections.

Your Majesty's decision is respectfully solicited at your pleasure; and, awaiting your Majesty's further commands, I am, with the deepest reverence,

Your Majesty's faithful servant,

V. MASSOW.

Memorandum by Mendelssohn, on the subject of a Music Academy to be established at Berlin.

Berlin, May, 1841.

It is proposed to establish a German Music Academy in Berlin, to concentrate in one common focus the now isolated efforts in the sphere of instruction in art, in order to guide rising artists in a solid and earnest direction, thus imparting to the musical sense of the nation a new and more energetic impetus; for this purpose, on one side, the already existing institutes and their members must be concentrated, and on the other, the aid of new ones must be called in.

Among the former may be reckoned the various Royal Academies for musical instruction, which must be united with this Musical Academy, and carried on as branches of the same, with greater or less modifications, in *one* sense and in *one* direction. In these are included, for example, the Institute for Élèves of the Royal Orchestra; the Organ Institute; that of the Theatre (limited to the theatre alone) for instruction in singing, declamation, etc. Further, the members of the Royal *Capelle* must be required to give instruction

20*

on their various instruments. A suitable locality can no doubt be found among the royal buildings, and also a library, with the requisite old and new musical works, scores, and books.

The new appointments to consist of—

1. A head teacher of composition; the best that can be found in Germany, to give regular instructions in theory, thorough-bass, counterpoint, and fugues.

2. A head teacher of solo singing; also the best to be had in Germany.

3. A head teacher of choral singing, who should strive to acquire personal influence over the scholars under his care, by good pianoforte-playing and steady direction.

4. A head teacher of pianoforte-playing, for which office a man of the most unquestionable talent and reputation must alone be selected. The other teachers for these departments could be found in Berlin itself; nor would there be any difficulty in procuring teachers of Æsthetics, the history of music, etc.

The complete course to last three years; the scholars, after previous examination, to be instructed *gratis;* no prize works to be admitted but at stated periods; all the works of the scholars, from the time of their admission, to be collected and criticized in connection with each other, and subsequently a prize (probably consisting of a sum sufficient for a long journey through Germany, Italy, France, and England) to be adjudged accordingly. Every winter a certain number of concerts to take place, in which all the teachers (including the above-named members of the Royal *Capelle*) must co-operate, and by which, through the selection of the music, as well as by its execution, direct influence may be gained over the majority of the publi '.

The following principle must serve as a basis for the whole Institute : that every sphere of art can only elevate itself above a mere handicraft, by being devoted to the expression of lofty thought, along with the utmost possible technical finish, and a pure and intellectual aim; that also solidity, precision, and strict discipline in teaching and learning should be considered the first law, thus not falling short in this respect of any handicraft; that in every department, all teaching and learning should be exclusively devoted to the thoughts intended to be expressed, and to that more elevated mood, to which technical perfection in art must ever be subordinate.

To Paul Mendelssohn Bartholdy.

Leipzig, July 9th, 1841.

Dear Brother,

I send you, with this, a copy of the Minister Eichhorn's letter, which I received this evening. It is evident from it that the King only intends to make me Capellmeister if the plan for the Academy is carried out; not otherwise. If this be his irrevocable determination, I have only to choose between two alternatives; to go to Berlin on the 1st of August without the title, and without any further public appointment, and merely receive the salary there, or at once to break off all further negotiations on the matter, and never to renew them.

Now, I must confess, first, that I could not without
unpleasant feelings enter on an office, after having considerably abated my own demands; secondly, that I
still find all those reasons valid, now as heretofore,
which made such a title necessary, in Herr Massow's
opinion, as well as in my own, in order to enable me to
give the desired concerts and performances in the course
of the winter; and, thirdly, it appears to me only just
that from the first I should receive a public proof of
the King's confidence; for, very possibly, after the lapse
of a year no renewal of the relation may be desired on
the *other* side, in which case I alone shall be the losing
party, for *they* only risk conferring a title for nothing,
while *I* lose my present situation, and you know that
this costs me no small sacrifice. I beg you will communicate this letter and Eichhorn's to Von Massow.
He will observe that his proposals, and the results of
my whole residence in Berlin, are again detailed, so that
I must go to Berlin under very different circumstances,
which, as I said, I am very unwilling to do. Hear what
Massow says, and let me know. Do not forget to place
strongly before him that I always thought it probable, and
now more likely than ever, that no definitive arrangement about the Academy would take place in one
year,—not, indeed, from any fault on my side, or from
any want of complaisance in me, but from want of decision on their part. I therefore wished at that time,
and wish now, that there should be something definite,
for which I am called to Berlin. I cannot say to any one
that the mere direction of the Academy is a sufficient
purpose. If they choose to make me "Geheimsecre-
tär," instead of Capellmeister, I am equally content,

but I should like to have some ostensible ground for going there, if I am to go at all; probably the affair will be now more complicated by my having in the mean while received the much-discussed title (deuce take it!) in Saxony; they will say, what is the use of a second? and pronounce it to be obstinacy on my part. I appeal, however, to the above reasons, and think, on the contrary, that it proves I did not, or do not, insist on this point from any love of a title.

Pray, pray forgive me, dear Brother; you have most cause to complain; for in any case I shall reap some advantage, having at the worst gained valuable experience, but you only much plague and lost time (even at the best, by which I mean my remaining in Berlin). Forgive me.—Ever your

FELIX.*

To CARL KLINGEMANN, LONDON.

Leipzig, July 15th, 1841.

My dear Friend,

To-morrow I go with some pleasant friends to Dresden to hear Ungher and Moriani sing, to see Raphael and Titian paint, and to breathe the air of that lovely region. A few days after my return I am off for a year

---

* Massow's proposals were finally accepted by Mendelssohn, who came to Berlin; there were many conferences held as to the remodelling of the musical class in the Academy, and the organization of the future Conservatorium; but, as Mendelssohn very justly foresaw, all this evaporated, though from no fault of his, which the beginning of Minister Eichhorn's letter of the 2d March, 1845, fully proves.

to Berlin, one of the sourest apples a man can eat, and yet
eaten it must be. Strangely enough, there seems to be a
misunderstanding between *us* on this affair, and hitherto
we have scarcely ever had one. You think I want your
advice, and mean to act according to it; but, in fact,
when I say anything to you, or discuss anything, I say
it and do it from no other reason than from instinct.
I *must* speak to you or discuss whatever is of importance
to me, or nearly concerns me; it cannot be otherwise,
and this proceeds so little from that tiresome asking for
advice, that I am convinced, if you had not answered me
at all, and if we had not spoken to each other for ten
years, I should have asked you the same questions, and
expected your answer as eagerly and received it with as
much pleasure as now. There is a curious misapprehension on your part with regard to the comparison between the two cities. You believe (and several of the re-
sidents here, as well as strangers, have told me the same)
that here in Leipzig we have comfort, domestic life, and
retirement, and in Berlin, public efficacy in and for
Germany, and active work for the benefit of others,
etc., etc.; whereas it is in truth exactly the reverse. It
is just because I am so unwilling to be burdened with
a sinecure, the public active efficiency which you so
urged on me formerly, and which seemed to myself so
necessary, having become gradually dear to me, and
nothing of the kind being possible in Berlin,—it is for
these very reasons I go there unwillingly. There, all
efforts are private efforts without any echo in the land,
and *this* they certainly do have here, small as the
nest is. I did not establish myself in Leipzig with a
view to a quiet life · on the contrary, I felt a longing

to do so, because here all is so gay and motley. On the other hand, I have mastered and learned many things which could only be thus mastered and learned; nor have I been idle, either; I think I am on a better footing with my countrymen in Germany, and have gained their confidence more than I should probably have done all my life long in Berlin, and that is worth something, too. That I am now to recommence a private life, but at the same time to become a sort of schoolmaster to a Conservatorium, is what I can scarcely understand, after my excellent vigorous orchestra here. I might perhaps do so if I were really to enjoy an entirely private life, in which case I should only compose and live in retirement; but the mongrel Berlin doings interfere,—the vast projects, the petty execution, the admirable criticism, the indifferent musicians, the liberal ideas, the Court officials in the streets, the Museum and the Academy, and the sand! I doubt whether my stay there will be more than a year; still I shall of course do all in my power not to allow this time to pass without some profit to myself and others. I shall have no solitude during the time, for I must bestir myself and write what I can; a couple of earlier melodies may bring up the rear-guard. Many others have come to light since their date; you see I defend myself vigorously, with claws and teeth. Believe me, Berlin is at the present day the city which is the least efficacious, and Leipzig the most beneficial to the public. Do you know what I have recently been composing with enthusiasm? Variations for the piano,— actually eighteen on a theme in D minor; and they amused me so famously, that I instantly made fresh ones on a theme in E flat major, and now for the third time on a theme in B flat major. I feel quite as if I must make up for lost time, never having written any before.

To CONCERT-MEISTER FERDINAND DAVID, LEIPZIG.

Berlin, August 9th, 1841.

Dear Friend,

You wish to hear some news about the Berlin Conservatorium: so do I; but there is none. The affair is on the most extensive scale, if it be actually on any scale at all, and not merely in the air. The King seems to have a plan for reorganizing the Academy of Arts; this will not be easily effected, without entirely changing its present form into a very different one, which they cannot make up their mind to do; there is little use of my advising it, as I do not expect much profit for music from the Academy, either in its present or future form. The musical portion of the new academy is, I believe, to become a Conservatorium; but to reorganize one part alone, is an idea which cannot be entertained under any circumstances, so it depends now on the three others. A director is not yet found for the architectural department, and in the four different departments the existing members cannot (or at least will not) be superseded, or their privileges diminished: so these members must first die off; but we must die off as well as they, and whether the reorganization will then take place in the wished-for manner is the question.

One service I have at all events accomplished here, in having placed these relations in a clear light, and free from all circumlocution,—so that there will be no longer any necessity to refer to these projects, or the discussions connected with them, until the obstacles are removed.

You will ask, then, what in the world do they want with me just now in Berlin? My answer is, on the one side, I really do not know; on the other, I believe that it is intended to give, during the winter, some great concerts, with the addition of all their best means, and that I am to direct them, some in church, and some in the concert-hall; but whether they will ever take place seems to me very doubtful; at all events these are, in my opinion, the only projects which can or will be carried out at this time.

To PRESIDENT VERKENIUS, COLOGNE.

Berlin, August 14th, 1841.

Dear and esteemed Herr President,

Though so much delighted by recognizing on the address of your letter of yesterday the well-known writing, I was equally grieved by the grave and mournful tone of your words, and I cannot tell you how much the intelligence of your continued illness alarms and distresses me. It is, indeed, often the case, that, in moments of indisposition, everything seems to us covered with a black veil,—that illness drags within its domain not only the body, but also the spirit and the

21

thoughts (thus it is always with me when I am ailing or ill), but with returning health these mournful images are chased away. God grant this may be the case with you, and soon, too, very soon; such sorrowful moments, however, are not less distressing at the time, though they quickly pass away and are forgotten. Would that I could do anything to make you more cheerful, or to drive away such sad thoughts! These are the moments when distance seems doubly painful; when cordially-loved and honoured friends are in suffering, and yet we must go on living apart from them, instead of being near to sympathize with them, even if unable to do them good or to alleviate their troubles.

You say that my letters are agreeable to you. I shall therefore frequently write; let me know if I do so too often; and Heaven grant that, in return, I may soon receive good news of your recovery, from yourself, or one of your family!

I have now been a fortnight here with my family, and am living with my mother and brother and sisters, in the very same house which I quitted twelve years ago with a heavy heart. The more unaccountable is it to me that, in spite of the delight of being with my mother and family once more, in spite, also, of every advantage, and many and glad memories, there is scarcely a place in all Germany where I feel so little at home as here. The reason of this may be, that all the causes which formerly made it impossible for me to begin and to continue my career in Berlin, and which drove me away, still subsist, just as they formerly did, and are likely, alas! to subsist to the end of time. There is the same frittering away of all energies and all people, the same unpoetical striving after outward results, the same superfluity of knowledge, the same failure in production, and the same want of nature, the same illiberality and backwardness as to progress and development, by which, indeed, though the latter are rendered safer and less dangerous, still they are robbed of all merit and of all life. I believe that these qualities will one day be reproduced here in all things; that it is the case with music, there can be no doubt whatever. The King has the best inclination to alter and to improve all this; but if he were to hold fast his will steadily for a succession of years, and were he to find none but people with the same will, working unweariedly in accordance with it,—even then, results and happy consequences could not be anticipated till *after* a succession of years had elapsed; yet here these are expected first and foremost. The soil must be entirely ploughed and turned up before it can bring forth fruit, at least so it seems to me in my department; the musicians work, each for himself, and no two agree; the amateurs are divided and absorbed into thousands of small circles; besides, all the music one hears is, at the best, only indifferent; criticism alone is keen, close, and well-studied. These are no very flattering prospects, I think, for the approaching period, and to " organize this from the foundation " is not my affair, for I am deficient both in talent and inclination for the purpose. I am, therefore, waiting to know what is desired of me, and probably this will be limited to a certain number of concerts, which the Academy of Arts is to give in the coming winter, and which I am then to direct. In my next letter, I will write you some musical details. Heaven grant that I may soon be tranquillized about your recovery, and may we meet again in cheerfulness and health; God grant it!—Ever your faithful

FELIX MENDELSSOHN BARTHOLDY.

To PRESIDENT VERKENIUS, COLOGNE.

Berlin, August 23d, 1841.

Dear Herr President,

You see that I take advantage of your permission, and write constantly; if it be too much for you, let me know it, or do not read my letters. May it please God that I shall soon receive good news of your returning health! I think of it every day, and I wish it every day! In my previous letter I promised you some details of musical life here, so far as I am acquainted with it. Unfortunately, there is very little that is cheering to relate. Here, as everywhere else, it is principally the committees which ought to be answerable for this; while, as these are appointed, more or less, by the public, I cannot make the distinction which seems so usual with the Berliners, who abuse and revile all committees, both musical and others, and yet like to see them remain in their old form. The whole tendency of the musicians, as well as of the *dilettanti*, is too little directed to the practical; they play chiefly that they may talk about it, before and afterwards: so the discussions are better and wiser than in most other places in Germany, but the music more defective. Unfortunately, there is very little to discuss with regard to music and its deficiencies; the only thing to be done is to feel, and to improve it; so I have not the least idea how it is ever to become better. In the orchestra (excellent as some individual members of it are) this is, alas! too perceptible. In operas and symphonies, I have heard blunders, and false notes constantly played, which could only proceed from the grossest carelessness. The people are royal functionaries, and cannot be brought to account, and if the conversation turns on these faults afterwards, they strive to prove that there is no such thing as time, or should be none,—what can I say? but *item*, it goes badly. I have played my trio ten or twelve times here; on each occasion the same mistakes were made in the time, and the same careless blunders in the accompaniment, though they were the first artists here who played with me. The blame of this state of things rests chiefly on Spontini, who was for so long a period at their head, and who rather oppressed than sought to elevate and improve the many excellent musicians in this orchestra. My conviction is, that Spohr would be the man to aid them, and to restore proper order; but just because he is so, he will not be elected; too many talk about it, and wish to have everything in ideal beauty; and this produces mediocrity. The *dilettanti* doings are even worse. Their chief organ and institution is the Academy for Singing, and there each individual considers himself far superior to the Director. But if they really did all know properly how things should be, they would sing better together,—whoever directed,—and the false notes, and errors in time, would disappear,—but they by no means disappear. So here, again, it is mostly

21*

all talk. I lately heard Pasta in "Semiramide." She sings now so fearfully out of tune, especially in the middle notes, that it is quite painful to listen to her; but, of course, the splendid remains of her great talent, the traces of a first-class singer, are often unmistakable. In any other city, this dreadful want of tune would have been felt first of all, and, afterwards, the remembrance that she was a great artist would have recurred; here every one said, beforehand, that here was the Pasta, she was old, she could not longer sing in tune, so this must be put out of the question. In other places, they would perhaps have unjustly abased her; here they as unjustly praised her to the skies, and after deliberate reflection, and entire consciousness of the state of things, they continued to be delighted: this is a bad kind of delight!

How hypochondriacal this letter is become! I ought rather to write to you in a gayer strain, to cheer you. Next time I shall try to find a more rose-coloured aspect; forgive the dark-brown hues of to-day.* With the most heartfelt and cordial wishes for your recovery, I am always, your loving

FELIX MENDELSSOHN BARTHOLDY.

---

* The death of President Verkenius ended the correspondence by this Letter.

To Franz Hauser,

(Present Director of the Conservatorium in Munich.)

Berlin, October 12th, 1841.

· . . . I do not know what you have been told about Berlin and its prospects. If, however, you allude to the project of which all.the people and all the journals are speaking, that of establishing a Musical Conservatorium here, then I regret to be obliged to say that I know no more about it than every one else seems to know. It is said the desire for it exists, and perhaps a remote prospect, but far too remote for anything to be told about it with the least certainty at present. Years may pass away, nothing may ever come of it (which is not at all improbable), and also it may soon be again discussed. During the last three months which I passed here I came to this conclusion, on seeing the proceedings more closely. I am so kindly received on every side, that personally I can wish for nothing better, and have only cause for gratitude. But though it is easy for a person here to do what he chooses, it is proportionably difficult to aid the cause; and yet that is, after all, the most important point, and should be the very first. If I only knew how to make this better! In the mean while I write music, and when asked a question I answer it.

To Concert-Meister Ferdinand David, Leipzig.

Berlin, October 21st, 1841.

Dear David,

Thanks for your having at once read through " Antigone." I felt assured beforehand that it would please
you beyond measure when you did so; and the very
impression which reading it made on me, is in fact the
cause of the affair being accomplished. There was a
great deal of talking about it, but no one would begin;
they wished to put it off till next autumn, and so forth;
but as the noble style of the piece fascinated me so
much, I got hold of old Tieck, and said "Now or
never!" and he was amiable, and said "Now!" and so
I composed music for it to my heart's content; we
have two rehearsals of it daily, and the choruses are
executed with such precision that it is a real delight to
listen to them. All in Berlin of course think that we
are very sly, and that I composed the choruses to
become a court favourite, or a court *musicus*, or a court
fool; while at the beginning I thought, on the contrary, that I would not mix myself up with the affair;
but the piece itself, with its extraordinary beauty and
grandeur, drove everything else out of my head, and
only inspired me with the wish to see it performed as
soon as possible. The subject in itself was glorious,
and I worked at it with heartfelt pleasure. It seems
to me very remarkable that there is so much in art
quite unchangeable. The parts of all these choruses
are to this day so genuinely musical, and yet so different
from each other, that no man could wish anything finer
for his composition. If it were not so difficult here to

come to any kind of judgment about a work ! There
are only shameless flatterers, or equally shameless critics, to be met with, and there is nothing to be done
with either, for both from the very first deprive us of
all pleasure. As yet I have had only to do with admiration. After this performance the learned will, no
doubt, come forward and reveal to me how I should
and must have composed, had I been a Berliner.—
Your .

FELIX MENDELSSOHN BARTHOLDY.

TO PROFESSOR DEHN, BERLIN.*

Berlin, October 28th, 1841,

Sir,

The kind and amiable feelings which your letter of
yesterday testified towards me caused me great pleasure, and I beg to thank you very sincerely and truly.
Although I entirely agree with you that my choruses
to "Antigone" will furnish an opportunity for a number of unfair and malignant attacks, still I cannot meet
these unpleasant probabilities by the means which you
are so good as to propose to me. I have always made
it an inviolable rule, never to write on any subject
connected with music, in newspapers, nor either directly or indirectly to prompt any article to be written
on my own compositions; and although I am well
aware how often this must be both a temporary and sen-

---

* In answer to the Professor's offer to write, or to cause to be written, something in his musical paper with regard to " Antigone."

sible disadvantage, still I cannot deviate from a resolution which I have strictly followed out under all circumstances. I decline, therefore, accepting your obliging offer; but I beg you will believe that my gratitude for the friendly intentions you expressed remains the same; and, in the hope of soon finding an opportunity to repeat this assurance in person, I am, etc.*

To Professor Köstlin, Tübingen.

Berlin, December 15th, 1841.

. . . When I was lately in society, I was seated next a lady at supper who spoke the South German dialect, and seemed at home in Stuttgart: so I thought I would ask her if she knew anything of Tübingen, and inquired about Professor Köstlin. She said she did not know him, but one of her acquaintances had written to her that he had been recently betrothed. This was the first happy news. She did not know the name of the bride, but so far she remembered, that she was from Munich, and a fine musical genius. I had instantly a presentiment. I vowed it must be Josephine Lang. She thought it was another name; but she would look at the letter when she went home. Next morning I got a note. " The bride of Herr Köstlin is Josephine Lang, after all, and he has been recently in Munich, and then in Stuttgart with her," etc. Had it not been for this last piece of intelligence, I would have written to you instantly, to offer you both my congratulations and

* Compare also his letter to Julius Stern of the 27th of May, 1844.

to express my most heartfelt joy. Now I have got your welcome letter, and the details of the piece of good news the South German lady told me; first, then, receive my thanks for it, and then accept my fervent prayers for a blessing on your fortunate union, my wishes for health for you and your bride (happiness and every other good you already have), and my cordial, most cordial sympathy in all connected with you both, now and for the future. Whatever concerns you concerns me also. If I were not the most miserable correspondent in the world, I should have written to your bride six months ago, to thank her for the two books of songs she published. I have done so in thought twenty times at least. It is long since I have seen any new music so genial, or which affected me so deeply, as these charming songs; their appearance was equally unexpected and welcome, not only to me, but to all those whose predilections are in accordance with my own, who participate in my love of music, and feel in a similar manner with myself. I sent my sister a copy at the time from Leipzig, but when it arrived she had already bought one, without our ever having corresponded on the subject. The " poem," in F sharp major, is, I think, best of all, and the " Lenau Meer," in C major, and the " Frühlingskinder " in E, and the " Goethe'schen geliebten Bäume " in D; I also think the " Blumauer'sche " in F major $\frac{3}{8}$ wonderfully lovely. Nothing more charming could be devised than the happy way in which they prattle together, one after the other telling their tale, and all so delicate and sportive, and a little amorous too. In so many passages in both books, I thought I heard Josephine Lang's voice, though it is a long time now since I have heard her sing; but there are many inflections peculiar to her, and which she inherits from the grace of God, and when such a turn occurred in the music, she made a little turn with her head; and in fact the whole form, and voice, and manner, were once more placed before my eyes by these songs. I intended to have written all this to her, and to have thanked her a thousand times in my name, and in that of all my friends. Now this will come sadly in the background, for our cordial congratulations must take place of everything else, and prevent any other topic being alluded to. But when you tell her of these, tell her at the same time what pleasure she caused us all.

For Heaven's sake, urge her to continue composing. It is really your duty towards us all, who continually long and look for good new music. She once sent me a collection of the music of various composers, with some of her own, saying that among so many masterworks she hoped I would view her attempts with indulgence, etc. Oh, Gemini! how petty many of these *chefs-d'œuvre* appear beside her fresh music! So, as I said, instigate her strongly to new compositions.

If I have still a wish to form, it is that your blissful betrothal mood may be continued in marriage; that is, may you be like me, who feel every day of my life that I cannot be sufficiently thankful to God for my happiness.

Do not punish me for my laziness as a correspondent. I really cannot contrive to write a tolerably sensible letter to-day; still, you must write to me from time to time. If it were by music I should not complain, for *your* music is speech, though probably you have other things to think of.

And now farewell for to-day, and remember kindly your devoted

FELIX MENDELSSOHN BARTHOLDY.

TO HIS MOTHER.

London, June 21st, 1842.

Dear Mother,

Your letter of yesterday was most charming, and gave us so much pleasure,* that I must thank you for it in detail to-day; I could scarcely do so as I wished for the previous one, containing quite a kaleidoscope of events in Berlin, which through the glasses of your description assumed constant novel and pleasing forms. If I could write half as well, you should receive to-day the most charming letter, for we are daily seeing the most beautiful and splendid objects; but I am somewhat fatigued by the incessant bustle of this last week, and for two days past I have been chiefly lying on the sofa reading " Wilhelm Meister," and strolling through the fields with Klingemann in the evening, to try to restore myself.

So, if the tone of this letter is rather languid and weary, it accurately paints my feelings. I have really been urged to do too much. Lately, when playing the organ in Christ Church, Newgate Street, I almost thought, for a few moments, I must have been suffo-

---

* Mendelssohn and his wife.

cated, so great was the crowd and pressure round my
seat at the organ; and two days afterwards I played in
Exeter Hall before three thousand people, who shouted
hurrahs and waved their handkerchiefs, and stamped
with their feet till the hall resounded with the uproar;
at the moment I felt no bad effects from this, but next
morning my head was confused and stupefied. Add to this
the pretty and most charming Queen Victoria, who looks
so youthful, and is so gently courteous and gracious, who
speaks such good German and who knows all my music
so well,—the four books of songs without words and
those with words, and the symphony, and the " Hymn
of Praise." Yesterday evening I was sent for by the
Queen, who was almost alone with Prince Albert, and
who seated herself near the piano and made me play to
her; first seven of the " songs without words," then
the serenade, two impromptus on " Rule Britannia,"
Lützow's " Wilde Jagd," and "Gaudeamus igitur." The
latter was somewhat difficult, but remonstrance was
out of the question, and, as they gave the themes, of
course it was my duty to play them. Then the splendid
grand gallery in Buckingham Palace where they drank
tea, and where two boars by Paul Potter are hanging,
and a good many other pictures which pleased me well.
I must tell you that my A minor symphony has had
great success with the people here, who one and all
receive us with a degree of amiability and kindness
which exceeds all I have ever yet seen in the way of
hospitality, though this sometimes makes me feel my
head quite bewildered and strange, and I am obliged
to collect my thoughts in order not to lose all self-
possession.

June 22*d.*—To-day, however, I can continue my letter in a more cheerful spirit; I have slept away my weary mood, and feel again quite fresh and well. Yesterday evening I played my concerto in D minor, and directed my "Hebrides" in the Philharmonic, where I was received like an old friend, and where they played with a degree of enthusiasm which caused me more pleasure than I can describe. The people make such a fuss with me this time that I feel really quite abashed; I believe they clapped their hands and stamped for at least ten minutes after the concerto, and insisted on the "Hebrides" being repeated. The directors are to give a dinner at Greenwich next week, and we are to sail down the Thames *in corpore* and to make speeches. They talk of bringing out "Antigone" at Covent Garden as soon as they can procure a tolerable translation. Lately I went to a concert in Exeter Hall where I had nothing whatever to do, and was sauntering in quite coolly with Klingemann,—in the middle of the first part, and an audience of about three thousand present, —when just as I came in at the door, such a clamour, and clapping, and shouting, and standing up ensued, that I had no idea at first that I was concerned in it; but I discovered it was so. On reaching my place, I found Sir Robert Peel and Lord Wharncliffe close to me, who continued to applaud with the rest till I made my bow and thanked them. I was immensely proud of my popularity in Peel's presence. When I left the concert they gave me another hurrah.

Oh! how splendidly Mrs. Butler, at Chorley's, lately read aloud Shakespeare's "Antony and Cleopatra;" we have always been on the most friendly terms since our

acquaintance twelve years ago, when she was Miss
Fanny Kemble; and she gave this reading in honour
of me, and quite too beautiful it was; and Lady Morgan
was there, and Winterhalter, and Mrs. Jameson, and
Duprez, who afterwards sang a French Romance of a
starving old beggar, and another of a young man losing
his reason, with the *refrain*, "Le vent qui vient à tra-
vers la montagne me rendra fou!" "Sweet!" said the
ladies; and Benedict,. and Moscheles, and the Grotes—
who can enumerate them all! This evening at seven
o'clock we dine with Bunsen, and, as we do not know
what to do with our evening afterwards, we shall probably drive to Charles Kemble's about eleven o'clock
and be among his early guests; the late ones will not
arrive till after midnight. We have, too, such invariably
bright and beautiful weather. One day lately we saw
first in the morning the Tower, then the Katharine
Docks, then the Tunnel, and ate fish at Blackwall, had
luncheon at Greenwich, and home by Peckham; we
travelled on foot, in a carriage, on a railway, in a boat,
and in a steamboat. The day after to-morrow we intend to go to Manchester for a couple of days, and next
week be on our way back to Frankfort. I have given
up the musical festival at the Hague, though they
pressed me very hard to go there for my "Hymn of
Praise." I wish to have nothing to do with music
during the next few weeks.

I have still a vast deal to say to Fanny about the
Bridgewater Collection, where pictures and sketches
by Hensel are hanging up, and Sutherland House, and
Grosvenor House, etc., etc.; and to Rebecca, about the
meeting of scientific men at Manchester, to which I

was invited, but unfortunately I could not go to greet Whewell. Jacoby and Enke were also there; I alone was absent.

But I must conclude. May we soon have a happy meeting, dearest Mother, and dearest Brother and Sisters.—Your

FELIX.

To CARL ECKERT, PARIS.

Berlin, January 26th, 1842.

Dear Eckert,

I have been long in your debt for an answer to your kind letter; pray forgive this. I have been living such a stirring, excited life this year, that I am more than ever unable to carry on any correspondence. I need not tell you the great pleasure I felt in hearing from you, and always shall feel every time that I do so. You know how entirely you won my regard during the years when you resided in Leipzig, and how highly I both honour and estimate your talents and your character. It is really difficult to say which, in the present day, should be considered most important; without talent nothing can be done, but without character just as little. We see instances of this day after day, in people of the finest capacities, who once excited great expectations, and yet accomplish nothing. May Heaven bestow on you a continuous development of both, in the same measure that within the last few years you have made progress; or, rather, *bestow all this on yourself*, for Heaven can do no more than endow you with

22*

the germs and capabilities for this end, with which it has already so richly endowed you: the rest becomes the affair, and the responsibility, of each individual. Such a preaching tone must sound very strange to you, living in joyous Paris; but it is a part of the world and of life, that every wild animal has its own special skin and roar, so I continue to roar in my old tones.

Hofrath Förster sent me yesterday your "Lieder ohne Worte," and your overture, so I have occupied myself with little else than with you and your compositions, and heartily rejoice in both; in the former from the memory of the past, and in the latter from the pleasure of the present. Both yesterday and to-day I have looked through, and played through, your charming "Lieder" with the greatest delight; they all please me, and are thoroughly genial, earnest music. More, more, a thousand times more, in this and every other style! The overture in F sharp major, too, caused me great pleasure, and suits me almost throughout; a few passages only seem to me rather too amplified: we must not write, however, but speak on this subject when we meet again, although the only really important thing I have to say with regard to your music, I have already said in this letter,—more, more! You have reached a standard that may in every relation well be called a mastership, which all musicians or friends of music must highly esteem, and beyond which nothing actually extrinsic (whether it be called erudition or recognition, facility and knowledge, or honour and fame) is any longer worth striving for; but this is, in my opinion, just the time when true work really first begins. The question is then solely what is felt and experienced within a man's own breast, and uttered from the depths of his heart, be it grave or gay, bitter or sweet,—character and life are displayed here; and in order to prevent existence being dissipated and wasted when brilliant and happy, or depressed and destroyed when the reverse, there is but one safeguard,—to work, and to go on working. So, for your sake, I have only *one* wish, that you may bring to light what exists within you, in your nature and feelings, which none save yourself can know or possess. In your works, go deeper into your inmost being, and let them bear a distinct stamp ; let criticism and intellect rule as much as you please in all outward questions and forms, but in all inner and original thought, the heart alone, and genuine feeling. So work daily, hourly, and unremittingly,—*there* you never can attain entire mastery or perfection ; no man ever yet did, and therefore it is the highest vocation of life.

I was three weeks in Leipzig not long since, where I was well amused, and both heard and assisted in much good music. One morning I went to the Klengels' ; it was on the Wednesday of the fast-week, at eleven o'clock in the forenoon ; the old gentleman was sitting in his dressing-gown at the piano. As during the whole week there had been no rehearsal of any concert, he had made Nanné sing a little. The conversation turned on Julius's " Lieder." " If we only had an alto !" said they. I offered to sing *falsetto ;* the music was brought, and good red wine beside. We sat round the table, and sang all his songs, which delighted me exceedingly, and some of yours also. I had a great deal to do that morning, but I stayed on till half-past one o'clock, and could not resolve to come away. See if you can find such mornings in Paris! " And you in Berlin," you will reply.

Now, farewell; continue your regard for me, and ever believe me your friend,

FELIX.

To his Mother.

Interlachen, August 18th, 1842.

My dearest Mother,

Do you still remember our staying, twenty years ago, in a pretty small inn here, shaded by large walnut-trees (I sketched some of them), and our lovely young landlady? When I was here ten years ago, she refused to give me a room, I looked so shabby from my pedestrian journey; I believe that was the only real vexation I at that time experienced during the whole course of my tour. Now we are living here again as substantial people. The Jungfrau, with her silver horns, stands out against the sky, with the same delicate, elegant, and pointed outlines, and looks as fresh as ever. The landlady, however, is grown old, and had it not been for her manner I should never have recognized her to be the same person. I have again sketched the walnut-trees, much better than I did at that time, but far worse than they deserve; the post in Untersee brings us letters from the same house as it did then, and many new houses are built; and the Aar gurgles and glides along as rapid, and smooth, and green as ever,—*time is, time was, time is past.* I have, in fact, nothing more to write about, except that we are all well, and think of you daily and hourly.*

Descriptions of Switzerland are impossible, and instead of a journal, such as I formerly kept, I this time sketch furiously, and sit in front of a mountain, and try to draw its likeness, and do not give it up till I have quite spoiled the sketch; but I take care to have at least one new landscape in my book every day. He who has not seen the Gemmi knows nothing of Switzerland; but this is what people say of every new object in this most incredibly beautiful country. With regard to this land, I feel just as I do about clever books; when one is exchanged for another, in every exchange a new phase presents itself, always equally fine and equally admirable. So now, when I see this country with my wife, I have quite a different impression from the previous times; then I wished forthwith to climb every crested mountain, and to run into every meadow; this time, on the contrary, I should like to stay everywhere, and to remain for months in one spot. I am by no means sure that some fine spring I may not set off, bag and baggage, not returning to the North till all the leaves are gone. Such, at least, are my daily thoughts, and castles in the air. In a few days we are going into Oberland; I rejoice at the thoughts of the full moon in Lauterbrunn. We then return here, across Furka and Grimsel to the Lake of Lucerne and the Righi, and thence away from the land of all lands, and back to Germany,—where it is not so bad, after all. I own there are many days when the world

* The party consisted of Mendelssohn and his brother, and their wives.

pleases me most exceedingly. I am writing fine novelties, dear Mother! Forgive me, for I have nothing better to say; besides, I know that Paul wrote to you at full length a few days ago. When we meet, I shall have a tale to tell that will know no end. I wish I only knew whether I am to remain in Berlin permanently, or merely for a few weeks. How gladly would I write to you that it was to be the former! but the whole affair has taken so many strange twists and turns of late, that I feel quite astray and bewildered when I try to think what is to be done. On my return it will all come right, no doubt. Do not be displeased with me, I entreat, on account of this prolonged uncertainty; it is no fault of mine.—Ever your

FELIX.

To his Mother.

Zurich, September 3d, 1842.

Dear Mother,

I am not so hard-hearted a correspondent as to rest satisfied with only writing to you once from Switzerland. Indeed, our Swiss expedition is drawing nearly to a close for the present. There are few more herdsmen's huts to be seen; neither glaciers, nor anything of the kind; rocks, and so forth, just as little; but we still have the greenish-blue lake, and the clean houses, and the bright gardens, and a chain of mountains, such as could only stand on the confines of a land like this. So my greetings to you all once more from Switzerland! How beautiful all has been, and most thoroughly have we enjoyed it! A gay mood, perfect health, and clear weather, combined to impress all the marvels indelibly on our souls. We were obliged to give up the expeditions we had planned the last few days, owing to the rain, and mists, and unfavourable weather; unfortunately the Righi was among the number, and the Schaffhausen Rheinfall, neither of which is there any chance of our seeing, for the weather continues cloudy, and the air very cold and comfortless for a journey. But, with these two exceptions, we have seen everything in as great beauty as we could have wished or expected; and I am particularly delighted that, on the last fine forenoon, I accomplished my expedition over the *Surene* ("Durch der Surener furchtbar Eisgebirg," *vide* "William Tell"). On the same afternoon it began to rain in Engelberg, and next day I was obliged to tramp through the whole of the Unterwalden under an umbrella, nor has it ever been fair since. I sought out my former guide, and we mutually recognized each other, to our great joy.* He is now the landlord of the "Crown" in Meiringen. Dearest Mother, recommend the man and his house to all your correspondents. I am quite determined to write to London and ask Murray to praise the "Crown" in Meiringen, in his next red Guide-book to Switzerland; he can do so with a clear conscience. Michael has a good house, an extremely pretty wife, and five fine children, for whom I bought a few little trifles and some toy soldiers in Untersee, and thus we had a happy meeting after the lapse of eleven years. He brought me the words of the song in G major he sang at that

---

* See Mendelssohn's Letters in 1831.

time, the melody of which I had retained, but always plagued myself in vain about the verses. When I told him that we wished to go to the Grimsel, he got very red, and said, " Then I must go too—I must go." He intrusted the public room (which is his department) to the care of a friend, and was ready next morning with his mountain staff and blouse, and led the horses past some awkward places, and the ladies past the most dangerous ones, and us too, when it was possible to cut off the distance by footpaths; and the people in Guttann laughed at seeing him again. " It is only for a little while," said he; and a man who was making hay called out to him, " Oho, Michael, so you can't give up being a guide yet?" He confided to me, that it did sometimes seem hard to be obliged to do so, and if he did not think of his wife and children, who knows what might happen? We separated on the Grimsel. This was a pleasant episode. I have sketched a great deal, and taken much trouble, but more than a mere scrawl cannot be accomplished here. Still, it may serve as a kind of diary, and as such I feel an attachment to all the old leaves in my book, and to the present ones also.

Kücken has just been with me; he is going to Paris, having composed an opera, which he is anxious to have performed first in Berlin; he got the *libretto* from a man in Vienna. The Faulhorn, Meyerbeer, Rungenhagen, the Brünig, the Lungernsee, Donizetti, and the drivers, enlivened the conversation by turns,—not forgetting the Conservatorium in Berlin, and the Grimsel and Furka in the snow. But what kind of letter is this? Paul is resolved to see Zurich, so I must conclude. I feel as if you must be provoked at my chit-chat, all about nothing. Well, then, we are all perfectly hale and hearty, and love you very dearly, and think of you always and everywhere, and send you a thousand greetings, and hope for a joyful meeting. Such is, after all, the chief substance of every letter we long for, and so it is of this one also. *Au revoir,* dearest Mother.—Ever your

FELIX

To A. Simrock, Bonn.

Dear Herr Simrock,

Frankfort, September 21st, 1842.

I write to you to-day on a particular subject, relying on your most entire discretion and perfect secrecy; but I know too well from experience your kindly feeling towards myself, to doubt the fulfilment of my wish, and in full confidence in your silence I shall now come to the point. During my stay here I heard by chance that my friend and colleague in art, Herr X——, had written to you about the publication of some new works, but hitherto had received no answer. Now, both in the interest of art, as well as in that of my friend, I should indeed be very glad if the answer were to prove favourable; and, as I flatter myself that you place some value on my opinion and my wish, it occurred to me to write to you myself on the subject, and to beg of you, if you possibly can, to make some of my friend's works known to the German public. My wish for the secrecy which I beg you to observe *to-*

23

wards every one and under *all circumstances,* is owing to
this: that I feel certain Herr X—— would be *frantic*
if he had the most remote idea that I had taken such a
step on his behalf. I know that nothing would be
more intolerable to him than not to stand absolutely on
his own ground, and therefore he *never* must know of
this letter; but, on the other hand, it is the positive
duty of one artist towards another to assist as much as
possible in overcoming difficulties and annoyances,
when such efforts are noble and in a good cause, and
both of these are so to the highest degree in this case.
I therefore beg you to publish some of his compositions,
and, above all, if possible, to enter into a more permanent connection with him. I am well aware that
the German publishers have not hitherto had any very
brilliant success (as it is called) with the works he has
written, and whether this may be otherwise in future
I cannot pretend to say; but that they *well deserve* to
succeed, is a point on which I have no doubt; and on
that account, and *solely* on that account, I now make
my request. Were it not so, however great a friend
he might be of mine, I would not do this. In fact, the
only consideration which ought to have any influence
is the *intrinsic* value of a work,—that being the only
thing which would *inevitably* insure success, if there
were any honesty in the world. It is too provoking to
hear the oft-told tale of clever, meritorious artists, who,
at the beginning of their career, are in such a state of
anxious solicitude that their works should be purchased
and made known, and when one of these chances to
make a good hit, and gains great applause and becomes
vastly popular, still this success does not cause him

satisfaction equal to all his previous anxiety and vexation; for this very reason I should like you to act differently, and to place more value on true worth than on any chance result. This system, in fact, must soon be abolished, and in such a case the only question is, how soon? and after how many more annoyances? and this is just the point where a publisher can be useful and valuable to an artist. When universal popularity ensues, they are all ready enough to come forward, but I think you are the very man to act differently, not losing sight of the ideal, but also doing what is practical and right. Forgive the liberty I have taken, and, if possible, comply with my wish. So far as I have heard, there is no pretension to any considerable sum for these works, but a very strong desire that they may be generally circulated and made known, and that the correspondence should be carried on in a friendly artistic spirit. If you will or can enter into the affair, I rely on your *sacred silence* as to my interference, my name, or my request. If I shortly hear from my friend that you have written to him in a kind manner, and have agreed to assist him in making the public familiar with his songs and pianoforte works, how heartily shall I then rejoice! Perhaps you will say, what does this lazy composer, and still more lazy correspondent, mean? But I have improved in the latter respect, as the *figura* proves; and with regard to the former, I mean to set to work shortly, and to overwhelm you with music-paper (as soon as it is well filled), and to request in my own name what I now so urgently and anxiously entreat in that of my friend.—Ever yours, with esteem,

FELIX MENDELSSOHN BARTHOLDY.

To A. Simrock, Bonn.

Berlin, October 10th, 1842.

Sir,

If I ever was agreeably surprised by any letter, it was by yours, which I received here yesterday. Your kind and immediate compliance with my request, and also the very handsome present you make me for my "Songs without Words," render it really difficult for me to know how to thank you, and to express the great pleasure you have conferred on me; I must confess that I had not expected such ready courtesy, and satisfactory compliance with my letter of solicitation. I now doubly rejoice in having taken a step which a feeling of false shame, and that odious worldly maxim, " Don't interfere in the affairs of others," which occurred to me while writing, nearly deterred me from carrying out. Your conduct, as displayed in your letter of yesterday, has confirmed me more than ever in what I esteem to be good and right; so I intend to lay aside for ever the (so-called) highly-prized worldly wisdom, and henceforth to pursue a straightforward course according to my own first impulse and feeling; if it fails a hundred times, still *one* such success is ample compensation. What artist, too, would not, at the same time, be highly delighted by the kind manner in which you allude to my compositions, and evince your approbation? Who would not prize and esteem this beyond all other recognition? I ought especially to feel thus, and, by hereafter producing better works, strive to deserve the good and friendly feeling shown to me for my present ones. I hope one day, in some degree at least, to succeed in doing so; and if not, you will at all events know that neither good will nor earnest efforts were wanting. So I thank you for the fulfilment of my request, I thank you for the flattering and handsome present, and, above all, I thank you for your kindly sentiments about myself and my music, both of which are so much indebted to you, and which will fill me with gratitude and pleasure so long as I live.—I am, with esteem, your

FELIX MENDELSSOHN BARTHOLDY.

To Marc-André Souchay, Lübeck.*

Berlin, October 15th, 1842.

. . . There is so much talk about music, and yet so little really said. For my part I believe that words do not suffice for such a purpose, and if I found they did suffice, then I certainly would have nothing more to do with music. People often complain that music is ambiguous, that their ideas on the subject always seem so vague, whereas every one understands words; with me it is exactly the reverse,—not merely with regard to entire sentences, but also as to individual words; these, too, seem to me so ambiguous, so vague, so unintelligible when compared with genuine music, which fills the soul with a thousand things better than words. What the music I love expresses to me, is not thought too *indefinite* to be put into words, but, on the

---

* Herr Souchay had asked Mendelssohn the meanings of some of his "Songs without Words."

23*

contrary, too *definite*. I therefore consider every effort
to express such thoughts commendable ; but still there
is something unsatisfactory too in them all, and so it is
with yours also. This, however, is not your fault, but
that of the poetry, which does not enable you to do
better. If you ask me what *my* idea is, I say—just the
song as it stands ; and if I have in my mind a definite
term or terms with regard to one or more of these
songs, I will disclose them to no one, because the words
of one person assume a totally different meaning in the
mind of another person, because the music of the song
alone can awaken the same ideas and the same feelings
in one mind as in another,—a feeling which is not,
however, expressed by the same words.* Resignation,
melancholy, the praise of God, a hunting-song,—one
person does not form the same conception from these
that another does. Resignation is to the one what
melancholy is to the other ; the third can form no lively
idea of either. To any man who is by nature a very
keen sportsman, a hunting-song and the praise of God
would come pretty much to the same thing, and to such
a one the sound of the hunting-horn would really and
truly be the praise of God, while we hear nothing in it
but a mere hunting-song ; and if we were to discuss it
ever so often with him, we should get no further.
Words have many meanings, and yet music we could
both understand correctly. Will you allow this to
serve as an answer to your question ? At all events, it

---

* Goethe also says, in the fourth part of " Dichtung und Wahrheit,"
" I have already but too plainly seen that no one person understands
another ; that no one receives the same impression as another from the
very same words."

is the only one I can give,—although these too are nothing, after all, but ambiguous words!

To WIRKLICH GEHEIMRATH HERR VON MASSOW.

Berlin, October 23d, 1842.

Your Excellency,

Permit me respectfully to ask whether you will be so good as to assist in procuring me an audience of his Majesty, to place before him my present position here, and my wishes with regard to it.

Your Excellency is aware that I am not so situated as to be able to accept the proposal of Herr Eichhorn to place myself at the head of the whole of the Evangelical Church music here. As I already told the Minister (and your Excellency quite agreed to this in our last conversation), such a situation, if considered *practically*, must either consist of a general superintendence of all the present organists, choristers, schoolmasters, etc., or of the improvement and practice of the singing choirs in one or more cathedrals. Neither of these, however, is the kind of work which I particularly desire. Moreover, the first of these functions is superfluous if such places are properly filled; and the second, to be really effectually carried out, demands more vast and comprehensive regulations and greater pecuniary resources than could be obtained at this moment.

With regard to the other plans which were proposed, partly for the reorganization of the present Institute, and partly for the establishment of a new one, difficulties have arisen which render the establishment of these plans void; and thus the case now occurs which your Excellency may remember I always anticipated, much to my regret, at the very beginning of our correspondence in December, 1840,—there is no opportunity on my side for a practical, influential, musical efficiency in Berlin.

Herr Eichhorn declared that this would be altered in the course of time,—that everything was being done in order to bring about a different state of things; and he requested me to wait with patience till the building was completed which it was proposed to erect.

I think, on the contrary, that it would not be responding properly on my part to the confidence the King has placed in me, if I were not at once to employ my energies in fulfilling what your Excellency at that time told me, in the name of the King, were his designs; if, instead of at least making the attempt to animate and ennoble my art in this country (as your Excellency was pleased to say), I were to continue to work for myself personally; if I were to wait instead of to act. The very depth of my gratitude for such flattering confidence constrains me to say all this candidly to his Majesty,—to state that circumstances, over which I have no control, now render the fulfilment of his commands impossible.

My wish is that his Majesty would permit me in the mean time to reside and to work and to await his commands in some other place, where I could for the moment be useful and efficient. As soon as the building is finished of which Herr Eichhorn spoke, or so soon as the King required any service from me, I should consider it a great happiness to hasten back and to exert my best energies for such a Sovereign, whose mandates are in themselves the highest rewards for an artist.

I would fain have written this to the King sooner, but when I reflected that my communication would only meet his Majesty's eye among a vast number of others, I thought I could express my views and feelings of most sincere gratitude more plainly and better verbally, even if only by a few words; and that your Excellency may be so obliging as to promote my wish is my present request, and the object of this letter.—I am, your Excellency's most devoted

FELIX M. B.

TO HIS MAJESTY THE KING OF PRUSSIA.*

Berlin, October 28th, 1842.

Your Majesty,

In the memorable words your Majesty was pleased to address to me, you mentioned that it was intended to add a certain number of able singers to the existing Royal Church choirs, to form a nucleus for these choirs, as well as for any amateurs of singing who might subsequently wish to join them, serving as a rallying-point and example, and in this manner gradually to elevate and to ennoble church music, and to insure its greater development.

Also, in order to support the singing of the congregation by instruments, which produce the most solemn and noble effects,—as your Majesty may remember,

---

* The following letter contains the result of the audience requested.

during the celebration of the Jubilee in the Nicolai Church,—it is proposed that a small number of instrumentalists (probably selected from the members of the Royal Orchestra) should be engaged, who are also intended to form the basis for subsequent grand performances of oratorios, etc.

The direction of a musical choir of this instructive nature, a genuine Royal Orchestra, your Majesty expressed your intention to intrust to me, but, till its formation, to grant me entire freedom of choice with regard to my place of residence.

The execution of this plan will fulfil to the utmost all my wishes as to public musical efficiency; I can never cease to be grateful to your Majesty for it, and I do not doubt that the organization of such an institution could be effected here without any serious difficulties.

But I would request your Majesty not to devolve this organization on me personally, but merely to permit me to co-operate with my opinion and advice, which I shall always be gladly prepared to give. Until, however, to use your Majesty's own expression, the instrument is ready on which I am hereafter to play, I wish to make use of the freedom of action so graciously accorded me, and shortly to return to Leipzig, for the direction of the Town Hall concerts. The orders which your Majesty was pleased to give me, I shall there with the utmost zeal and to the best of my abilities carry into execution; at the same time I entreat your Majesty, as I am engaged in no public sphere of action here till the organization of the Institute, and am till then to enjoy entire liberty, to be allowed to give up one-half of the salary previously granted to me, so long as I take advantage of this entire freedom from work.

In repeating my heartfelt thanks for all the favours which your Majesty has so liberally bestowed on me, I am, till death, your Majesty's devoted servant,

FELIX MENDELSSOHN BARTHOLDY.

To CARL KLINGEMANN, LONDON.

Leipzig, November 23d, 1842.

We are now again settled in Leipzig, and fairly established here for this winter and till late in the spring. The old localities where we passed so many happy days so pleasantly are now rearranged with all possible comfort, and we can live here in great comfort. I could no longer endure the state of suspense in Berlin; there was in fact nothing certain there, but that I was to receive a certain sum of money, and that alone should not suffice for the vocation of a musician; at least I felt more oppressed by it from day to day, and I requested either to be told plainly I should do *nothing* (with which I should have been quite contented, for then I could have worked with an easy mind at whatever I chose), or be told plainly what I was to do. As I was again assured that the results would certainly insure my having employment, I wrote to Herr von Massow begging him to procure me an audience of the King, that I might thank him verbally, and endeavour to obtain my dismissal on such and such grounds, requesting him to communicate the contents of this letter to his

Majesty; this he did, and appointed a day for the audience, at the same time saying that the affair was now at an end, the King very much displeased with me, and that it was his intention to take leave of me in very few words. He had made me some proposals in the name of the King to which I could not altogether agree, and with which I do not now detain you, as they led to nothing, and could lead to nothing. So I was quite prepared to take my leave of Berlin in very bad odour, however painful this might be to me. I was at length obliged also to speak to my mother on the subject, and to break to her that in the course of eight days I must return to Leipzig; I could not have believed that this would have affected her so terribly as it actually did. You know how calm my mother usually is, and how seldom she allows any one to have a glimpse of the feelings of her heart; and therefore it was doubly and trebly painful to me to cause her such a pang of sorrow, and yet I could not act otherwise; so next day I went to the King with Massow,—the most zealous friend I have in Berlin—and who first took a final leave of me in his own house. The King must have been in an especial good humour, for, instead of finding him angry with me, I never saw him so amiable and so really confidential. To my farewell speech he replied: he could not indeed compel me to remain, but he did not hesitate to say that it would cause him heartfelt regret if I left him; that, by doing so, all the plans which he had formed from my presence in Berlin would be frustrated, and that I should leave a void which he could never fill up. As I did not admit this, he said if I would name any one capable of carrying such and such plans into execution as well as he believed I could do, then he would intrust them to the person I selected, but he felt sure I should be unable to name one whom he could approve of. The following are the plans which he detailed at full length; first of all, to form a kind of real *capelle*, that is, a select choir of about thirty very first-rate singers, and a small orchestra (to consist of the *élite* of the theatrical orchestra); their duties to consist in church music on Sundays and at festivals, and, besides this, in performing oratorios and so forth; that I was to direct these, and compose music for them, etc. etc. "Certainly," said I, "if there were any chance of such a thing here, if this were only accomplished;" it was the very point at issue on which I had so much insisted. On which he replied, again, that he knew perfectly well I must have an instrument to make music on, and that it should be *his* care to procure such an instrument of singers and players; but when he had procured it, he must know that I was prepared to play on it; till then I might do as I liked, return to Leipzig, or go to Italy, —in short, be entirely unfettered; but he must have the certainty that he might depend on me when he *required* me, and this could only be acquired by my remaining in his service. Such was at least the essential substance of the whole long conversation; we then separated. He said I was not to give him my decision *immediately*, because all difficulties could not be for the moment entirely obviated; I was to take time to consider, and to send my answer to Massow, who was present during the whole of this conversation of an hour and a quarter. He was quite flushed with excitement

24

when we left the room, repeating over and over again, "Surely you can never *now* think of going away!" and, to tell you the truth, I thought more of my dear mother than of all the rest. In short, two days afterwards I wrote to the King, and said that after his words to me I could no longer think of leaving his service, but that, on the contrary, my best abilities should be at his command so long as I lived. He had mentioned so and so (and I repeated the substance of our conversation), that I would take advantage of the liberty he had granted me, and remain in Leipzig *until* I was appointed to some *definite* sphere of work; on which account I begged to relinquish one-half of my salary, so long as I was not really engaged in active work. This proposal he accepted, and I am now here again with my wife and child. I have been obliged definitively to decline the offers of the King of Saxony ; but, in order to do so in the most respectful manner, I went to Dresden a few days after my return here, thanked the King once more verbally, and entreated him not the less to bestow the twenty thousand *thalers* (which an old Leipziger bequeathed in his will to the King for the establishment of an Academy of Art) to found a school for music in Leipzig, to which he graciously acceded. The official announcement came the day before yesterday. This music school is to be organized next winter, at least in its chief features ; when it is established, I may well say that I have been the means of procuring a permanent advantage for music here. If they begin anything solid in Berlin, I can settle there with a clear conscience ; if they allow the matter to stand over, it is probable that I may go on

with my half-salary and my situation here for more
than a year, and my duties be confined, as now, to
executing particular commands of the King: for instance, I am to supply him with music for the "Midsummer Night's Dream," the "Tempest," and "Œdipus Coloneus."

Such, then, is the desired conclusion of this long,
long transaction. Forgive all these details; but I wished
to inform you minutely of every particular.

A request occurs to me which I long ago intended to
have made to you. In Switzerland I saw my former
guide, Michael, whom on my previous mountain-ex-
peditions I always found to be an excellent, honest,
obliging fellow, and on this occasion I met with him
again, married to a charming pretty woman; he has
children, and is no longer a guide, but established as
landlord of the "Krone." During our first visit to
Meiringen this summer, we lived at the Hôtel de Reichenbach, but the second time we were at the "Krone,"
and quite delighted with the cleanliness and neatness,
and the civil behaviour of all the people in the house.
It is a most genuine Swiss village inn, taken in its best
sense. Now, Michael's greatest wish is to be named
among the inns at Meiringen in the new edition of
Murray's "Switzerland," and I promised to endeavour
to effect this for him.* Is it in your power to get this
done? The first inn there is the "Wilde Mann," the
second the "Reichenbach," and the third undoubtedly
the "Krone;" and if Murray recommends it as such, I
am convinced it will do him credit. He might also
mention that it is most beautifully situated, with a full

---

* See Letter to his Mother of the 3d of September, 1842.

view of the Engelhorn, and the glacier of the Rosenlaui.
Michael said that the editor of the Handbook had been
there, and very much *fêté* by the other landlords; his
means did not admit of this, still he would give him a
good round sum of money if he would only mention
him. I was indignant, and said, " *Without money, or
not at all.*" But I thought of many musical newspapers
and composers, so I did not lecture him much on the
subject, from the fear that he might one day hear something of the same sort from one of my colleagues, and
take his revenge. There is now a general complaint,
that the large town hotels have superseded the smaller
comfortable genuine Swiss inns; this is one of the
latter sort. Murray must really recommend it. Pray,
do what you can about this, and tell me if you succeed.
Forgive my troubling you, the secretary to an embassy,
with such things, but if you knew Michael you would
like him, I know. I would fain draw a great deal now,
and gladly devote myself to all manner of *allotria*, including composition; but I see lying before me an
enormous thick packet of proofs of my A minor symphony, and the "Antigone," which must absorb all my
leisure time; and then the frightful heap of letters!

My dearest friend, may these lines find you in good
health, and in a happy frame of mind; may you think
of me, as I shall of you, so long as life lasts; and may
you also soon be able to tell me yourself that it is so,
and again rejoice your true friends by your presence,
for Cecile writes this letter from first to last along with
me, and knows all I have said, and is, like myself, for
ever and ever your friend.

F. M. B.

To his Mother.

Leipzig, November 28th, 1842.

Dearest Mother,

As pen and paper must again serve instead of our usual evening hour for tea, I begin by making a suggestion, which is, whether you would like me to write to you regularly every Saturday (perhaps only a few words, but of this hereafter), and that one of the family, as often as you cannot or will not write, should undertake to send me a punctual reply. In addition to the joy of knowing beforehand the day when I am to hear of you, it is in some degree indispensable to insure my writing to you, for time *must* be found for a weekly letter; while, were this not the case, I should be ashamed to send you only a few lines, should it happen that I could not accomplish more. You can have no idea of the mass of affairs—musical, practical, and social—that have accumulated on the table in my study since my return here. The weekly concerts; the extra ones; the money the King has at length bestowed at my request on the Leipzigers, and for the judicious expenditure of which I only yesterday had to furnish the prospectus; the revisal of "Antigone" and of the A minor symphony, its score and parts; and a pile of letters. These are the principal points, which, however, branch off into a number of secondary ones. Besides, Raupach has already sent me the first chorus of "Athalia." The "Midsummer Night's Dream" and "Œdipus" daily work more busily in my head; I am really anxious at last to make the "Walpurgis Nacht" into a symphony cantata, for which it was originally

24*

intended, but did not become so from want of courage on my part; and I must also complete my violoncello sonata.

Old Schröder's concert took place three days ago, in which I played, and directed the overture to " Ruy Blas;" the old *déclamatrice* delighted us all exceedingly by the great power and spirit of her voice, and every gesture. In particular passages I thought she laid rather too much stress on the expression of the words, and gave too much preference to details over the voice; but as a whole her genius was highly remarkable. In her youth, had she the reputation of laying more stress on effect than was admissible? and what were her best parts in those days? Her daughter (looking younger, and wilder, and more of a madcap than ever) sang also, and sings this evening in Döhler's concert; she will also probably sing in our subscription concert next Thursday; the days which she passes in any town are not of the most quiet description for her acquaintances. We had, besides, Tichatschek, Wagner, Döhler, Mühlenfels: so there was a continual hurry and excitement last week.

Make them read aloud to you at the tea-table the passage from the last of Lessing's " Antiquarian Letters,"—" Wenn ich Kunstrichter wäre," etc. etc.,—and tell me whether any of you dispute the point, or whether you all agree with me, that it is the most exhaustive address which can be made to a critic, indeed to every critic. At this moment, when so many artists, old and young, good and bad, come here, this passage daily recurs to me.—Your

FELIX.

To Paul Mendelssohn Bartholdy.

My dear Brother,

Leipzig, December 5th, 1842.

As we agreed (and indeed very properly) that I was to take no step with regard to my affairs in Berlin without informing you immediately of every detail, I write you these lines to-day, although I am over head and ears in business. I received yesterday from the King the following communication:—

" By the enclosed written document you will perceive the tenor of the communication I have this day made on the subject of an Institute for the Improvement of Church Singing; it is addressed to the Special Commissioners, W. G. R. von Massow and W. G. R. General Intendant of Court Music, Graf von Redern. I have also, in compliance with your own wish, informed the Minister of State, Eichhorn, and the Finance Minister, Von Bodelschwingh, that, until you enter on your functions, you decline receiving more than fifteen hundred *thalers*, instead of three thousand. I nominate you General Music Director, and intrust to you the superintendence and direction of church and sacred music as your appointed sphere of action.—Charlottenburg, November 22d, 1842."

The enclosure consists of a Cabinet order, which is drawn up in a most clear and judicious style, entirely in the spirit of our interview, and thoroughly in accordance with my wishes, manifestly with the co-operation of Herr von Massow, and with the true and honest purpose of carrying out the affair. That no material obstacles exist, is again evident from this Cabinet order, but whether I may consider the accomplishment of the project as certain, I cannot say with any security till I actually see it. The affair of the Conservatorium was still further advanced, and seemed even more decided. On the other hand, I adhere to my former views, and do what I can to promote the project and to display my good will towards it.

Herr von Massow writes to me (only yesterday) that I had better soon come again to Berlin, to converse with him and Graf von Redern, and that only one or two days would be required; I shall, however, answer him that I mean to go there on the 17th, and have arranged to remain till the 23d. A longer stay is unfortunately impossible; still you and I can have some political gossip together, and be inseparable during my stay.

The king having on this occasion conferred on me a new title,* almost embarrasses me; I am unwilling to be of the number of those in the present day who possess a greater number of decorations than they have written good compositions, and yet it seems rather like it; at all events, I really have no idea what return I can possibly make for all this; still, as I have not in any way sought it, I may be excused. To refuse such a thing is out of the question, and there is no one who does not rejoice in being over-estimated, because on some other occasion the balance is sure to be made even by depreciation.—Ever your

FELIX.

* See Letter to the King of the 28th of October, 1842.

To his Mother.

Leipzig, December 11th, 1842.

Dearest Mother,

On the 21st or 22d, we give a concert here for the King, who has sworn death and destruction to all the hares in the country round. In this concert we mean to sing for his benefit (how touching!) the partridge and hare hunt out of the " Seasons." My " Walpurgis Nacht " is to appear once more in the second part, in a somewhat different garb indeed from the former one, which was somewhat too richly endowed with trombones, and rather poor in the vocal parts; but to effect this I have been obliged to re-write the whole score from A to Z, and to add two new arias, not to mention the rest of the clipping and cutting. If I don't like it now, I solemnly vow to give it up for the rest of my life. I think of bringing with me to Berlin a movement from the " Midsummer Night's Dream," and one from " Œdipus." The music school here, please God! will make a beginning next February; Hauptmann, David, Schumann and his wife, Becker, Pohlenz, and I, are to be the teachers at first. Ten scholars are received gratis; the rest who may wish to have instruction must pay seventy-five *thalers* a year. Now you know all that I know; the rest can only be taught by experience and trial.

I wished for you recently at a subscription concert. I think I never played the Beethoven G major concerto so well,--my old *cheval de bataille ;* the first cadence especially, and a new return to the solo, pleased me exceedingly, and apparently the audience still more.

What you write to me about the *répertoire* of your
Berlin concerts does not inspire me with any wish to
hear more about them.   The arrangement of the " Auf-
forderung zum Tanz," and the compositions of English
ambassadors,—these are valuable things !   If experi-
ments are to be thus made and listened to, it would be
advisable to be rather more liberal towards the works
of our Fatherland.   You will again say that I am cynical ; but many of my ideas are so intimately connected
with my life and my views on art, that you must be
indulgent with regard to them.

The monument to old Sebastian Bach is now very
handsome.*   Bendemann was here the day before yesterday, to inspect it once more.   All the inner scaffold-
ing had been removed; so the pillars and smaller col-
umns, and scrolls, and above all the bas-reliefs, and the
grand, antiquated old features, sparkled clearly in the
sun, and caused me great delight.   The whole structure,
with its numerous elegant decorations, is really typical
of the old fellow.   It is now covered up again, and will
remain so till March, when it is to be inaugurated on
his birthday, by one of his motetts.   Cedars are to be
planted round the monument, and a Gothic seat placed
in front of it.   We are anxious, however, not to make
too much fuss on the subject, and to avoid the present
pompous style of phraseology, and the worship of art
and artists, which is so much the fashion.

Here, the outward aspect of things is now as much
too flourishing as it formerly was too miserable for artists, which would be very pleasant for us, but it does
harm to the cause.   Art is becoming spoiled and slug-

---

* See Letter of 10th August, 1840.

gish, so we should rather be grateful to our present enemies than be angry with them. I also consider it too much good fortune that the King of Prussia has nominated me General Music Director. This is another new title and new honour, whereas I really do not know how to do enough to deserve the old ones.

This is a hallowed day for us all, with its delightful and memorable recollections;* think of me too on this anniversary, as I do of you and of him, so long as life endures.—Your

FELIX.

TO PASTOR JULIUS SCHUBRING, DESSAU.

Leipzig, December 16th, 1842.

My dear Schubring,

I now send you, according to your permission, the text of " Elijah," so far as it goes. I do beg of you to give me your best assistance, and return it soon with plenty of notes on the margin (I mean Scriptural passages, etc.). I also enclose your former letters on the subject, as you wished, and have torn them out of the book in which they were. They must, however, be replaced, so do not forget to send them back to me. In the very first of these letters (at the bottom of the first page), you properly allude to the chief difficulty of the text, and the very point in which it is still the most deficient,—in universally valid and impressive thoughts and words; for of course it is not my intention to com-

---

* The birthday of Mendelssohn's father.

pose what you call " a Biblical Walpurgis Night." I
have endeavoured to obviate this deficiency by the passages written in Roman letters; but there is still something wanting, even to complete these, and to obtain
suitable comprehensive words for the subject. This,
then, is the first point to which I wish to direct your
attention, and where your assistance is very necessary.
Secondly, in the "dramatic" arrangement. I cannot
endure the half operatic style of most of the oratorio
words (where recourse is had to common figures, as,
for example, an Israelite, a maiden, Hannah, Micaiah,
and others, and where, instead of saying " this and
that occurred," they are made to say, " Alas! I see
this and that occurring"). I consider this very weak,
and will not follow such a precedent. However, the
everlasting "he spake," etc., is also not right. Both
of these are avoided in the text; still this is, and ever
will be, one of its weaker aspects.

Reflect, also, whether it is justifiable that no positively dramatic figure except that of Elijah appears.
I think it is. He ought, however, at the close, at his
ascension to heaven, to have something to say (or to
sing). Can you find appropriate words for this purpose? The second part, moreover, especially towards
the end, is still in a very unfinished condition. I have
not as yet got a final chorus; what do you advise it to
be? Pray, study the whole carefully, and write on
the margin a great many beautiful arias, reflections,
pithy sentences, choruses, and all sorts of things, and
let me have them as soon as possible.

I also send the "Méthode des Méthodes." While
turning over its leaves, I could not help thinking that

you will here and there find much that will be useful. If that be the case, I beg you will keep it as long as you and your young pianoforte player may require it. I don't use it at all. If it does not please you, I can send you, instead a sight of Zimmermann's " Pianoforte School," which is composed pretty much on the same ·principle, and has only different examples, etc.

Speaking is a very different thing from writing. The few minutes I lately passed with you and yours were more enlivening and cheering than ever so many letters.—Ever your

FELIX M. B.

To Paul Mendelssohn Bartholdy.

Leipzig, December 22d, 1842.*

My dear brother,

I wrote to you the day after our arrival here that we were all well, and living in our sorrow as we best could, dwelling on the happiness we once possessed. My letter was addressed to Fanny, but written to you all; though it seems you had not heard of it, and even this trifle shows, what will day by day be more deeply and painfully felt by us, that the point of union is now gone, where even as children we could always meet, and though we were no longer so in years, we felt that we were still so in feeling. When I wrote to my Mother, I knew that I wrote to you all, and you knew it too ; we are children no longer, but we have

---

* After the death of his mother.

enjoyed what it really is to be so. Now this is gone for ever! At such a time, with regard to outward things, we are as if in a dark room, groping to find the way, hour after hour. Tell me if we cannot arrange that I should write to one of you by turns once every week, and get an answer from you, so that we may at least hear of each other every three weeks, independent. of more frequent letters; or say whether any better arrangement occurs to you. I thank you a thousand times for your kind question about the house. I had thought of asking you for it, and now you offer it to me. But before we finally settle this, I should like you to bring the subject cautiously on the *tapis*, in the presence of our sisters and brother-in-law. If you perceive that any unpleasant feeling is awakened in their minds by such a proposal, when for the first time, in Berlin, I am not to live under the same roof with them, and if they give any indication of such a feeling, even by a single word or remark (you will quickly observe this, and I rely entirely on you), then we must give it up. In any other event, I shall thankfully accept your kindness. My next visit to Berlin will be a severe trial to me; indeed, all I say and do is a trial to me,— anything, in short, that is not mere patient endurance. I have, however, begun to work again, and that is the only thing which occupies me a little. Happily I have some half-mechanical work to do,—transcribing, instrumentation, and similar things. This can be accomplished by a kind of almost animal instinct, which we can follow, and which does us more good than if we had it not. But yesterday I was obliged to direct. That was terrible. They told me that the first time would be terrible, but sooner or later it must be done. I thought so too, but I would fain have waited for a few weeks. The first thing was a song of Rochlitz's; but when in the rehearsal the alto sang, *piano*, " Wie der Hirch schreit,"* I was so overcome that I was obliged afterwards to go out of the room, to give free vent to my tears.

To-day, Heaven be praised, I am not required to see or speak to any one, and my cough is better. Thus time glides on; but what we have once possessed is not less precious, and what we have now lost not less painful, with time. Farewell, dearest Brother. Continue to love me.—Your

FELIX.

To PROFESSOR KÖSTLIN, TÜBINGEN.

Leipzig, January 12th, 1843.

Dear Herr Köstlin, or rather, dear Herr Godfather,

You have caused me much joy by your kind letter of yesterday, and by the happy intelligence it contained, and, above all, by your wish that I should be godfather! Indeed, you may well believe that I gladly accede to the request, and after reading your letter it was some moments before I could realize that I could not possibly be present at the baptism. In earlier days, no reasoning would have been of any avail; I would have taken post-horses and arrived in your house for the occasion.

---

* From his own Psalm, op. 42.

This I cannot now do; but if there be such a thing as to be present in spirit, then I shall indeed be so. The remembrance of me by such well-beloved friends, and this proof of your regard, which causes a still more close and enduring tie between us, cannot fail to cause true joy and exhilaration of heart; and, believe me, I feel this joy, and thank you and your wife for it.

That I am to be godfather is then settled; but there are a thousand things I still wish to know, and if, when the christening is over, you do not write me all the details which you omit in this letter, you must expect a good scolding. You forget that I have myself three children, so I am doubly interested in such things. You do not even mention the name the boy is to have, and whether he is fair or dark, or has black or blue eyes. My wife is as desirous as I am to know all this, and we hope that after the christening you will write to us every particular. You were rather displeased with me for being so bad a correspondent. I earnestly entreat of you never to be displeased with me on that account; I cannot remedy this; it is a fault which, in spite of the best resolutions on my part, I constantly fall into, and which I shall never be cured of so long as I live. There is so much that stands in my way; first, a really instinctive dislike to pen and paper, except where music is concerned; then the various scattered branches of a perfect maze of professional and other avocations, which I am obliged to undertake partly for myself and partly for others, so that I really sometimes can only carry on life like a person in a crowd pushing his way, and shoving along with both his elbows, using his feet too, as well as his fists and teeth, etc. This is in fact, my mood many a week ; I extort the time for writing music, otherwise I could not go on from day to day ; but I cannot find leisure to write letters.

We have had recently a bitter heavy loss to bewail, —that of my dear Mother. I intended to have written in a gay mood all through this letter, and not by a single word to allude to anything that by its melancholy nature might disturb your happiness, but I feel that I must write this to you, otherwise all that I say would appear mere hypocrisy. You must therefore take part in my sorrow, for I could not conceal from you the event that during the last few weeks has so bowed us down from grief, and which it will be long before we can recover from. Yet such a letter as yours is welcome at all times, and in all sorrow, and just as I know how you will feel towards me on hearing this, so you know how cordially I sympathize with your joy; this may well be called sincere attachment! Give your wife a thousand greetings and congratulations from me. Tell me if she has composed new songs or anything else ; what I should like best would be to receive one from her in a letter ; they always delight me so much, when I hear and play them.—Ever your devoted

FELIX MENDELSSOHN BARTHOLDY.

TO FANNY HENSEL, BERLIN.

Leipzig, January 13th, 1843.

. . . We yesterday tried over a new symphony by a Dane of the name of Gade, and we are to perform it in

25*

the course of the ensuing month; it has given me more
pleasure than any work I have seen for a long time.
He has great and superior talents, and I wish you could
hear this most original, most earnest, and sweet-sound-
ing Danish symphony. I am writing him a few lines
to-day, though I know nothing more of him than that
he lives in Copenhagen, and is twenty-six years of age,
but I must thank him for the delight he has caused me;
for there can scarcely be a greater than to hear fine
music; admiration increasing at every bar, and a feeling of congeniality; would that it came less seldom!

To N. W. GADE, PROFESSOR OF MUSIC, COPENHAGEN.

Leipzig, January 13th, 1842.

Sir,

We yesterday rehearsed for the first time your symphony in C minor, and though personally a stranger,
yet I cannot resist the wish to address you, in order
to say what excessive pleasure you have caused me by
your admirable work, and how truly grateful I am for
the great enjoyment you have conferred on me. It is
long since any work has made a more lively and favourable impression on me, and as my surprise increased at
every bar, and yet every moment I felt more at home,
I to-day conceive it to be absolutely necessary to thank
you for all this pleasure, and to say how highly I esteem
your splendid talents, and how eager this symphony
(which is the only thing I know of yours) makes me
to become acquainted with your earlier and future com-

positions; but as I hear that you are still so young, it is the thoughts of those to come in which I particularly rejoice, and your present fine work causes me to anticipate these with the brightest hopes. I once more thank you for it and the enjoyment I yesterday had.

We are to have some more rehearsals of the symphony, and shall probably perform it in the course of three or four weeks. The parts were so full of mistakes, that we were obliged to revise them all, and to have many of them transcribed afresh; next time it will not be played like a new piece, but as one familiar and dear to the whole orchestra. This was indeed the case yesterday, and there was only one voice on the subject among us *musicians*, but it must be played so that *every one* may hear it properly. Herr Raymond Härtel told me there was an idea of your coming here yourself in the course of the winter. I hope this may be the case, as I could better and more plainly express my high estimation and my gratitude to you verbally, than by mere empty written words. But, whether we become acquainted or not, I beg you will always look on me as one who will never cease to regard your works with love and sympathy, and who will ever feel the greatest and most cordial delight in meeting with such an artist as yourself, and such a work of art as your C minor symphony.—Your devoted

FELIX MENDELSSOHN BARTHOLDY.

To CARL KLINGEMANN, LONDON.

Leipzig, January 13th, 1843.

I cannot as yet at all reconcile myself to distraction of thought and every-day life, as it is called, or to life with men who in fact care very little about you, and to whom what we can never forget or recover from, is only a mere *piece of news.* I now feel, however, more vividly than ever what a heavenly calling Art is; and for this also I have to thank my parents; just when all else which ought to interest the mind appears so repugnant, and empty, and insipid, the smallest real service to Art lays hold of your inmost thoughts, leading you so far away from town, and country, and from earth itself, that it is indeed a blessing sent by God. A few days previous to the 11th, I had undertaken to transcribe my " Walpurgis Nacht," which I had long intended to do, and caused the voice parts of the whole of the voluminous score to be written out and copied afresh. Then I was summoned to Berlin, and after an interval of some weeks, I have now begun to write the instru mental parts in my little study, which has a pretty view of fields, and meadows, and a village. I sometimes could not leave the table for hours, I was so fascinated by such pleasant intercourse with the old familiar oboes and tenor violins, which live so much longer than we do, and are such faithful friends. I was too sorrowful, and the wound too recent, to attempt new composi- tions; but this mere mechanical pursuit and employ- ment was my consolation the whole time that I was alone, when I had not my wife and children with their beloved faces, who make me forget even music, and cause me daily to think how grateful I ought to be to God for all the benefits he bestows on me.

You have not quite understood my previous letter. You say "I *could not act otherwise* in my official position." It was not *that*, it was my Mother I alluded to. All the plans and projects have since then been dragging on slowly; I have my half-salary, and begun the music for the "Midsummer Night's Dream," "Œdipus," and others for the King. My private opinion is, still, that he is resolved to allow things to rest as they are; in the mean time, I have established the Conservatorium here, the official announcement of which you will read in the newspapers, and it gives me a great deal to do.

To Madame Emma Preusser.

Leipzig, February 4th, 1843.

Dear Lady,

I send "Siebenkäs," according to your desire. May it cause you half the pleasure it caused me when I first read it, and very frequently since. I believe that the period when we first learn to love and to know such a glorious work, is among the happiest hours of our lives. As you have read very little of Jean Paul, were I in your place, I would not concern myself much about the prologues, but at first entirely discard the "Blumen-stücke," and begin at once at page 26, and follow the story of "Siebenkäs" to its close. When you have read this, and perhaps also the "Flegel Jahre," and some more of his wonderful works, then no doubt you will like and prize all he has written,—even the more laboured, the less happy, or the obsolete,—and then you will no longer wish to miss the "Blumenstücke," the prologues, and the "Traum im Traum," etc. etc.

As soon as you wish for anything new, you will always find me at the service of you and yours.—Your devoted

FELIX MENDELSSOHN BARTHOLDY.

To N. W. GADE, PROFESSOR OF MUSIC, COPENHAGEN.

Leipzig, March 3d, 1843.

Sir,

Your C minor symphony was performed for the first time yesterday at our eighteenth subscription concert here, to the lively and unalloyed delight of the whole public, who broke out into the loudest applause at the close of each of the four movements. There was great excitement among the audience after the scherzo, and the shouting and clapping of hands seemed interminable; after the adagio the very same; after the last, and after the first,—in short, after all! To see the musicians so unanimous, the public so enchanted, and the performance so successful, was to me a source of delight as great as if I had written the work myself, or indeed I may say greater,—for in my own compositions the faults and the less successful portions always seem to me most prominent, whereas in your work I felt nothing but pure delight in all its admirable beauties.

By the performance of yesterday evening you have gained the whole of the Leipzig public, who truly love music, as permanent friends; none here will ever henceforth speak of you or of your works but with the most heartfelt esteem, and receive with open arms all your future compositions, which will be assiduously studied, and joyfully hailed, by all friends of music in this town.

"Whoever wrote the last half of this scherzo is an admirable genius, and we have a right to expect the most grand and glorious works from him." Such was the universal opinion yesterday evening in our orchestra and in the whole hall; and we are not fickle here. Thus you have acquired a large number of friends for life by your work; fulfil, then, our wishes and hopes by writing many, many works in the same style, and of the same beauty, and thus imparting new life to our beloved art; and, to effect this, Heaven has bestowed on you all that He can bestow.

Besides the rehearsal which I formerly wrote to you about, we recently had two others, and, with the exception of some trifling unimportant mistakes, the symphony was played with a degree of spirit and enthusiasm which at once showed how highly enchanted the musicians were with it. I hear that it is to be published by Kistner: so permit me to ask whether the heading of the first introduction, $\frac{6}{4}$ time, afterwards repeated, may not give rise to misapprehension? If I am not mistaken, it is marked *moderato sostenuto*. Instead of this *sostenuto*, ought it not rather to be printed *con moto*, or *con molto di moto*? That heading would, it seems to me, lead to the right *tempo*, if it were $\frac{6}{8}$ time instead of $\frac{6}{4}$; but in $\frac{6}{4}$ time it is so very customary to count the separate crotchets slowly and deliberately, that I think the movement would be taken too slow, which I found to be the case at the first rehearsal, until I no longer paid any attention to the notes or the heading, but adhered to the sense alone. As many musicians cling so closely to such headings, I was resolved at all events to mention to you my doubts on this subject.

Allow me to thank you once more for your obliging letter, and the friendly intention which you inform me of in it;* but I thank you still more for the pleasure which you have caused me by the work itself; and pray believe that no one will follow your future course with warmer sympathy, or anticipate your future works with more anxiety and hope, than your

FELIX MENDELSSOHN BARTHOLDY.

To I. Moscheles, London.

Leipzig, April 30th, 1843.

. . . Our Music Academy here has made a famous beginning; fresh notices of students arrive almost daily, and the number of teachers, as well as of lessons, has been necessarily very much increased.

Two serious maladies, however, are apparent, which I mean vigorously to resist with might and main so long as I am here : the Direction is disposed to increase and generalize,—that is, to build houses, to hire localities of several stories; whereas I maintain that, for

---

* Gade dedicated his C minor symphony to Mendelssohn.

the first ten years, the two rooms we have, in which simultaneous instruction can be given, are sufficient. Then all the scholars wish to compose and to theorize; while it is my belief that practical work, thorough steady practising, and strict time, a solid knowledge of all solid works, etc., etc , are the chief things which can and must be taught. From these, all other knowledge follows as a thing of course, and anything further is not the affair of learning, but the gift of God. I need not, however, I am sure, say that, notwithstanding this, I am far from wishing to render Art a mere handicraft.

To M. Simrock, Bonn.

Sir,

Leipzig, June 12th, 1843,

Herr Herrmann, some time since, inquired of you once, in my name, about the printed score of the " Zauberflöte ;" but I now apply to yourself to know whether any copy of it still exists in the original German, or if any ever did exist. And if neither be the case, I should like to know whether you are disposed to allow the original correct text to be substituted in your plates of this opera, and some proofs to be taken. It appears to me almost a positive duty that such a work should descend to posterity in its unvitiated form ; we indeed all know perfectly well, for instance, the aria beginning with the words " Dies Bildniss ist bezaubernd schön," but if in the course of a few years the younger musicians always see it printed thus, " So reizend hold,

26

so zaub'risch schön," they will acquire a false idea of Mozart's thoughts; and I go so far as to assert that even the most undeniably bad passages in such a text deserve to be retained, as Mozart composed music for them, and they have thus become household words all through Germany. If improvements are to be proposed, it is all very well, but in that event they ought to stand *side by side* with the original words; in no case must they be entirely banished, otherwise fidelity towards the great deceased master is not properly observed. I beg you will say a few words on this point when you write to Herr Herrmann; and if you resolve to alter your plates, then I shall be the first, but certainly not the last, of your customers to thank you for it.—Your obedient

FELIX MENDELSSOHN BARTHOLDY.

TO G. OTTEN, HAMBURG.

Leipzig, July 7th, 1843.

Sir,

My best thanks for your obliging letter, which contains much that is really far too kind and flattering about myself and my music. Gladly, in compliance with your friendly invitation, would I at some future time come to express my thanks to you personally, and to play to you as you wish me to do. Since we met in Dessau I have learnt a good deal more, and have made progress. But you must not compare my playing with my music; I feel quite embarrassed by such an idea, and I am certainly not the man to prevent people worshipping the golden calf, as it is called in the fashion of the day. Moreover, I believe that this mode will soon pass away, even without opposition. True, a new one will certainly start up; on this account therefore it seems to me best to pursue one's own path steadily, and especially to guard against an evil custom of the day, which is not included in those you name, but which, however, does infinite harm,—squandering and frittering away talents for the sake of outward show. This is a reproach which I might make to most of our present artists, and to myself also more than I could wish; I have no great inclination therefore to extend my travels, but rather to restrict them far more, in order to strive with greater earnestness for my own improvement instead of the good opinion of others.

I conclude by thanking you for your friendly letter, and pray remember kindly your obedient

FELIX MENDELSSOHN BARTHOLDY.

TO PAUL MENDELSSOHN BARTHOLDY.

Leipzig, July 21st, 1843.

Dear Brother,

I had almost hoped to be able to answer your letter in person, for I was very nearly taking a journey to Berlin again. Herr von Massow has sent me a communication connected with that tedious everlasting affair, which irritated me so much that it almost made me ill, and I do not feel right yet. In my first feeling of anger, I wished to go to Berlin to speak to you and break off the whole affair; but I prefer writing, and so I am now writing to you. Instead of receiving the assent to the proposals on which we had agreed in the interview of the 10th,* Herr von Massow sends me a commission to arrange for orchestra and chorus, without delay, the chorale, " Herr Gott, Dich loben wir," the longest chorale and the most tiresome work which I ever attempted; and the day after I had finished it and sent it off, I receive an official document which I must sign before the assent of the King can be solicited; when I had signed it, the others present at that conference would also subscribe their names. In this deed all the stipulations are correctly stated, but six or eight additional clauses are written on the margin not one syllable of which had ever been named during the conference, invalidating the whole intention of the above stipulations, and placing myself and the Institute in the most entire subservience to Herr von Küstner,—and, in short, showing in the clearest light all the difficulties to which I formerly alluded, and the existence of which Herr von Massow denied. Among other things, it is said, the appointment of the orchestra for all church music is to be devolved on the *theatrical* music direction; before every concert there must be an application made to the General *Intendancy,* whether the day, which according to our agreement was to be settled once for all at the beginning of the winter, is to con-

---

* This conference was held in order to hasten the performance of the plans of the King. See the letters of 28th October, 1842, and 5th December, 1842.

tinue the same or be altered, etc.; all things of which *not one syllable* had been alluded to in the conference. As I told you, I fretted myself till I was quite ill about it. Remembering your words, I thought it the most judicious plan to write direct to the King and break off the affair. After two days' consideration, I did not think I was justified in doing so; I therefore wrote to Herr von Massow, why and wherefore I could not give my signature, requesting him to inform me whether the King intended to carry out our former agreement. If he did not feel disposed to do so, or if he, Herr von Massow, considered it necessary to insert new clauses in the agreement, I should then consider the affair impracticable, and must act accordingly. In the other view of the case, he knew that I was prepared to come; I was also to say how far I had got with " Œdipus." I answered that, in accordance with Tieck's wish, I had arranged the "Midsummer Night's Dream" with music, to be performed in the new palace; that I had also, by special commission from the King, written choruses,* and that I had not resumed the choruses of " Œdipus" since the previous autumn, because another Greek piece had been appointed to be performed. I said all this in a friendly manner, but I do assure you that the affair cost me four most angry, disturbed, and irksome days. If I could only have spoken to you for a single hour! I should have been glad to know whether you approved of my course,—that is, of my letter, —or whether you would have preferred a short letter resigning the appointment. It is really too provoking

* Neither of these works, however, had yet been performed.

26

that in all and everything the same spirit prevails; in this case, too, all might be smoothed over and set to rights by a few words, and every moment I expect to hear them spoken, and then there would be a possibility of something good and new; but they are not spoken, and they are replaced by a thousand annoyances, and my head at last is so bewildered that I think I become almost as perverted and unnatural as the whole affair is at last likely to turn out. Forgive me for causing you to have your share of annoyance, but now I have told you all,—and enough. I have not been able to work during these days. To make up for this, I have done the "Jungfrau" for you in Indian ink; the mountain I think is excellent, but I have again utterly destroyed the pines in the foreground. I mean now, too, to resume your sonata.—Your

FELIX.

To PAUL MENDELSSOHN BARTHOLDY.

Leipzig, July 26th, 1843.

Dearest Brother,

I have just received your kind letter, and indeed at the very moment when I was about to write to you and beg you to give me quarters. Next Tuesday, the 1st of August, I am obliged to return to Berlin to rehearse and perform the "Tausendjährige Reich," and to hear from the King his views with regard to the composition of the Psalms. He yesterday summoned me for this purpose, and of course I must go, and of course I must live with you; but is it also of course that

my visit is convenient to you? This time I shall
remain at least eight days; on the sixth is the celebration of the above-mentioned " Reich." Give me a
line in answer.

I have a reply to my letter from Von Massow, who
writes me the King's invitation; he says we are sure
to agree, and that some matters of form are the only
things in question; that I shall spare myself the
annoyance and vexation which such a tiresome correspondence must entail, and that as I am coming at all
events for the " Tausendjährige Reich," I can also reply
personally to the *zehntausendjährige* affair. Herr von
Massow, in fact, says pretty plainly, " Asking and bidding make the bargain;" that he wished to see whether I would sign; and this not being the case, the
others would no doubt give way, etc., etc. All this is
very confusing, and I do not at all like it. To be sure,
it is true that his head must also be in a maze, and he
appears to take all imaginable trouble about the affair.
I mean to bring you the whole of the everlasting papers
for your inspection; we can read them together when
we meet. I hope on this occasion not merely to have
a Court dinner with the King, but a satisfactory discussion on business,—probably the easiest mode of
bringing about a result. I wish, if possible, to defer
this till after the celebration of the *tausendjährig* festival; the chorale that I wrote for it is, I believe, just
what the King wishes; at all events, it furnishes an
opportunity for a complete understanding.

My anger, which was indeed greater on this occasion than for a long time past, I shook off in a defile on
the way to Naumburg, close to Rippach, where you

drive down to Meissenfels; and a couple of good talks
and walks with Mühlenfels fairly banished every trace
of it. Kösen was a pretty sight; we met Mlle. F——
and Herr C—— under the hazel-bushes and lovely
lime-trees, and from every shrub, instead of glow-
worms glittered the order of the red eagle, of different
classes; but it was really beautiful. And now I am
writing music once more instead of painting fir-trees;
therefore I cannot positively promise to finish the
"Jungfrau" before eight days. I have washed out the
forest recently, for the second time. It is a year the
day after to-morrow since we set off to Switzerland.—
Your

FELIX.

To PAUL MENDELSSOHN BARTHOLDY.

Dear Brother,
Leipzig, August 26th, 1843.

I yesterday received a letter from Herr von Massow
containing the intelligence that the King had fully
sanctioned the affair of the Wirklich Geheimrath; I
wished to write this to you instantly.* To-day I got
a second letter, with the information that the King desires to have three representations in the New Palace
in the second half of September, namely, 1, "Antigone;"

---

* The execution of this project, also, was not completed; and
Mendelssohn, after some time had elapsed, requested the King to
relieve him from all public duties, and to be permitted to remain only
in an artistic and personal relation to his Majesty, to which the King
was graciously pleased to accede.

2, " The Midsummer Night's Dream; " 3, " Athalia "
(" Medea " is to be given between Nos. 1 and 2, and all
the four within fourteen days) ; and I am invited to
Berlin for the purpose. Now, I would rather not write,
for I have a frightful quantity of things to do before
then, as not one of the scores is yet fit for the transcriber, and the overture to "Athalia" still wanting, as
well as the instrumentation of the whole, etc., etc. I
have written nevertheless that I would come, and the
music should be finished.—Ever your

FELIX.

To PAUL MENDELSSOHN BARTHOLDY.

Leipzig, September 16th, 1843.

Dear Brother,

Six days ago, Herr von Küstner (after a silence of
ten days, in spite of all my letters and messages) wrote
to me, that the whole project of the representations in
the New Palace was postponed till October. So of
course I receive from him a letter to-day, saying that
" on Tuesday, the 19th, 'Antigone' is to be given."
Luckily I smelt a rat, and shall set off to Berlin by the
first train the day after to-morrow.

I defer all else till we meet. You gave me permission
to occupy the only hotel in Berlin that I like, so I mean
to go to you. *Au revoir*.—Your

FELIX.

To THE HOCH EDELRATH OF LEIPZIG.

(*The Corporation.*)

Leipzig, October 3d, 1843.

To the Corporation of the City of Leipzig I am indebted for the privilege of considering myself as in every sense belonging to that city. I therefore take the liberty to address myself to the Corporation on a subject which, though it does not personally concern me, is closely connected with the interests of Art in this place, and with the city itself. I hope on this account for their indulgence, and esteem it my plain, bounden duty as a citizen, not to be idly silent on such an occasion, but to express my dutiful wish, and request, in confidence to the Corporation.

The town orchestra here has communicated to me a memorial, in which they beg that some alterations may be made in the terms of their contract with the lessee of the theatre. Their chief object is an increase of their salaries, which have for many years remained the same, and also an improvement in the deputy regulations; and for the attainment of this purpose the intervention of the Corporation is requested.

The petition has been rejected in its most essential points; for, instead of the increase of salary demanded, the reply is that the lessee of the theatre means to expend three hundred thalers more yearly on the orchestra (which three hundred thalers must be divided among thirty-one persons), and that "if he is satisfied with the performances of the orchestra, and if his receipts admit of it, he may possibly be disposed to grant a donation to the orchestra."

I can only attribute such a proposal to some indistinct statement in the memorial, or some obscure expressions. For, in my opinion, it is not a question of alms, but of just claims.

I am well aware that it may be no easy matter to apply a scale of payment to an intellectual body like that of the orchestra, and to tax it in thalers and groschen; but in days like the present, when so much is said about intellectual qualifications, there is one thing absolutely certain, that it is possible for *justice* and *injustice*, *fairness* and *unfairness*, to exist in the remuneration of intellectual services; that this does not depend upon the good will, more or less, or on the favour of those who pay, but that a positive *right* exists, which he has the privilege of claiming who devotes his life to an intellectual vocation, and can therefore legitimately demand that his life should be sustained, if he carries out his calling well and blamelessly. This the orchestra here do in the most admirable manner; and under such a conviction I do, in my inmost heart, consider that the salaries fixed in the contract between the lessee of the theatre and the orchestra are unjust. Perhaps they were so even at the time they were settled, but are now, owing to the change in the times, infinitely more so; the evidence of which is so clearly set forth in the first memorial of the orchestra, that I believe only a glance at it is necessary to prove the justice of my assertion.

If the Corporation be also of this opinion, and convinced of the unfairness of these points, the question would then be, in how far it is *possible* for the lessee of the theatre to comply with the wishes of the orchestra;

if by his consent to increase the salaries he would not
become bankrupt himself; and whether, in endeavour-
ing to obtain justice for the orchestra, injustice might
not be done to the lessee ?

Three things may form a criterion on this point,—the
average receipts of the lessee hitherto, the comparison
between other theatrical salaries and those of this orchestra, and, lastly, the pay of other German orchestras
in cities of the same standing as Leipzig.

With regard to the receipts of the lessee, it will be
difficult to obtain exact information. In spite of all the
official documents and rendering of accounts, I venture
to assert that there is not a person in Leipzig who is
thoroughly acquainted with the fact, except the former
lessees themselves, who will at once decline answering
any such questions. In so far as I have seen of similar
official documents, here and in other cities, it seems an
undeniable truth that, in an undertaking of the kind, a
yearly additional payment of two thousand thalers
would not cause the speculation to become a losing
instead of a good one. This is evident by a glance at
the variable and sometimes enormous salaries of the
singers, male and female, for whose engagement no
theatre *entrepreneur* would grudge an outlay like the
above, in order to cast greater lustre on his stage.

These salaries also furnish a complete answer to the
second point; being almost everywhere so greatly increased during the years when the orchestra here have
only received the old scale of payment, that a theatrical
lessee of the former date would perhaps also have
declared that such an amount of money was utterly
irreconcilable with any profits to himself. Singers,

after a certain number of years, deteriorate; their places must be supplied, new contracts made, and thus they can obtain for themselves that justice which the members of the orchestra in vain demand. Singers are paid in Leipzig at the same rate as in other places; but not so the orchestra. If it be said, singers are only selected and paid according to the requirements and fashion of the day, whereas, with regard to the orchestra, it is so in a minor degree, for whether it be better or worse constituted or paid, the public know nothing, —then this is an additional reason for my writing this letter; for I consider it my duty, and that of every friend of music, to protest against such a theory. Just because the orchestra is not an article of luxury, but the most necessary and important basis for a theatre,— just because the public invariably regard with more interest articles of luxury than more essential things,— on this very account, it is a positive duty to endeavour to effect that what is legitimate and necessary should not be disparaged and superseded by a love of glitter. Indeed, this was why the Corporation took under their protection this orchestra, in the new theatre contracts. If, however, they sanction the lessee of the theatre making a contract with the orchestra, and permit the old and obsolete salaries to remain as they are, then such protection would be no benefit, but rather an injury to the orchestra. Things would thus necessarily remain, year after year, in a position which has no parallel in any German city of the same rank as Leipzig.

This leads me to the third point. It has been said that a comparison of the salaries here with those in

27

other towns is inadmissible. But how is it possible to
arrive in a better manner at a scale of justice or injustice, in similar payment?   As in other towns orchestras
are better paid, as, in spite of this, lessees do not
become bankrupt (and I believe no instance was ever
known of a theatrical manager being ruined by the high
salaries of an orchestra), as the same pretensions with
regard to services are made by the musicians here as
elsewhere,—is it not clear from all this that the same
mode of acting is possible here as elsewhere ?   The pay
which the orchestra in Frankfort-on-the-Maine receives
from the *theatre alone* is not only higher than it would
be here were the increase in question granted, but it is
almost without exception *higher than it is here for the
theatre, concert, and church music combined,* even if the
demand in question were complied with.   Should not
this prove that the prayer of the orchestra here is not
unreasonable,—that the theatre lessee may accede to it
without any risk ?   Indeed, may not a refusal on his
part lead to the inference that this city considers its
own musicians inferior to those of other towns of a
similar class?   And yet such cannot be the case, for
the performances of our orchestra are not only equal to
that of Frankfort, but to those of every other German
city ; indeed, undeniably superior to most of those with
which I am acquainted ! The favourable and wide-
spread musical reputation which Leipzig enjoys through
the whole of Germany, it owes entirely and solely to
this orchestra, the members of which must get on as
they best can, in the most sparing and scanty manner.
Such a good reputation is certainly not without material advantage for the town of Leipzig, even indepen-

dent of the intellectual benefit to art. Shall, then,
those individuals to whom such happy results are
owing, remain in a state of privation, now as formerly,
irrespective of these services, and the change in the
times, while the whole community thrives by their
merits, and the city itself derives honour and profit
from them?

I shall only add a few words with regard to the
deputy rule, or rather *misrule*, as it ought more properly
to be called; for it is really difficult to form an idea of
the confusion in this department, without knowing it
from personal experience, which I had an opportunity
of doing.   This also has been minutely stated in former
memorials, and I now add an example from my own
knowledge.   In the concert of the day before yesterday,
the clarionet players were obliged to pay a silver thaler
each to their theatre deputy, so that each of them, for
his services at the rehearsal, and performance in the
first subscription concert, *paid* eight groschen.   It may
be suggested to raise the prices of the concert-tickets;
but this would not check the mischief.   A strict rule
as to deputies can alone effect this.   On the contrary,
it is very desirable that the scale adopted for payment
of the concerts should equally be applied to the payment of extra performances in the theatre, which
demand the same amount of time and energy.

This brings me to the last point on which I wish to
touch.   If there be the greatest difficulties in the way
of repairing these evils, what difficulty can there be in
greatly raising the former fixed salaries for extra performances?   It is notorious that they are in no degree
in proportion to the increased receipts of the lessee;

they are not in proportion to the remuneration for other extra services, such as concerts, church music, etc.; they are not even in proportion to the set price fixed for the town musicians for balls, weddings, and so forth. I am perfectly convinced that such an augmentation could be effected without difficulty, and without any injury to the theatre lessee, and a portion of the just complaints of the orchestra would thus be obviated. May they all meet with that consideration to which their equity and justice entitle them!

In conclusion, I beg forgiveness from the Corporation for the great liberty which I have taken in writing this letter; it regards a matter which does not personally concern me, and from which neither evil nor good can accrue to me, and which only affects me in so far as it relates to the interests of artists whom I so highly prize and esteem; it is of importance to art also in this city; and I certainly can never see with calmness or indifference the increasing or decreasing reputation of such an artistic institution as Leipzig possesses in this admirable orchestra. May my words accordingly prove the heartfelt love and esteem with which, so long as I live, I must ever regard all that affects the honour of Leipzig in her artistic and musical sphere.—I am always the devoted servant of the Corporation,

FELIX MENDELSSOHN BARTHOLDY.

To the King of Prussia.

Berlin, 1844.

Your Majesty,

I venture in these lines to bring before you a petition which I have much at heart.

Among the vast number of compositions sent to me from musicians here and in other places, I lately received some works of a young man of the name of G——, in which I perceived such unmistakable talent and such genuine musical feeling that they seemed to me like an oasis in the desert. They consisted of a set of songs, and a grand piece of music for Good Friday, which (each in its own peculiar style) displayed genuine conceptions, and a true artistic nature. Indeed, the sacred music inspires me with a strong hope that the composer may accomplish something really important in this sphere. Nothing is wanting for the full development of his talents save that he should reside for some time in a large city, in order to hear music and to become acquainted with musicians; for since his youth he has for the last eight years been a teacher in the country, and during all that long period has lived entirely apart from music, with no one but himself to rely on.

His most anxious wish is, therefore, to come to Berlin, there to pursue his musical studies and compositions, and to cultivate his talents for future practical efficacy. But for the fulfilment of this wish all pecuniary resources are wanting, and gladly as I would lend him a helping hand to attain his aim in a musical point of view, as far as my ability goes, and willing as he is

27*

by his own labours in giving lessons to endeavour to gain his own livelihood, still this latter resource is always very precarious, and especially just at first, accompanied by so many difficulties, that I could scarcely advise him to give up the situation of tutor, by which he now gains his living.

If your Majesty were graciously pleased to furnish the young man with the means of residing here, where he could hear and practise music till he could become familiar with the musical world, from which he has been so long estranged, then all obstacles would be removed, and your Majesty have made one happy man the more.

I believe if he were allowed for two years two hundred thalers each year, this would suffice, with his modest ideas and simple mode of living, to enable him to accomplish the visit to Berlin he so eagerly desires, and, along with what he could and would make by his own industry, secure his existence in the mean time.

His Excellency Herr von Massow, to whom I had an opportunity of detailing personally the circumstances of the young man, encouraged me to approach your Majesty with this petition. May, in any event, my presumption be forgiven. The fulfilment of my request will be a fresh reason, among many others, to feel the most heartfelt gratitude and thankfulness towards your Majesty, and I need not say that such a fulfilment would make the young man happy for life.*

---

* Mendelssohn's request was graciously granted by the King.

---

*From Wirklich Geheimrath Ritter Bunsen, to Felix Men-
delssohn Bartholdy, Frankfort-on-the-Maine.**

Berlin, Sunday morning, April 28th, 1844.

My dear and esteemed Friend,

I hope that these lines may find you free from all
cares and anxieties. I send them to you in a kindly
spirit for the sake of the cause and yourself.

You have *hurt* the feelings of the King by your refusal to compose music for the "Eumenides." I was
with him when Graf Redern gave him back the book
with this decision. As I saw this touched the King
very nearly, though he was not in the least *excited*, I
remarked that perhaps you conceived that the whole
trilogy was to be set to music. His Majesty answered,
"That would be all the better, but it could not prevent
Mendelssohn composing for the 'Eumenides,' which,
in itself, may be regarded as a splendid whole." I really
did not know what to say, and I confess to you that
your answer has deeply grieved myself. The affair,
too, is much talked of *here*, and minutely discussed. In
this good town it is thought "very wrong" in you to
go to England instead of composing for the King. The
King himself is quite determined not to let the affair
drop. It has been suggested to him to intrust the work
to another artist, who, it seems, has promised to undertake the affair at once. You neither *must* nor *can*
permit this; you neither can nor will annoy the King.
I also heard Tieck speaking of the affair the day before

---

* The letter of Herr von Bunsen to Mendelssohn is inserted here, in
order to render the following reply intelligible.

yesterday, who began to talk of it when I was with
him. The King sent him also a message on the subject.
You can understand that his Majesty, taking into consideration the short span of life remaining to the great
Chorodidascalos, and knowing that *he* alone can put it
on the stage here, is somewhat impatient. Tieck shares
the universal opinion about you here, although with
the most entire recognition of your character and of
your genius. I may also further say to you, quite in
confidence, that your declining to compose some songs
for " Wie es euch gefällt " has left a painful impression
on Tieck, and elsewhere; he is of opinion that your
reason for this, " to allow some time to elapse between
this and the Midsummer Night's Dream," is a very in-
sufficient one; for the more and the oftener the public
are offered good food, the sooner will they turn away
from the wretched stuff on which they are now
nourished.

But this is immaterial compared with the chief point.

Rejoice me soon by the intelligence that the whole
thing is a misunderstanding, and that you are willing
to compose music for the " Eumenides." Tieck himself says that the choruses might be here and there
shortened; a trilogy, too, might be accomplished with
great curtailments. But the " Eumenides," as a whole,
with any curtailments which may appear advisable to
you, must first be separately performed. What a glorious subject! What an unparalleled effect! Your
"Antigone" choruses are making the tour of Europe;
those of Æschylus would do the same. You will aid
in establishing a new phase in art. Reflect that the
King loves you; that your refusal affected him very

painfully ; that after having endured so much mis-apprehension, so many bitter disappointments, so many obstacles in the noblest paths of his reign, he is not prepared to meet with difficulties in this quarter also. " Et tu Brute fili." Pour out your heart to me as I have done to you. You know that you may depend upon me. We must all assist in supporting this noble Prince in his good and grand ideas. The world requires new elements of life; happy he who can help to create them!—Unchangeably your faithful friend,

BUNSEN.

To the WIRKLICH GEHEIMRATH BUNSEN.

Frankfort-a.-M., May 4th, 1844.

Your Excellency's kind letter I received here when on the point of setting off for England. First of all, I hasten to thank you in the most heartfelt manner for this fresh proof of your friendly feelings towards myself. I wish I may one day be able to express more clearly my gratitude for all your kindness and friendship! I know how to appreciate these to the fullest extent, and am proud of them, as the best and dearest which can ever be my portion in this world.

To all those who have discussed with me the performances of Æschylus's " Eumenides," to the King, to Graf Redern, and more particularly to Geheimrath Tieck, I have declared that I consider this representation, and, above all, the composition of the choruses, a most difficult and perhaps impracticable problem, *but*

that I would nevertheless make the attempt to solve it. I
asked Herr Geheimrath Tieck what time was allowed
me to make my decision; whether my attempt would
be considered by the King worthy of being performed,
or if it were likely to be permitted to rest in my desk.
He answered me that the representation could only
take place in the *large Opera-House;* that pieces of this
kind could not be produced in small localities; this was
a very different affair from the "Antigone," etc., and as
the opening of the Opera-House was fixed for the 15th
of December, it would be time enough if I occupied
myself with the music during my stay in England, or
after my return thence.   Moreover, it was signified to
me that in the event of my not undertaking the commission, some other composer would be selected.   In
accordance with truth I was obliged to answer that it
would certainly be more agreeable to me if another
person were chosen for this purpose, as in my eyes the
difficulties were immense; but I always and everywhere declared my entire readiness to attempt the composition, adding that my decision on the point should
at all events be made early enough to give ample time
to any other composer who could more easily solve the
difficulties, so that no obstacles should be thrown in the
way on my side.

What your Excellency therefore has written to me
about this affair, comes upon me the more unexpectedly
and vexatiously since Herr Geheimrath Tieck, in the
conversations we held together on the subject, thoroughly agreed in my views of the difficulties attending
its execution,—acknowledging them in his turn to be
almost insuperable; and yet, to his express question,

whether I would not undertake the composition of the choruses, he received from me, agreeably to the above-mentioned explanations, the following answer,—that I was, *on the contrary*, ready to make the *attempt*, and I should certainly *not be any hindrance* in the matter. Indeed, with a view to facilitate the idea, I suggested *to him* that some of the choruses, which appeared to me unsuitable, should be curtailed, a proposal which, as you write to me, he fully concurs in.

I have always spoken only of an attempt, and must now do the same. My not being able at once to accept and consent to the request as I would to any other, is partly owing to the novel nature and extraordinary difficulty of the piece itself (I can appeal to the judgment of any musician as to the fact), and partly to the high estimation in which I hold the refined artistic feeling of the King,—to whom it is impossible to offer indiscriminately failures and successes,—and, lastly, owing to a certain duty that I owe to myself, which makes me unwilling to undertake music in the success of which I, at least to a considerable degree, place no faith. I thought I might hope that this should not cause my good-will to be doubted, which I have already proved in the course of this year by the accomplishment of various very difficult tasks, which were demanded in the *shortest* time.

The key of the riddle seems to me to be, that my views as to the difficult nature of the representation are shared by many who may probably have wished to convince the King also of the fact; for this purpose they have selected me as the origin of these difficulties, which I am not, and never will be; they lie, unluckily,

far more in the piece itself. And now permit me a few
words on this point also.

Because I owe so much gratitude to the King,—because I honour him in the depths of my soul as an
admirable, noble prince and man,—on this very account
I think that all I do by his command should be done
with a good conscience and in a cheerful spirit. If I
were to accept his ideas *without that*, were I to produce
them before people without being myself really and
truly inspired by them, were I to use his commands as
a cloak for my failure, and, further, to represent my
failure as the result of his ideas,—then I should utterly
ruin these ideas, and then I should utterly ruin the
good opinion which I trust he still has of me; *then* he
would have a right to apply to me the words, "Et tu
Brute." For thus it appears to me most of those seem
to act who entail on him, as you say, so many obstacles
and deceptions, and I never will join such " assassins."

I will always obey the commands of a sovereign so
beloved by me, even at the sacrifice of my personal
wishes and advantage. If I find I cannot do so with a
good artistic conscience, I must endeavour candidly to
state my scruples or my incapacity, and if that does not
suffice, then I must go. This may sound absurd in the
mouth of a musician, but shall I not feel duty as much
in *my* position as others do in *theirs ?* In an occurrence
so personally important to me, shall I not follow the
dictates of integrity and truth, as I have striven to do
all my life ?

After this fresh experience, I fear even what I verbally mentioned to your Excellency already,—that my
stay on such slippery ground, and under such perplexing

circumstances, is impossible. But by this mode of act-ing, and this *alone*, can I hope, independently of mo-mentary impressions, to preserve the good opinion of his Majesty, which is more important to me than all the rest; indeed, it is only thus that I can hope *really* to serve the King and his ideas. I cannot be an indiffer-ent, doubtful, or secretly discontented servant to such a monarch; he could not employ me *thus*, and *thus* I would not only be useless to him, but sacrifice myself.

<hr/>

To Julius Stern, Paris,

(*Now Professor in Berlin.*)

London, May 27th, 1844.

Dear Herr Stern,

You well know the very great pleasure your kind letter was sure to cause me; at the same time I was perfectly aware that in the first moments after the representation* you would view in far too favourable a light, and far too highly prize, my music and its success. But that you should do so, and feel yourself thus rewarded for the many and great efforts which this representation has cost you, is indeed to me a source of the highest gratification. Accept my most cordial thanks. May I, by better works, deserve your too partial opinion! May all my works find friends as loving to adopt them, and to bring them to a satisfac-tory execution! May this also be the case at all times

<hr/>

* Herr Stern had accomplished the production of "Antigone," in the Odéon Theatre, in Paris.

with your own works; I cannot desire anything better for you.

I am also exceedingly indebted to you for having been so kind as to thank the performers in my name. According to your suggestion, I am writing some lines to Herr Morel, who directed the music, requesting him to be assured of my gratitude, and to express this also to Herr Boccage; but do not be displeased with me if I decline taking the other hint,—as to making a present to the leading performers. This would be contrary to the fixed principles which I adopted at the beginning of my musical career,—never in any way to mix up my personal position with my musical one, or ever to improve the latter by the influence of the former, or in any manner to bribe public or private opinion with regard to me, or even attempt to strengthen it. Precisely owing to the heartfelt gratitude I entertain towards all those who interest themselves in my music, it would be impossible for me to follow the fashion of giving similar presents, without for ever embittering for the future the gratitude and the joy emanating from it. And although this fashion may have been introduced by great authorities, I must always remain true to myself, and to what I deem to be right and feel to be right: so you must excuse me for not complying with this practice.* I trust that you will not be angry with me, and rather defend me against those who may attack me on this account. You will acknowledge that every man must fix certain rules by which he is to live and act, and will not, therefore, misconstrue my adhering to mine. My hearty greeting to all my friends, and

* See also the Letter to Dehn, of the 28th of October, 1841.

may we have a happy meeting in our Fatherland.—
Your devoted

FELIX MENDELSSOHN BARTHOLDY.

———— ————

To CARL KLINGEMANN, LONDON.

Soden, near Frankfort-a.-M , July 17th, 1844.

My dearest Friend,

I found all my family well, and we had a joyful
meeting when I arrived here on Saturday, in health
and happiness, after a very rapid journey. Cécile looks
so well again,—tanned by the sun, but without the
least trace of her former indisposition ; my first glance
told this when I came into the room, but to this day I
cannot cease rejoicing afresh every time that I look at
her. The children are as brown as Moors, and play all
day long in the garden. I employed yesterday and the
day before entirely in recovering from my great fatigue,
in sleeping and eating ; I did not a little in that way,
and so I am myself again now, and I take one of the
sheets of paper that Cécile painted for me to write to
you. Once more I thank you from my very heart for
the past happy time,—all that is good and imperishable
in it comes from you ; so I feel most grateful to you,
and pray continue to love me, as I shall you so long as
I live.

I am sitting here at the open window, looking into
the garden at the children, who are playing with their
" dear Johann."* The omnibus to Königstein passes

———————————————————————————————————

* Mendelssohn's servant.

this twice every day. We have early strawberries for breakfast, at two we dine, have supper at half-past eight in the evening, and by ten we are all asleep. Hoffmann von Fallersleben is here, and paid me a visit yesterday. All those who are entitled to do so, wear a bit of ribbon in their button-holes, and are called "Geheimrath;" all the world talking of Prussia and blaming her,—in fact, they speak of nothing else. The country is covered with pear-trees and apple-trees, so heavy with fruit that they are all propped up; then the blue hills, and the windings of the Maine and the Rhine; the confectioner, from whom you can buy thread and shirt-buttons; the well-spring No. 18, which is also called the Champagne Spring; the Herr Medicinalrath Thilenius; the list of visitors, which comes out every Saturday, as "Punch" does with you; the walking-post, who, before going to Frankfort, calls as he passes to ask what we want, and next day brings me my linen back; the women who sell cherries, with whom my little four-year-old Paul makes a bargain, or sends them away, just as he pleases; above all, the pure Rhenish air,—this is familiar to all, and I call it Germany!

To Paul Mendelssohn Bartholdy.

Soden, July 19th, 1844,

My dear Brother,

I am once more on German ground and soil; well, fresh, and happy at home, having found all my family in the best health possible; and we now pass our days pleasantly here, in this most lovely country.

My visit to England was glorious; I never was anywhere received with such universal kindness as on this occasion, and I had more music in these two months than elsewhere in two years. My A minor symphony twice, the "Midsummer Night's Dream" three times, "St. Paul" twice, the trio twice; the last evening of my stay in London the "Walpurgis Nacht," with quite wonderful applause; besides these, the variations for two performers on the piano, the quartett twice, the D major and E minor quartett twice, various songs without words, Bach's D minor concerto twice, and Beethoven's G major concerto. These are some of the pieces which I played in public. Then, in addition, the direction of all the Philharmonic and other concerts, the innumerable parties, the publication of "Israel in Egypt," which I worked at for the Handel Society, and revised from the manuscript; and in the midst of all this the composition of the overture to "Athalia," which, being excessively troublesome, was no slight task.*

You can gather from this how gay and stirring my life was. My chief aim—to do a service to the Philharmonic Society—succeeded beyond all expectation; it is the universal opinion that they have not had such a season for years past. This, to be sure, does not cure the radical evil which I this time amply experienced, and which must prevent the Society continuing to prosper,

---

* Mendelssohn was desired by the Berlin Theatre Intendancy to compose this overture as quickly as possible (which he consequently did in a few days), because "Athalia" was to be performed immediately. The performance, however, did not take place till the 1st of December. 1845.

—the canker in its constitution,—musical *rotten boroughs*, etc. But more of this and many other points when we meet. One thing I must also mention, which I regretted chiefly on your account. I was invited to go to Dublin, to be made a Doctor by the University there, and Morgan John O'Connell wished to give me a letter to his uncle in prison; but I could not accept it, on account of the short time, and the intense excitement of such a journey, in five days. The thought of the great pleasure you would have felt in my doing so was constantly present with me, and I gave up the idea with sincere regret. What a strange contrast this quiet little spot forms to all the previous immense excitement! Here a walk of ten minutes brings you to the heights of the Taunus, with a view over the valleys of the Maine and Rhine, as far as Frankfort, Worms, and Mayence. Here I can look all around for days and days, and require nothing further, and yet do as much, or, in fact, more, than in the midst of the excitement in London.—Your

FELIX.

To FANNY HENSEL, BERLIN.

Soden, July 25th, 1844.

If you refuse to come to Soden for a fortnight, to enjoy with me the incredible fascinations of this country and locality, all my descriptions are of no avail; and alas! I know too well that you will not come. I therefore spare you many descriptions. My family improve every day in health, while I lie under apple-trees

and huge oaks. In the latter case, I request the swine-
herd to drive his animals under some other tree, not to
disturb me (this happened yesterday); further, I eat
strawberries with my coffee, at dinner and supper; I
drink the waters of the Asmannshäuser spring, rise at
six o'clock, and yet sleep nine hours and a half (pray,
Fanny, at what hour do I go to bed?). I visit all the
wondrously beautiful environs, I generally meet Herr
B. in the most romantic spot of all (happened yesterday), who gives me the latest and best report of you
all, and addresses me as General Music Director, which
sounds as strange here as Oberursel, and Lorschbach,
and Schneidheim would to you. Then towards evening
I had visits from Lenau, and Hoffmann von Fallersleben, and Freiligrath, when we stroll through the fields
for a quarter of an hour near home, and find fault with
the system of the world, utter prophecies about the
weather, and are unable to say what England is prepared to do in the future. Further, I sketch busily,
and compose still more busily. (*A propos*, look for the
organ piece in A major, that I composed for your wedding, and wrote out in Wales, and send it to me here
immediately; you shall positively have it back, but I
require it. I have promised an English publisher to
furnish him with a whole book of organ pieces, and as
I was writing out one after another, that former one
recurred to me. I like the beginning, but detest the
middle, and am rewriting it with another choral fugue;
but should like to compare it with the original, so pray
send it here.) Further, I must unluckily go to-morrow
to Zweibrücken,* and I don't feel much disposed for

* To direct the musical festival there.

this; still, there is first-rate wine at Dürkheim (as credible witnesses inform me), and I hear the country is very beautiful, and to-morrow week (God willing) I shall be here again, when I shall once more lie under the apple-trees, etc., *dal segno*. Ah! if this could go on for ever!

Jesting apart, the contrast of these days with my stay in England is so remarkable, that I can never forget it. The previous three weeks *not a single hour* unoccupied, and here the whole of the bright days free, without an employment of any kind, except what I choose for myself (which is the sole fruitful and profitable kind), and what is not done to-day is done to-morrow, and there is leisure for everything. In England this time, it was indeed wonderful; but I must describe to you when we meet each concert there, and each bramble-bush here.

Now, tell me what you are doing, and *he*, and all of you. It is high time that Sebastian* should write me a letter. Read him these lines from his uncle (no other part of the letter; he ought to think it contained something worth reading), and do really make him write to me. But I stipulate beforehand, that none of you are to read his letter, or he would be on ceremony, and write in a fine style, or even write first a rough copy.

Farewell, dear Sister; may we soon meet again. Do not forget the piece for the organ, and still less its author; forget, however, the stupidity of this letter, and that I am such a lazy correspondent.—Your

FELIX.

---

* The son of his sister Fanny.

To Fanny Hensel, Berlin.

Soden, August 15th, 1844.

Look again in the music shelves, in the compartment
where there is a great deal of loose music lying; among
it you will find an open red portfolio, which contains
a quantity of my unbound manuscript music—songs,
pianoforte pieces, printed and unprinted; there you will
positively find the organ piece in A major. It is just
possible that I may in so far be mistaken; that it is in
a *bound* music-book which lies in "*my* compartment,"
and in which many similar pieces are bound together.
I found the piece, however, in one of the two last
winter, and *stans pede in uno* (Sebastian will explain
this) looked through it, marvelled at the odious middle
part, and also at the charming commencement (between
ourselves, all from modesty). Now, pray search dili-
gently, and send it off to Soden as soon as you find it.
I shall laugh heartily if, by describing to you at the
distance of Soden where the piece is, you find it. I
must tease you about this for the rest of my life.

I am going to make an expedition on foot to Wiesbaden to-morrow, to visit Uncle Joseph; and the day
after to Hamburg, also on foot, to attend Döhler's concert. Prume is to call for me, and we are to go
together. I heard Döhler and Piatti in their last concert in London, and clapped and shouted for them; and
now I mean to do the same at Hamburg, which will be
diverting enough. The day before yesterday I was at
Eppstein, where there was a new organ and a church
festival, and where the Vocal Associations of Frank-

fort, Wiesbaden, and Mayence offered to sing, and were present; but a letter came from the Amtmann in Königstein forbidding them to sing, so they set off, and went to Hofheim (do you know the white chapel, which is visible in the whole country round? Paul will tell you about it), and there they sang. Towards evening, as I was driving quietly with the ladies and all the children on the high-road through Hofheim, we saw heads innumerable peeping out of the windows of the inn,—all, I suspect, more or less tipsy,—shouting out loud *vivats* to me. The ladies wished to stop there to have some coffee, but I opposed this strongly, so we ate pound-cake in the carriage.

But I must now tell you of my works; there is little enough to say about them as yet. With the exception of five great organ pieces, and three little songs, nothing is finished; the symphony makes but slow progress; I have resumed a Psalm. If I could only continue to live during half a year as I have done here for a fortnight past, what might I not accomplish? But the regulation and direction of so many concerts, and attending others, is no joke, and nothing is gained by it. I feel always at home among cows and pigs, and like best to be with my equals,—the one is the result of the other, you will say; but, to let bad jokes alone, I am not a little pleased with your new songs. Would that I could hear them forthwith! But it will certainly be September before we see each other again, as Madame Bunsen has written that she has been charged to inform me the King does not expect me back in Berlin till the end of September. We have had for some days past such abominable weather, that this is

the first day I have been able to cross the threshold
since I left Eppstein. My letter, therefore, is not so
cheerful as you could desire; but I cannot help it, for
the Altkönig looks too stern and gloomy. I must
describe to you my journey back from Zweibrücken.
My landlord drove me the first stage in his carriage;
there the Landrath von Pirmaseus received us with a
breakfast, and very fine wine (this was at eight o'clock
in the morning), and drove us a stage further in his
carriage, to a grand old castle in the Vosges, where we
dined, and ascended a hill in the afternoon. Cannons
were fired there to show the echo, and champagne
drunk, and at every fresh toast the cannons were dis-
charged. He then drove us another stage, where the
proprietor of St. Johann took us under his charge, and
gave us quarters for the night, and good wine; and
next morning came another Zweibrückner with his
carriage, and, after drinking a little more good wine, we
drove on to Deidesheim, where Herr Buhl was waiting
to receive us in his vaults; but who and what Herr
Buhl and his vaults are, it is quite impossible for me to
describe to you,—you must come and taste for yourself, I mean the Forster of 1842, which he fabricates.
The cellars were lighted up, and there lay all the valuable
hogsheads; and the rooms above these cellars were as
elegant as possible, adorned with paintings by "Lo Spasi-
mo" and the great Roberts, and Winterhalter's "Deca-
meron;" and a fine new grand pianoforte, by Streicher;
and a pretty woman, who in autumn selects the particular grapes in the bunches to be used in making the wine,
which—but excuse the rest. Still, those who have not
paid a visit to Herr Buhl (or to his brother-in-law,

Herr Jordan) do not know what Forster is here below
They insisted on our dining with them, though we
ought not to have done so, being expected to dinner at
Dürkheim; still, we dined all the same (Richard
Boeckh will fully confirm all this, for he was with us
the whole time), and when dinner was over, Herr
Buhl drove us in his phaeton to Dürkheim (three-quar-
ters of a German mile) in twenty minutes, so that we
might not arrive too late for dinner; and in Dürkheim
we found half the musical festival again assembled, and
wreaths, and inscriptions, and ripe grapes; only we
could drink no more wine after that of Herr Buhl!

    This is the national song of the Palatinate, called
"Der Jäger aus Kurpfalz." It is sung the whole live-
long day, blown on horns by postilions, played as a serenade by regimental bands, and used as a march; and,
if a native of the Palatinate comes to see you, and you
wish to give him pleasure, you must play it to him;
but with *abandon*, and with great expression,—that is,
jovially.
    Such was my journey back from the Palatinate; and

if you find this description somewhat inebriated, I have certainly hit on the right key, for from nine o'clock in the morning we were never really quite steady, though I can assure you that until the evening I invariably displayed great dignity and propriety. (I refer you to Richard Boeckh.) After the performance of "St. Paul," he suddenly and unexpectedly emerged from among the public, and you may imagine with what joy I recognized my *Boccia* comrade from the Leipziger Strasse, No. 3,* among all the strange faces; and to use an expression of the Palatinate, I held him fast. As to the performances themselves,—now I must of course resume my usual sober style, for the other forms too great a contrast to my *métier*,—but no! I think I must continue my tipsy tone, and tell you that amid a great many deficiencies, we had the best St. Paul and Druid Priest there whom I have yet met with in Germany, namely, a Herr Oberhofer, a singer from Carlsruhe, who was formerly in the capital. I do not know what he may be on the stage, but it is impossible for any one to sing, or to deliver the music which I heard, better, with more intelligence, or more impressively, than he did. He made the third in our merry return journey. How the Landrath Pirmaseus was thrown into a brook, how Herr Sternfeld used a sausage to conduct the orchestra, and how, in the first part of the oratorio, the player of the kettle-drum beat it in two, and his remark on the subject, when sitting in the street with the others, at half-past two o'clock in the morning, drinking punch,—all this you must hear from my own lips.

---

* Mendelssohn's paternal home, in which the Boeckh family also resided.

Keep the whole of this letter strictly private from Sebastian; but thank him repeatedly from me for his nice letter. Tell him that I care very little about his No. 1, and that he ought not to be in any hurry to come to *Untersecunda*. When all number *ones*, and classes, and examinations, come to an end, and when no man living either asks for or gives testimonials, then learning will first begin in good earnest, and all our energies will be called forth, and yet we shall obtain no red certificates; and that would indeed be delightful, and that would indeed be life itself. And thus it is that I care so little about No. 1 of *Untertertia*, or for No. 1 of the Order of the Red Eagle, or for all the other numbers in the world. Or, if this be too philosophical for you, or too unphilosophical, then keep it from him also; but it forms a part of my creed. May we have a pleasant, happy, speedy meeting!—Your

FELIX.

To PROFESSOR VERHULST, THE HAGUE.

Berlin, November 17th, 1844.

Sir,

Pray accept my thanks for your kind letter, and the accompanying parcel, with its rich and valuable contents.

If you are like me, you can hear nothing more welcome about your works than when you are told that you have made progress in them; and in those you have now sent me, this is very manifest throughout them all. They are almost in every respect masterly and defined, and devoid of all that is false or incongruous, in individual passages; and when taken as a whole, if one piece appears more finished or more sympathetic than another, what is so fine in Art is precisely that it gives no mastery so entire as to *rise superior* to this; and one of the secrets of honest assiduous work is, that what is less successful does not give rise to despair, and what is more successful does not give rise to arrogance; and thus others may get a just insight into the workshop of the soul of an artist. Such a survey of your present production you have enabled me to make, by the valuable packet you have sent me. A succession of many works displays decidedly what one solitary work cannot do, that you have won for yourself a higher and loftier position by the cultivation of your talents, which rejoices me much, and for which I owe you my sincere and heartfelt thanks.

May your praiseworthy endeavours to diffuse the knowledge of songs in your mother-tongue prove successful, and meet with that grateful acknowledgment which they so well deserve! I know of no more noble aim that any one could propose to himself, than to give music to his own language and to his own country, as you have done and still design to do. These works are a fine commencement for such a purpose; but, that their tones may not die away unheard by your fellow-countrymen, many, many more must yet follow, and with ever-increasing progress. Vocation and endowments are your own. So, may Heaven grant you also health and steady perseverance, and a happy life!

This is the wish of your devoted

FELIX MENDELSSOHN BARTHOLDY.

From Minister Eichhorn,* to Felix Mendelssohn Bartholdy, at Frankfurt-am-Main.

Berlin, March 2d, 1845.

Sir,

You may remember that I made a report to his Majesty, some years since, on proposals which had been suggested for the establishment of a Conservatorium here; his Majesty, however, was pleased to declare that the establishment of such a Conservatorium was not at present in accordance with his Majesty's views. The affair has, consequently, remained since that time in abeyance. The absolute necessity of a reform in the Royal Academy of Arts seems daily to be more urgent; it therefore becomes a duty to obtain as clear a view as possible of the measures to be pursued, and to settle the preliminary arrangements for the best mode of fulfilling this design. The musical section of the Academy, which cannot be continued under its present regulations, must form one of the most essential points in this reform. As, however, in accordance with the good pleasure of his Majesty, the eventual enlargement of this section to a real Conservatorium is not at present to take place, it seems most advisable not to lose sight of the principle which forms the basis of the present section, and to direct every effort to secure its most perfect development. This principle assumes that the chief object of the musical section should be especially to form a school for *musical composition*. For this purpose, it is, in my opinion, above all expedient that a

---

* Inserted in order to make Mendelssohn's reply more clear.

master should stand at the head of such a section who, by his own energetic, creative powers, may become a guiding star for others, and thus be enabled to exercise a genuine and stimulating influence; possessing also the ability to examine critically the productions of the scholars, and by his zealous co-operation to guide them on the right path, in the very same way that in the plastic arts the master of the *atelier* stands in relation to his scholars. Instruction in the theory and history of music might be shared by other teachers. Steps should besides be taken, by a closer connection with other institutes, or by any other suitable means, to endeavour to form a limited choir and orchestra, which might furnish an opportunity for the performance of classical *chefs-d'œuvre*, as well as of the works of the scholars, and likewise for practice in conducting,—an arrangement which, in the event of an urgent and manifest necessity for such a thing, might perhaps at some future day lead to a real Conservatorium.

You will, Sir, earn my best thanks by being só good as to transmit to me your sentiments on these suggestions, and more especially if, in case you agree to these proposals in their general outline, you could also assure me that you are eventually disposed yourself to undertake the direction and the situation of teacher of composition, in the said musical section. Should this latter proposal, however, not be in conformity with your plans in life, may I request you to name the person among our composers here or elsewhere who, according to your competent judgment, is best suited to superintend with success the situation in question, as it seems to me very desirable to discuss any further measures

that may be necessary with the director selected foi
that section.—Accept, Sir, etc.,

EICHHORN.

To Minister Eichhorn, Berlin.

Frankfurt-am-M., March 6th, 1845.

I must first of all thank your Excellency for the flattering proof of confidence contained in the letter I have
received from your Excellency, and also for your wish
to hear my opinion in so important a matter. That the
reform of the Academy of Arts and its musical section,
which your Excellency refers to in your letter, will be
of the greatest value to the whole musical condition
of Berlin, does not admit of the smallest doubt. Your
Excellency informs me that it is your intention to
effect this by placing a composer at the head of the
musical section to be a guiding star to the pupils by
his own energetic creative powers, like the master of
the *atelier* in the plastic arts, and you do me honour to
mention my name on this occasion, or, in the event of
my being prevented accepting this offer, you commission me to point out one of my colleagues in art whom
I consider best suited for such a situation. But, in
order to form a decided opinion on the matter, I must
beg for an explanation of various points which, in this
and every other affair of the same kind, appear to me
the most important, and before which all personal questions must retire into the background.

Is the reform which you have in view in the musical

section, to consist solely in the appointment of such a
composer, and the musical section to continue in the
same shape as formerly? If this be the case, what relation will such a director assume to the former members of the senate or section, and to the director of the
whole Academy? Is the distribution of the different
branches of instruction to remain the same, or is a
reform proposed in this respect also? In what does
the actual practical efficacy of such a teacher consist?
It is not possible to show the act of composition, as the
master in an *atelier* does the design of a picture or the
form of a model; and, according to your Excellency's
words, an intellectual influence is what is chiefly required. Such an influence, according to my conviction,
is only to be obtained in the School of Art, when the
whole course of instruction has already laid a sound
foundation, when all the teachers in their positive departments strive towards the same point, when no
actual deficiency is anywhere overlooked in the education, and, finally, when, as a key-stone, the corresponding impulses of this education are combined
and placed before the scholars in their practical application, and thus more strongly impressed on their minds.
In this sense I could well imagine such a new active
situation fruitful for good and for influence; but it
seems to me that for this purpose it is not merely the
situation itself which is to effect it, but in reality a
reform of the whole *inner* constitution of the Academy;
and I do not know whether this enters into your Excellency's views, or indeed be within the range of possibility. Without this, the position, though undoubtedly
highly honourable, would be devoid of all real, practical

utility; a merely universal excitement, however great, can at best only call forth an unfruitful enthusiasm in the minds of the scholars, if indeed it calls forth anything whatsoever. The teachers of positive science alone would, in such a case, acquire a decided influence on the development of young artists; the professor at the head, influencing only by example, would, on the other hand, be like a mere airy phantom, and the connection between the head and the limbs fail, without which neither the head nor the limbs can live or thrive.

If your Excellency will be so good as to give me some more precise information on this matter, I shall then be in a position to form a clearer view of the affair itself, as well as of the personal questions connected with it; and I shall esteem it my duty, on this as on every other subject, to state my opinion candidly to your Excellency.*—Your devoted

FELIX MENDELSSOHN BARTHOLDY.

To Felix Mendelssohn Bartholdy, from the Geheim Cabinetsrath Müller.†

Berlin, March 5th, 1845.

It is proposed to set to music the choruses of the trilogy of "Agamemnon," the "Choëphoroe," and the "Eumenides," to be combined and curtailed for performance. According to Tieck's information, you de-

---

* This communication also led to no results.

† Here also this letter to Mendelssohn seems necessary to render his reply intelligible.

clined the composition in this form. The King can
scarcely believe this, as his Majesty distinctly remem-
bers that you, esteemed Sir, personally assured him
that you were prepared to undertake this composition.
I am therefore commissioned by the King to ask,
whether the affair may not be considered settled by
your verbal assent, and whether, in pursuance of this,
you feel disposed to be so kind as to declare your
readiness to undertake the composition, which will be
a source of much pleasure to the King, and in accordance with your promise, gladly to comply with any
wishes of his Majesty.—I am, Sir, your obedient,

MÜLLER.

To GEHEIM CABINETSRATH MÜLLER, BERLIN.

Frankfort, March 12th, 1845.

His Majesty the King never spoke to me on the
subject of the choruses in the combined and curtailed
trilogy of "Agamemnon," the "Choëphoroe," and the
"Eumenides." His Majesty certainly was pleased to
appoint me the task last winter of composing music for
the choruses in Æschylus's "Eumenides." I could
not promise to supply this music, because I at once
saw that the undertaking was beyond my capabilities;
still I promised his Majesty to make the attempt, not
concealing at the same time the almost insuperable
difficulties which caused me to doubt the success of
the attempt.*

---

* See the Letter to Bunsen of May 1st, 1844.

Since then, I have occupied myself for a considerable
time, in the most earnest manner, with the tragedy. I
have endeavoured by every means in my power to extract a musical sense from these choruses, in order to
render them suitable for composition, but I have not
succeeded, and have not been enabled to fulfil the task
in the case of one of them, in such a manner as is demanded by the loftiness of the subject, and the refined
artistic perceptions of the King. Of course the question
was not that of writing tolerably suitable music for the
choruses, such as any composer conversant with the
forms of art could write for almost every word, but the
injunction was to create for the Æschylus choruses
music in the good and scientific style of the present
day, which should express their meaning, with life and
reality. I have endeavoured to do this in my music to
"Antigone," with the Sophocles choruses; with regard,
however, to the Æschylus choruses, in spite of all my
strenuous efforts, I have not hitherto succeeded even
in any one attempt.

The contraction of these pieces into one, exceedingly
augments the difficulty, and I venture to assert that no
living musician is in a position to solve this giant task
conscientiously; far less, then, can I pretend to do so.

In requesting your Excellency to communicate this
to his Majesty, I also beg you at the same time to
mention the three compositions of mine, which, by his
Majesty's commands, are now ready for performance,
namely, the "Œdipus Coloneus," the "Athalie" of
Racine, and the "Œdipus Rex" of Sophocles. The entire full scores of the two former are completed, first
and last, so that nothing further is required for their

representation, except the distribution of the parts to
the actors and singers.   The sketch of the " Œdipus
Rex" is also completed.   I mention these, in the hope
that they may furnish a proof that I always consider
the fulfilment of his Majesty's commands as a duty and
a pleasure, so long as I can entertain any hope of performing the task worthily; and to show that when I
allow even one to remain unfulfilled, it arises solely
from want of ability, and never from want of intention.

ANSWER FROM MÜLLER.

Berlin, March 19th, 1845.

Immediately on receipt of your esteemed letter of
the 12th instant, I took an opportunity to inform his
Majesty of its contents.   The King laments being
obliged to resign the great pleasure it would have
caused his Majesty to see the Æschylus choruses composed by you, but rejoices in the completion of the
Sophocles trilogy, and also in that of "Athalie."   The
King hopes for your presence here in the approaching
summer, as his Majesty wishes to become acquainted
with these new compositions under your direction
alone.

To I. Moscheles, London

My dear Friend,

It is so good and kind of you to write me a gossip-ing letter again, as in the good old times. I leave everything undone and untouched till I have answered you, and thanked you for all your continued friendship and kindness towards me. What you say of the English musical doings certainly does not sound very satisfactory, but where are they really satisfactory? Only within a man's own heart; and there we find no such doings, but something far better. So little benefit is derived even by the public itself from all this direct-ing and these musical performances,—a little better, a little worse, what does it matter? how quickly is it forgotten! and what really influences all this and advances and promotes it, are after all the quiet calm moments of the inner man, taking in tow all these pub-lic fallacies and dragging them to and fro as they well deserve. Probably you will say this is the way in which a domestic animal, or a snail, or an old-fashioned grumbler, would speak; and yet there is some truth in it; and one book of your studies has had more influ-ence on the public and on Art, than I do not know how many morning and evening concerts during how many years. Do you see what I am aiming at? I should like so very much to get the sonata as a duett, or the "Études" as duetts or solos, or, in short, some-thing.

I much regret the affair with the *Handel Society,**

* Referring to his edition of "Israel in Egypt," for this Society.

but it is impossible for me to alter my views on the subject. Though quite ready to yield in non-essential points, such as the mode of marking accidentals,— though in this, even, owing to the long bars, I prefer the old fashion,—yet on no account whatever would I interpolate marks of expression, *tempi*, etc., or anything else, in a score of Handel's, if there is to be any doubt whether they are mine or his; and as he has marked *pianos* and *fortes* and figured bass whenever he thought them essential, I must either leave these out altogether, or place the public under the impossibility of discovering which are his marks and which are mine. To extract these signs from the pianoforte edition, and transfer them to the score, *if mine are to be inserted*, would cause very little trouble to any one who wishes to have the score thus marked; while, on the other hand, the injury is very great if the edition does not distinguish between the opinion of the editor and the opinion of Handel. I confess that the whole interest I take in the Society is connected with this point, for the edition of the Anthems which I formerly saw was of a kind, precisely owing to the new marking, that I could never adopt for performance. Above all, I must know exactly and beyond all doubt what is Handel's and what is not. The Council supported me in this opinion when I was present, now they seem to have adopted a contrary one; if this is to be followed out, I, and I fear *many* others, would much prefer the old edition with its false notes, to the new, with its different readings and signs in the text I have already written all this to Macfarren. I am sure you are not angry with me for stating my opinion so candidly? it is too closely

connected with all that I have considered right, during
the whole course of my life, for me now to give it up.

André has just sent me the original score, to look
over, of Mozart's symphony in C major, "Jupiter;" I
will copy for you something out of it that will amuse
you.   The eleven bars at the close of the adagio were
formerly written thus:—

and so on to the end.

He has written the whole repetition of the *thema* on
a separate leaf, and struck out this passage, bringing
it in again only three bars before the end.   Is not this
a happy alteration ?   The repetition of the seven bars
is to me one of the most delightful passages in the
whole symphony !

Give my kind remembrances to your family, and retain a kindly regard for your

FELIX MENDELSSOHN BARTHOLDY.

TO REBECCA DIRICHLET, FLORENCE.

Frankfort, March 25th, 1845.

Dear Sister,

I continue faithful to the new custom I have adopted,
and answer your welcome letter on the spot; it is just
come, and brings spring with it. For the first time to-
day we have, out of doors, that kind of atmosphere in
which ice and winter cold melt away, and all becomes
mild, and warm, and enjoyable. If, however, you have
no driving ice in Florence, you ought to *envy us*, instead
of the reverse, for it is a splendid spectacle to see the
water bubbling under the bridge here, and springing
and rushing along, and flinging about the great blocks
and masses of ice, and saying, "Away with you! we
have done with you for the present!" it also is celebrating its spring day, and showing that under its icy
covering it has preserved both strength and youth, and
runs along twice as rapidly, and leaps twice as high, as
in the sober days of other seasons. You should really
see it for once! The whole bridge and the whole quay
are black with people, all enjoying the fine sight gratis,
with the sun shining on them gratis too. It is very
pitiable in me, that, instead of speaking of the poetry
of spring, I only talk of the economy she brings in
wood, light, and overshoes, and how much sweeter

everything smells, and how many more good things there are to eat, and that the ladies have resumed their bright gay-coloured dresses, and that the steamboats are going down the Rhine, instead of diligences, etc. etc. From above you will perceive, and Fanny also (for you must send *her* all my letters to Rome), that, God be praised, there is nothing new with us, which means that we are all well and happy, and thinking of you. I came with S—— last night at one o'clock from a punch party, where I first played Beethoven's sonata 106, in B flat, and then drank two hundred and twelve glasses of punch *fortissimo;* we sang the duett from "Faust" in the Mainz Street, because there was such wonderful moonlight, and to-day I have rather a headache. Pray cut off this part before you send the letter to Rome; a younger sister may be intrusted with such a confidence, but an elder one, and in such a Papal atmosphere,—not for your life!

I have only seen X——· three times this winter; he is, unfortunately, very unsociable; I cannot get on with him even with the best will on my side, and I believe he is going on worse now than for many years past. Any one who at all enters into the religious squabbles of the moment, and does not steadily refuse to listen to them, one and all, will get so deeply involved, as to be ere long severed unawares from both friends and happiness, and instances of this begin to be manifest in Germany in all circles. In my inmost heart I feel uncertain as to which extreme is the most repugnant to me, and yet I cannot clearly decide between them.

In Düsseldorf they announced, on the second day of

the Musical Festival, Mozart's "Requiem," my "Walpurgis Nacht," and finally Beethoven's choral symphony. "O tempora! O mores!" If you ask what this
letter contains, the answer is, that we are all well, and
hope you are the same, and rejoice at the thoughts of
our meeting again.—Your (in spring weather) very
pleased

FELIX.

To Emil Naumann,

(Now Music Director at Berlin.)

Leipzig, March, 1845.

Dear Herr Naumann,

I have observed with much pleasure very important
progress in the compositions which you have sent me,
and essential improvement in your whole musical
nature and efficiency. I consider these works in every
particular preferable to your earlier ones, and, consequently, they cause me most extreme gratification.
There is much in them to be unreservedly commended;
almost all, when compared with your productions of
past years, awaken in me a fresh hope that you will
one day be able to produce something really vigorous
and good, and that it only rests with yourself to fulfil
this hope.

I have nothing special to say to you with regard to
the works, and indeed, owing to the mass of affairs and
occupations which crowd on me here, I can now less
than ever find time to write. But it is not necessary,

30*

for throughout I see traces of the good advice of your present instructor,* and feel increased respect for him in consequence of your progress. You are certainly, with him, in the best hands possible; attend assiduously therefore to his advice, and take advantage of his instructions, and of the time in which you can and must learn.

I should like to hear you play the capriccio in C, for if you can play it with steadiness and clearness, and keep correct time, you must have improved very much. I like this capriccio better than the one in E minor, and it seems to me more original. On the other hand, there is a great deal that pleases me in the sonata; particularly the beginning and end of the first movement, and the *tempo di marcia*, etc. etc. As I said before, you must *continue* to work: I must also beg you to place the same reliance henceforth on me, that you so kindly express in your letter. And as you apply Goethe's words to me, and call me a *master*, I can only reply once more in Goethe's words:—

> "Learn soon to know wherein he fails;
> True Art, and not its type, revere."

The advice in the first line is not difficult to follow, and the latter is not to be feared with you. Towards Whitsunday, when I am to be at Aix, I intend to pass through Frankfort, and hope then to see and hear something new of yours.—Always yours sincerely,

FELIX MENDELSSOHN BARTHOLDY.

---

* Franz Messer, at Frankfort-on-the-Main.

To Senator Bernus, Frankfort.

Leipzig, October 10th, 1845.

. . . I cannot tell you how often, indeed almost daily, I think of the last winter and spring which I passed so pleasantly with you in Frankfort. I could scarcely myself have believed that my stay there would have caused such a lasting and happy impression on my mind! So strong is it, that I have often pictured to myself, in all earnest, giving you a commission (according to your promise) to buy or to build for me a house with a garden, when I would return permanently to that glorious country with its gay easy life. But such happiness cannot be mine; some years must first elapse, and the work I have begun here must have produced solid results, and be a good deal further advanced (at least I must have tried to effect it), before I can think of such a thing.

But I have the same feeling as formerly, that I shall only remain in this place so long as I feel pleasure and interest in the outward occupations which *here* seem the most agreeable to me. As soon, however, as I have won the right to live solely for my inward work and composing, only occasionally conducting and playing in public just as it may suit me, then I shall assuredly return to the Rhine, and probably, according to my present idea, settle at Frankfort. The sooner I can do so, the more I shall be pleased. I never undertook external musical pursuits, such as conducting, etc., from inclination, but only from a sense of duty; so I hope, before many years are over, to apply myself to building a house.

Before then, probably, either a true and solid nucleus will have been formed among the German Catholics in favour of enlightenment and other new German ideas, and free ground and soil won for these, or the whole movement will have vanished and been superseded by other catastrophes. If neither the one nor the other occurs, I fear we run the risk of losing our finest national features, solidity, constancy, and honourable perseverance, without gaining any compensation for them. A collection of French phrases and French levity would be too dearly bought at such a price. It is to be hoped that something better will ensue!

To Pastor Bauer, Beszig.

Leipzig, May 23d, 1846.

Your kind letter and the book caused me great pleasure. I received the parcel some weeks since, but as I have very little time left for reading, and as a work like yours cannot be quickly perused by a layman, you will be able to understand the delay in expressing my thanks. I have learnt much from your book, for it is in fact the first summary of Church history that I ever read; but from this very circumstance you are mistaken in my position if you think I could attempt either verbally or in writing to maintain my own opinions on such a matter, when opposed to yours, and that I might see it in a different light as a musician, etc. The only point of view from which I can consider

such questions is that of a learner, and I confess to
you that the older I become, the more do I perceive
the importance of *first* learning and *then* forming an
opinion; not the latter previous to the former, and not
both simultaneously. In this I certainly differ much
from very many of our leading men of the present day,
both in music and theology. They declare that he
alone can form a right judgment who has learned
nothing, and indeed requires to learn nothing; and my
rejoinder is, that there is no man living who does not
require to learn. I think, therefore, that it is more
than ever the duty of every one to be very industrious
in his sphere, and to concentrate all his powers to accomplish the very best of which he is capable; and thus
the recent Church movements are more unknown to
me than you probably believe (perhaps more than you
would approve), and I rejoice that the very reverse is
the case with you. I cannot, in fact, understand a
theologian who at this moment does not come forward,
or who feels no sympathy in these matters; but just
as little, many of those *non*-theologians whom I often
see, and who talk of reformation and of improvement,
but who are equally incompetent to know or to comprehend either the present or the past, and who, in short,
wish to introduce *dilettanteism* into the highest questions.

I believe it is this very *dilettanteism* which plays us
many a trick, because it is of a twofold nature,—necessary, useful, and beneficial, when coupled with sincere
interest and modest reserve, for then it furthers and
promotes all things,—but culpable and contemptible
when fed on vanity, and when obtrusive, arrogant, and
self-sufficient. For instance, there are few artists for

whom I feel so much respect as for a genuine *dilettante*
of the first class, and for no single artist have I so little
respect as for a *dilettante* of the second class. But
where am I wandering to? . . .

To Pastor Julius Schubring, Dessau.

Leipzig, May 23d, 1846.

Dear Schubring,

Once more I must trouble you about "Elijah;" I
hope it is for the last time, and I also hope that you
will at some future day derive enjoyment from it; and
how glad I should be were this to be the case! I have
now quite finished the first part, and six or eight numbers of the second are already written down. In various places, however, of the second part I require a
choice of really fine Scriptural passages, and I do beg
of you to send them to me! I set off to-night for the
Rhine, so there is no hurry about them; but in three
weeks I return here, and then I purpose forthwith to
take up the work and complete it. So I earnestly be-
seech of you to send me by that time a rich harvest of
fine Bible texts. You cannot believe how much you
have helped me in the first part; this I will tell you
more fully when we meet. On this very account I entreat you to assist me in improving the second part
also. I have now been able to dispense with all historical recitative in the form, and introduced individual
persons. Instead of the Lord, always an angel or a
chorus of angels, and the first part and the largest half

of the second are finely rounded off. The second part
begins with the words of the queen, " So let the gods
do to me, and more also," etc. (1 Kings xix. 2); and
the next words about which I feel secure are those in
the scene in the wilderness (same chapter, fourth and
following verses); but between these I want, *first*,
something more particularly characteristic of the persecution of the prophet; for example, I should like to
have a couple of choruses *against* him, to describe the
people in their fickleness and their rising in opposition
to him; *secondly*, a representation of the third verse of
the same passage; for instance, a duett with the boy,
who might use the words of Ruth, "Where thou goest,
I will go," etc. But what is Elijah to say before and
after this? and what could the chorus say? Can you
furnish me with, first, a duett, and then a chorus in this
sense? Then, till verse 15, all is in order; but there a
passage is wanted for Elijah, something to this effect:—
" Lord, as Thou willest, be it with me;" (this is not in
the Bible, I believe?) I also wish that *after* the manifestation of the Lord he should announce his entire
submission, and after all this persecution declare himself to be entirely resigned, and eager to do his duty.
I am in want, too, of some words for him to say at, or
before, or even after his ascension, and also some for the
chorus. The chorus sings the ascension historically
with the words from 2 Kings ii. 11, but then there
ought to be a couple of very solemn choruses. " God
is gone up" will not do, for it was not the Lord, but
Elijah who went up; however, something of *that* sort.
I should like also to hear Elijah's voice once more at
the close.

(May Elisha sing soprano ? or is this inadmissible, as
in the same chapter he is described as a "bald head"?
Joking apart, must he appear at the ascension as a prophet, or as a youth?)

Lastly, the passages which you have sent for the
close of the whole (especially the trio between Peter,
John, and James) are too historical and too far removed
from the grouping of the (Old Testament) story; still
I could manage with the former, if, instead of the trio,
I could make a chorus out of the words; it would be
very quickly done, and this will probably be the case.
I return you the pages that you may have every necessary information, but pray send them back to me.
You will see that the bearing of the whole is quite
decided; it is only the lyric passages (from which arias,
duetts, etc., could be composed) which fail towards the
end. So I beg you will get your large Concordance,
open it, and bestow this time on me, and when I return
three weeks hence at latest, let me find your answer.
Continue your regard for your

FELIX.

To I. MOSCHELES, LONDON.

Leipzig, June 26th, 1846.

My dear Friend,

The cause of this letter is a line in a recent communication from Mr. Moore, who writes, "Nearly the
whole of the Philharmonic band are engaged;* a

---

* For the Musical Festival in Birmingham, where "Elijah" was per
formed for the first time.

few only are left out who made themselves unpleasant when you were there."* This is anything but pleasing to me, and as I think that you have the principal regulation of such things, I address my remonstrance to you, and beg you to mention them to Mr. Moore.

Nothing is more hateful to me than the revival of old worn-out squabbles; it is quite bad enough that they should ever be in the world at all. Those of the Philharmonic I had quite forgotten, and they *must on no account* have any influence on the engagements for the Birmingham Festival. If people are left out because they are incapable, that is no affair of mine, and I have nothing to say against it; but if *any one* is to be left out because "he made himself unpleasant" to me, I should consider it a piece of injustice, and beg that this may not be the case. There is certainly no cause to fear that those gentlemen will again be troublesome; at least, I feel none, and do not believe that any one can do so. So I beg you earnestly to let the affair proceed exactly as it would have done if I had no thoughts of coming to England; and if it be really desired to show me *consideration*, the greatest favour that can be conferred on me would be *not* to take notice of any such personal considerations.

I know you will be so good as to bring this subject under the notice of Mr. Moore, and I hope I shall hear nothing further of these obsolete stories; that is, if my wishes are complied with, and *no kind of vindictiveness*

---

* In relation to a couple of members of the orchestra, who took the liberty to make some saucy remarks on Mendelssohn coming in rather late one morning to direct a rehearsal at the Philharmonic.

exercised. Otherwise I shall protest against it ten times at least by letter.—Ever your

FELIX.

To HERR VELTEN, CARLSRUHE.

Leipzig, July 11th, 1846.

Sir,

When I received your letter of May the 10th, I felt most anxious to convey to you a word of consolation, and the assurance of my heartfelt sympathy; but I could find no words for such a loss as yours, or adequately express what I wished to say.

Far more could I appreciate the extent of this loss when I had become acquainted with the musical compositions which you so kindly sent me, in the name of your deceased son. Every one who is in earnest with regard to Art must indeed mourn with you, for in him a true genius has passed away, a genius that only required life and health to be developed, and to be a source of joy and pride to his family, and a benefit to Art. How very superior many of these works are to those we every day see, even by better musicians, and how there shines forth, in every part, a striving after progress, and the promise of a genuine vocation, along with the most perfect development! And all this was not to be! and everything in Art and in life remains so inscrutable? And thus *we* lament him, who only know a few compositions of this young artist; so how could suitable words of comfort be found for you, his father?

But I must *thank* you for having made me acquainted

with those works, and for having written me those few lines; and I will waft my thanks after your son also, for having destined these works for me. May Heaven grant you consolation, and alleviate your grief, and one day permit you to rejoin your son, where it is to be hoped there is still music, but no more sorrow or partings.—Yours,

FELIX MENDELSSOHN BARTHOLDY.

To PAUL MENDELSSOHN BARTHOLDY.

Birmingham, August 26th, 1846.

My dear Brother,

From the very first you took so kind an interest in my "Elijah," and thus inspired me with so much energy and courage for its completion, that I must write to tell you of its first performance yesterday. No work of mine ever went so admirably the first time of execution, or was received with such enthusiasm, by both the musicians and the audience, as this oratorio. It was quite evident at the first rehearsal in London, that they liked it, and liked to sing and to play it; but I own I was far from anticipating that it would acquire such fresh vigour and impetus at the performance. Had you only been there! During the whole two hours and a half that it lasted, the large hall, with its two thousand people, and the large orchestra, were all so fully intent on the one object in question, that not the slightest sound was to be heard among the whole audience, so that I could sway at pleasure the enormous orchestra and choir, and also the organ accompaniments. How often I thought of you during the time! More especially, however, when the " sound of abundance of rain" came, and when they sang and played the final chorus with *furore*, and when, after the close of the first part, we were obliged to repeat the whole movement. Not less than four choruses and four airs were encored, and not one single mistake occurred in the whole of the first part; there were some afterwards in the second part, but even these were but trifling. A young English tenor sang the last air with such wonderful sweetness, that I was obliged to collect all my energies not to be affected, and to continue beating time steadily. As I said before, had you only been there! But to-morrow I set off on my journey home. We can no longer say, as Goethe did, that the horses' heads are turned homewards, but I always have the same feeling on the first day of my journey home. I hope to see you in Berlin in October, when I shall bring my score with me, either to have it performed, or at all events to play it over to you, and Fanny, and Rebecca, but I think probably the former (or rather both). Farewell, my dear Brother; if this be dull, pray forgive it. I have been repeatedly inter rupted, and in fact it should only contain that I thank you for having taken such part in my "Elijah," and having assisted me with it.—Your

FELIX.

After the first performance of the " Elijah " in London, Prince Albert wrote the following in the book of words which he used on that occasion, and sent it to Mendelssohn as a token of remembrance :—" To the noble artist who, though encompassed by the Baal-worship of false art, by his genius and study has succeeded, like another Elijah, in faithfully preserving the worship of true art; once more habituating the ear, amid the giddy whirl of empty, frivolous sound, to the pure tones of sympathetic feeling and legitimate harmony;—to the great master who, by the tranquil current of his thoughts, reveals to us the gentle whisperings, as well as the mighty strife of the elements,—to him is this written in grateful remembrance, by

" ALBERT.

" Buckingham Palace."

To Frau Doctorin Frege, Leipzig.

London, August 31st, 1846.

Dear Lady,

You have always shown such kind sympathy in my " Elijah," that I may well consider it incumbent on me to write to you after its performance, and to give you a report on the subject. If this should weary you, you have only yourself to blame; for why did you allow me to come to you with the score under my arm, and play to you those parts that were half completed, and why did you sing so much of it for me at sight? Indeed, on this account you in turn should have considered it incumbent on you to go with me to Birmingham; for it is not fair to make people's mouths water, and to disgust them with their condition, when you cannot remedy it for them; and really the state in which I

31*

found the s prano solo parts here was most truly miserable and forlorn.

There was, however, so much that was good to make up for this, that I shall bring back with me a very delightful impression of the whole; and I often thought what pleasure it would have caused you.

The rich, full sounds of the orchestra and the huge organ, combined with the powerful choruses who sang with honest enthusiasm, the wonderful resonance in the grand giant hall, an admirable English tenor singer; Staudigl, too, who took all possible pains, and whose talents and powers you already well know, and in addition a couple of excellent second soprano and contralto solo singers; all executing the music with peculiar spirit, and the utmost fire and sympathy, doing justice not only to the loudest passages, but also to the softest *pianos*, in a manner which I never before heard from such masses, and, in addition, an impressionable, kindly, hushed, and enthusiastic audience,—all this is indeed sufficient good fortune for a first performance. In fact, I never in my life heard a better, or I may say so good a one, and I almost doubt whether I shall ever again hear one equal to it, because there were so many favourable combinations on this occasion. Along, however, with so much light, as I before said, there were also shadows, and the worst was the soprano part. It was all so neat, so pretty, so elegant, so slovenly, so devoid both of soul and head, that the music acquired a kind of amiable expression, which even now almost drives me mad when I think of it. The voice of the contralto, too, was not powerful enough to fill the hall, or to make itself heard beside such masses, and

such solo singers; but she sang exceedingly well and
musically, and in that case the want of voice can be
tolerated. At least to *me, nothing* is so repugnant in
music as a certain cold, soulless coquetry, which is in
itself so unmusical, and yet so often adopted as the
basis of singing, and playing, and music of all kinds. It
is singular that I find this to be the case much less
even with Italians than with us Germans. It seems to
me that our countrymen must either love music in all
sincerity, or they display an odious, stupid, and affected
coldness, while an Italian throat sings just as it comes,
in a straightforward way, though perhaps for the sake
of money,—but still not for the sake of money, *and*
æsthetics, *and* criticism, *and* self-esteem, *and* the right
school, and twenty-seven thousand other reasons, none
of.which really harmonize with their real nature. This
struck me very forcibly at the Musical Festival. Moscheles was ill on the Monday, so I conducted the rehearsals for him.* Towards ten o'clock at night, when
I was tired enough, the Italians lounged quietly in,
with their usual cool *nonchalance.* But from the very
first moment that Grisi, Mario, and Lablache began to
sing, I inwardly thanked God. They themselves know
exactly what they intend, sing with purity and in time,
and there is no mistaking where the first crotchet
should come in. That I feel so little sympathy for
their music is no fault of theirs. But this digression is
out of place here. I wished to tell you about the Birmingham Musical Festival, and the Town Hall, and
here I am abusing the musical execution of our country-

---

* Moscheles recovered sufficiently to direct the rest of the performances at the festival, except " Elijah."

men. You will say, I have often enough, and too often, been obliged to listen to you on that subject already. So I prefer reserving all further description of the festival till I can relate it to you in your own room.

May I soon meet you in health and happiness, and find you unchanged in kindly feelings towards myself. —Your devoted

FELIX MENDELSSOHN BARTHOLDY.

TO PAUL MENDELSSOHN BARTHOLDY.

My dear Brother,

Leipzig, October 31st, 1846.

From my only being able to-day to wish you joy of yesterday, that is, in writing and by words, you will at once see that I have even more than my full share of affairs at this moment. What I wish most to do, 1 cannot accomplish all day long, and what I most particularly dislike often occupies my whole day,—but no more *Jérémiades*, and now for true heartfelt good wishes. A thousand good wishes, which may all be summed up in one,—health for you and yours, and all those you love; in this wish lies the continuance of your happiness, in this lies your enjoyment of it, in this lies all that is good, all that I can possibly desire for you, and no human being could possibly wish or desire anything better for any man? Were you very happy on the day? were all your family well? (this, however, is included in my previous question;) had you a cake

decorated with lights ? This is certainly an entirely
novel question, but not absolutely indispensable to the
happiness of life (like the last). Did you drink chocolate ? were my sisters with you, or you with them, at
dinner or supper ? did you think of us ? May God
bless you, my dear Brother, on that day, and on every
day of your life !

It is shameful in me, not to have thanked you yet for
the beautiful copy of Dahlmann, but it is still more
shameful that such ordinary—not extraordinary—but
honest, able, true words, are so seldom to be met with
in our Fatherland; and the cause of this is, that mediocrity, or, what is still worse, vapid superficiality, is so
prevalent in Germany, parading itself till we would
fain drive out of sight; and this is also why I have
been hitherto prevented from even thanking you. I
never yet encountered such an accumulation of strangers, of inquiries and proposals, and almost all entirely
worthless; many so modest—and many so immodest!
Singers, players, a fine heap of compositions, and
scarcely one that can be called even tolerably good, but
at the same time overflowing with the longest words,
full of patriotic ardour, full of—anything but striving
after higher aims, though laying claim to the highest
of all; and then the impossibility of fulfilling even *one*
of these demands with a good conscience, or recom-
mending them to others. But why should I tell you
all this ? you, no doubt, know it by experience in your
own department, for it pervades every department.
All this, however, confirms me in my resolution not to
continue in this public official situation more than a
few years; and just as it formerly was my duty to fill

such an office to the best of my ability, it is now equally my duty to give it up. Everything here is gradually assuming a pleasant aspect. Moscheles has set to work very vigorously with the Conservatorium; the concerts also pursue their steady course now as ever; when all this is secure and certain, I daily meditate on the possibility of being able to pass the summer in some pretty country (somewhere near the Rhine), and the winter in Berlin, and this I hope to be able to do, without any public duties to perform in Berlin, and without all that has now irrevocably passed away there; I intend to live entirely with you in all happiness, and to write music. *Ainsi soit-il.*

I should have been glad to bring the "Elijah" with me, but I am still at work on two passages, which I am striving to remodel, and they cause me great tribulation. In the mean time, I have been obliged to compose afresh the whole Liturgy for the King. He has desired that I should be repeatedly written to on the subject, and now at last it is finished. I am often, too, in no happy mood, for poor Johann* is very seriously ill, and causes us really very great anxiety. "May I be so bold as to ask who is to play the part of the servant?" says Goethe, and lately these words often recurred to me. May God soon restore the poor faithful fellow! Love me as ever, and may you be happy in the approaching year.—Your

FELIX.

---

* Mendelssohn's servant.

To Professor Edward Bendemann.

Leipzig, November 8th, 1846.

. . . Have I already thanked you for your excellent contributions, and advice about "Elijah"? All your notes on the margin are most acceptable, and are a fresh proof that you have not only a different but a much deeper insight than almost any one else into a subject of this kind. You recommend that the "Sanctus" should be followed by the command of God to Elijah to resume his mission; such was indeed my original intention, and I think of replacing it, but I cannot dispense with an answer from Elijah; and I think *both* can and ought to be there. I shall not, however, be able to bring in King Ahab again. The greatest difficulty in the whole undertaking, was after the manifestation of the Lord in the "still small voice," to discover a conclusion for the whole, with sufficient breadth (and yet not long); and if Elijah were to be *afterwards* introduced again in person as a zealous and avenging prophet (in a dramatic aspect) it would in my opinion be difficult to represent, without great circumlocution, his significance for the new dispensation (which, however, must necessarily be alluded to), while I think it most important, that from the moment of the appearance of the Lord, all should go on in grand narrative to the close. But when you say that one of these passages should relate how he came down, and again came down in vain, you are quite right, and I will try to accomplish it, as I am at this moment revising the whole, and re-writing several passages before sending it to the engraver. It is singular that the passage which caused me the greatest trouble is the very one that you would like to see omitted,—that of the widow. To me it seems that by introducing some phrases (either by the chorus or otherwise) the part might become more significant and comprehensive, whereas you prefer its being a simple narrative. After all, you are possibly right, which would be unfortunate, for I believe that in the distribution of the whole, the passage in its present expansion could not possibly be spared. This is a point, therefore, which I shall weigh well.

To Carl Klingemann, London.

Leipzig, December 6th, 1846.

. . . Montaigne says, and so does Vult, that a man can have but *one* friend ; you will find this too in the " Flegeljahre." I also said this from my heart when I received your letter, my *one* friend !

How gladly would I have burst forth into joy and gratitude at the news it contained, and have replied in a gay and happy spirit ! but this was impossible, as at the time your letter arrived, we were in great anxiety about our servant Johann, who had been confined to bed for the last two months, with a species of dropsy, becoming daily worse, and when, about a fortnight since, the improvement took place that we had been so anxiously longing for during three weeks, his vital powers suddenly sank, and to our great sorrow he died.

You know that I valued him very highly, and can well understand that during the whole time when I saw him suffer so much, and become worse and worse, and then the momentary hope that ensued, followed by his sudden and inevitable death, must cause me to be in a very grave mood for long, long to come. His mother and sister did not arrive here till the day after his funeral. It distressed us also very much, not to be able to say one consolatory word to them! Among his things, which were all in the most exemplary order, we found a letter to me containing his last will; I must show you this the next time we meet,—no man, no poet indeed, could have written anything more heartfelt, earnest, and touching; then there was a great deal to do and to regulate, until all the trunks, with his clothes, etc., were sent off to his mother, and his brothers and sisters ; and this was why I have been unable to write to you during the last few weeks. I relate all this to you in detail, because you are my *one* friend, and because you sympathize in all that really affects and concerns me. Happily, I was able to work the whole time (though, indeed, not to compose). I got the parts of Bach's B minor Mass from Dresden. (Do you remember it on Zelter's Fridays ?) It is chiefly in his own writing, and dedicated to the Elector of that day. (" To his Royal Highness the most noble the Elector of Saxony, the accompanying Mass is dedicated, with the most respectful devotion of the author, J. S. Bach." This is inscribed on the title-page.) From it I have gradually corrected all the mistakes in my score, which were innumerable, and which I had frequently remarked, but never had a proper opportunity

32

to rectify. This occupation, mechanical, though now and then interesting enough, was most welcome to me. For the last few days, however, I have again begun to work with all my might at my "Elijah," and hope to amend the greatest part of what I thought deficient in the first performance. I have quite completed one of the most difficult parts (the widow), and you will certainly be pleased with the alterations,—I may well say, with the improvements. "Elijah" is become far more impressive and mysterious in this part, the want of which was what annoyed me. Unluckily I never find out this kind of thing till *post festum,* and till I have improved it. I hope, too, to hit on the true sense of other passages that we have discussed together, and shall seriously revise all that I did not deem satisfactory; so that I hope to see the whole completely finished within a few weeks, and then be able to begin something new. The parts that I have hitherto remodelled prove to me that I am right, not to rest till such a work is as good as I can make it, although in these matters very few people either remark or wish to hear about them, and yet they cost a very, very great deal of time; but, on the other hand, such passages make a very different impression when they are really made better, both in themselves, and with regard to all other portions,—you see I am still so very much pleased with the part of the widow, that I completed to-day,—so I think it will not do to rest satisfied with them just as they are. Conscience, too, has a word to say on this matter.

To his Brother-in-Law, Professor Dirichlet,
Berlin.

Leipzig, January 4th, 1847.

Dear Dirichlet,

I write you these lines to say that I wish for my sake, I might say for your sake also, that you should remain at Berlin.* Jesting apart, I would gladly repeat in writing, and at this new year's time, all that I said to you about it personally. The more I reflect on this plan *here* (not in Berlin), the more I feel convinced that its execution would grieve me, first, for your own sake, and secondly, for mine (which comes to one and the same thing); for when I look repeatedly around here, and thus try to discover what kind of weather there is in Germany (and you know that it is often long, long before this can be perceived in Berlin), I everywhere see the current setting in towards large cities, but receding from the smaller ones. It might be said, then, a residence in small towns will now become really agreeable; but they, too, will not be content to remain in their state of quiet comfort, but strive to become great cities : and this is why I could not see any one, far less yourself, leave a large city at this moment to settle in a small one, without the most extreme concern. There are a thousand wants, both material and spiritual, which these smaller places are at this moment seeking to supply (thus making these wants only more perceptible), a thousand pleasant things in life and knowledge,—all linked for many long years with your-

---

* Dirichlet was engaged in a negotiation about a situation at Heidelberg.

self and with Rebecca's early days,—which you value
less than they deserve, because you have always been
accustomed to have things in one fashion and in no
other, and because you are uneasy about the present,
and dissatisfied with what is going on. But, in truth,
you will find the same uneasiness, and the same dissatisfaction, prevailing everywhere through all Germany; at present, indeed, only in those whom you
meet, and not in yourself, the new-comer; but, alas!
alas! in these days such contamination spreads hourly
in our Fatherland, where these evils daily strike deeper
root, and you will and must experience them also,
wherever you go, and not in any respect improve your
condition in this chief point. By your change of residence, you cannot effect any cure in the prevailing malady, and I as little with my subscription concerts; it
can only be done by very different means, or by a very
sharp crisis; and, in any event, it would then be best
not to be placed in new, but in old familiar circumstances. A third thing may happen, and, alas! not
the most improbable; all may remain in its old form.
In that case also, however, it is best not to begin a new
life, which holds out no prospect of any improvement
in itself. I do wish, then, that you would remain in
Berlin.

That you, by any kind of promise, however well
meant or positive, are now in the hands of the people
of Heidelberg, and *must* say Yes, if *they* say Yes also, I
cannot believe. Such a connection as yours with Berlin is not to be dissolved by a letter and a few words;
and if these people believe that by your answer they
have acquired any right over you, it is not to be denied

that the others have at least an equal right. Simply from an overweening sense of justice, and from too much delicacy, a person often chooses that which costs him the greatest sacrifice, and thus, I believe, you would at last rather choose Heidelberg; but they will not be sensible of this; they only wish to conclude a bargain, and you must do the same, and no more. In the mean while they have the *præ*, because they wish to acquire something new for themselves, and the people of Berlin only to keep what they have, and the former is always more tempting and pleasant; but, as I said before, it is a mere matter of business,—do not forget that; and you know quite as well as I do that all the *Berliners* are anxious to keep you. Forgive my strange lecture, but remain.

I ask it for my sake also; for I have now, I may say, decided soon to go for the winter to Berlin. Don't let us play at the game of " change sides." I preferred a residence in a smaller town, under very favourable circumstances; I always liked it, and am accustomed to no other, and yet I feel compelled to leave it, to rejoin those with whom I enjoyed my childhood and youth, and whose memories and friendships and experiences are the same as my own. My plan is, that we should *form all together* one pleasant united household, such as we have not seen for long, and live happily together (independent of political life or *non-life*, which has swallowed up *all* else). For some time past everything seems to contribute to this, and, as I said, *I* shall not be found wanting, for I consider it the greatest possible good fortune that could ever befall me; so do not frustrate all this by one blow, but remain in Berlin, and

32*

let us be together there. These are my reasons, badly expressed, but better intended than expressed; and don't take this amiss.—Your

FELIX.

To FRAU GEHEIMERÄTHIN STEFFENS,* *née* REICHARDT, BERLIN.

Leipzig, February, 1847.

Dear Madam,

When I meet any one who knew my Father, and who loved and esteemed him as he deserved, I immediately look on such a one as a friend, and not as a stranger, and a meeting of this kind always makes me glad and happy. As you no doubt feel the same, I trust you will excuse the liberty I take in addressing you. I wish to relate to you how touched and delighted the friends of music in Leipzig were yesterday by the composition of your father; we felt as if his spirit were still living and working among us, and indeed it is so. In the concert of yesterday (which, like the previous and both the ensuing ones, was dedicated to a kind of historical succession of the great masters) there was an opportunity of bringing before the public some of your father's songs. A symphony of Haydn's was followed by the Reichardt song, "Dem Schnee, dem Regen," and his duett, "Ein Veilchen auf der Wiese stand;"

---

* Daughter of the distinguished composer Reichardt, and widow of Prof. Heinrich Steffens, whose delightful autobiography has been translated by Rev. W. L. Gage, and published in Boston (Gould & Lincoln) under the title of "The Story of my Career."

and then the same poem set to music by Mozart. You
will perceive that your father's music was by no means
in a very easy proximity, but I wish you could have
heard how he maintained his honourable position. The
very first song sounded charming and effective; but
when the little duett was given by two very fresh
pure voices, in great simplicity and perfection, many a
lover of music could not suppress his tears, so charming
and genial was *that* music, so genuine and touching.
Such applause as we seldom hear, and a *da capo* of all
three verses, followed as a matter of course. This was
not for a moment doubtful after the three first bars had
been sung, and I felt as if I could not only listen to the
song twice, but during the whole evening, and to
nothing else. It was the true genuine German song,
such as no other nation has, but even ours nothing better; perhaps grander, certainly more complicated, more
elaborate, and more artificial, but not on that account
more artistic,—thus, not better. This must happily be
the case for all time, and it must cause you much joy
thus once more to meet your father's spirit in its still
living influence; for many a young musician who
heard his music yesterday (if, indeed, he can feel such
things at all) will now know better what a song should
be, than from all the books of instruction, all the lectures, and all the examples of the present day; "and
thus is life won," as Goethe says. Forgive me for
writing nothing in this letter, except that the Reichardt
songs were so lovely, and the Leipzig public so enchanted. The first you have long known, though the
second in itself may be a matter of indifference; but as
I was seated at the piano accompanying yesterday and

feeling such delight, I said to myself that I must write to you about it.

Begging you to recall me to the remembrance of your daughter, I am your

FELIX MENDELSSOHN BARTHOLDY.*

To HIS NEPHEW, SEBASTIAN HENSEL.

Leipzig, February 22d, 1847.

Dear Sebastian,

I thank you very much for the drawing, which, as your own composition, pleases me extremely, especially the technical part, in which you have made great progress. If, however, you intend to adopt painting as a profession, you cannot too soon accustom yourself to study the *meaning* of a work of art with more earnestness and zeal than its mere *form*,—that is, in other words (as a painter is so fortunate as to be able to select visible nature herself for his substance), to contemplate and to study nature most lovingly, most closely, most innately and inwardly, all your life long. Study very thoroughly how the outer form and the inward formation of a tree, or a mountain, or a house always *must* look, and how it *can* be made to look, if it is to be beautiful, and then produce it with sepia or oils, or on a smoked plate; it will always be of use, if only as a testimony of your love of substance. You will not take amiss this little sermon from such a screech-owl as I often am, and, above all, do not forget

* See letter about Reichardt, of December 28, 1833.

the substance; as for the form (my lecture), the devil may fly away with it, it is of very little value.

Tell your mother that I quite agree with her about the scherzo. Perhaps she may one day compose a *scherzo serioso;* there may be such a thing.—Your Uncle,

FELIX M. B.

To General von Webern, Berlin.*

Frankfort, May 24th, 1847.

Your letter did me good, even in the depths of my sorrow, when I received it; above all, your hand-writing, and your sympathy, and every single word of yours. I thank you for it all, my dear, kind, faithful friend. It is indeed true that no one who ever knew my sister can ever forget her through life; but what have not we, her brothers and sister, lost! and I more especially, to whom she was every moment present in her goodness and love; her sympathy being my first thought in every joy; whom she ever so spoiled, and made so proud, by all the riches of her sisterly love, which made me feel all was sure to go well, for she was ever ready to take a full and loving share in all that concerned me. All this I believe we cannot yet estimate, just as I still instinctively believe that the mournful intelligence will be suddenly recalled, and then again I feel that it is true,—but never, never can I inure myself to it! It is consolatory to think of such a beautiful, harmonious nature, and that she has been spared

---

* After Fanny Hensel's death.

all the infirmities of advanced age and declining life; but it is hard for us to bear such a blow with proper submission and fortitude.

Forgive me for not being able to say or write much, but I wished to thank you.

My family are all well; the happy, unconcerned, cheerful faces of my children alone have done me good in these days of sorrow. I have not as yet been able to think of music; when I try to do so, all seems empty and desolate within me. But when the children come in I feel less sad, and I can look at them and listen to them for hours.

Thanks for your letter; may Heaven grant health to you, and preserve all those you love.—Your

FELIX M. B.

TO HIS NEPHEW, SEBASTIAN HENSEL.

Baden-Baden, June 13th, 1847.

Dear Sebastian,

I must send you my good wishes on your birthday, the most mournful one you have yet known. The retrospect of its celebration last year will deeply grieve you, for then your mother was still by your side; may, however, the anticipation of the future birthdays which you may yet be spared to see, comfort and strengthen you! for your mother will stand by your side in these also, as well as in everything that you do or fulfil. May all you do be estimable and upright, and may your daily steps be directed towards that path to which

your mother's eyes were turned for you, and in which
her example and her being went with you, and always
will go with you so long as you remain true to her,—in
other words, I trust, all your life long. Whatever
branch of life, or knowledge, or work you may devote
yourself to, it is indispensable to *will* (not to wish, but
to *will*) something good and solid ; but this is sufficient.
In all employments and in all spheres there is now and
always will be a want of able honest workmen, and
therefore it is not true when people declare it now more
difficult than formerly to achieve anything. On the
contrary, in a certain sense, it is and always will be
easy, or altogether *impossible ;* a genuine, faithful heart,
true love, and a brave, determined will, are alone
required for this, and you will not assuredly fail in
these, with such a bright and beloved example steadily
shining before you. And even if you follow this, and
do all, all in your power, still nothing is done, nothing
is attained, without the fulfilment of one fervent wish,
—may God be with you !

This prayer comprises consolation and strength, and
also cheerfulness in days to come. I often long to be
able to pass those days with you and your aunt Rebecca. We expect your father ten or twelve days hence ;
I wish you could come with him, and we might sketch
from nature together. I lately *composed* a sketch of an
old mountain castle in a forest, with a distant view of
a plain ; another of a terrace, with an old lime-tree and
an image of the Virgin under it; and a third, of a solitary mountain lake between high hills, with reeds in
the foreground. I mean to wash them in with Indian
ink. Are you inclined to try the same three subjects,

that we may compare our compositions? Do so, I beg, dear Sebastian, and show them to me when we meet again,—soon, very soon, I hope. May God bless you. —Ever your

FELIX M. B.

To REBECCA DIRICHLET, BERLIN.

Thun, July 7th, 1847.

Dear Sister,

In your letter of yesterday to Paul,* you said you wished I would write to you again; I therefore do so to-day, but what to write I cannot tell. You have often laughed at me and rallied me because my letters assumed the tone around me or within me, and such is the case now, for it is as impossible for me to write a consistent letter as to recover a consistent frame of mind. I hope that as the days pass on they will bring with them more fortitude, and so I let them pursue their course, and in the society of Paul, and in this lovely country, they glide on monotonously and rapidly.

We are all well in health, and sometimes even cheerful. But if I return within myself, which I am always inclined to do, or when we are talking together, the ground-tint is no longer there,—not even a black one, far less one of a brighter hue.

A great chapter is now ended, and neither the title nor even the first word of the next is yet written. But

---

* Mendelssohn and his brother, with their families, went together to Switzerland after Fanny Hensel's death.

God will make it all right one day; this suits the beginning and the end of all chapters.

We intend going to Interlachen in a few days, and towards the end of the month Paul will have begun his journey thence towards home. He enjoys with me the *old* familiar mountain-summits, which look as hoary as five or twenty-five years ago, and on which Time makes little impression! We shall probably stay in Interlachen for another month, and establish ourselves there; I will, and must, soon attempt once more to begin some regular work, and should like to have made some progress in a composition before my journey home. I hope to find you and yours in good health in September. May we soon meet again, my dear, good Sister! and do not forget your

FELIX M. B.

To PAUL MENDELSSOHN BARTHOLDY.

Interlachen, July 19th, 1847.

My dear Brother,

Scarcely were you gone, when a storm arose, and the thunder and rain were tremendous. Then we dined, and found an unfilled place at table. Then I reflected for two hours on Schiller's chorus in the "Bride of Messina," "Say what are we now to do?" and then the children brought the two enclosed letters for you, and said, "I wonder where our Uncle is now!"

But it is no longer any use telling you such commonplace, indifferent things, and yet life is made up chiefly

33

of these. So adieu, till we meet again on the plains or on the mountains. We shall be as happy there as we were here.

It is still thundering, and this is the most dreary day we have had here for many weeks—in every sense!—Your

FELIX.

To REBECCA DIRICHLET.

Interlachen, July 20th, 1847,

Dear Sister,

When your dear letter arrived, I was writing music; I force myself now to be very busy, in the hope that hereafter I may become so from inclination, and that I shall take pleasure in it. This is "weather expressly calculated for writing, but not for gipsying." Since Paul left us, the sky has been so dismal and rainy that I have only been able to take one walk. Since the day before yesterday, it has been quite cold besides, so we have a fire in-doors, and, out-of-doors, streaming rain. But I cannot deny that I sometimes rather like such downright, pouring wet days, which confine you effectually to the house. This time they give me an opportunity of passing the whole day with my three elder children; they write, and learn arithmetic and Latin with me,—paint landscapes during their play-hours, or play draughts, and ask a thousand wise questions, which no fool can answer (people generally say the reverse of this, still it is so). The standing reply is, and always will be, " You do not yet understand such things," which still vibrates in my ears from my own mother, and which I shall soon hear in turn from my children, when they give their children the same answer; and thus it goes on.

As for Sebastian's profession, I think he is now at the age, and period, when he is not likely to feel conviction or enthusiasm for anything that cannot be laid hold of by the hand, or counted by numbers, or expressed by words, and he must be kept from everything—as a life aim—which might forestal such convictions. He knows that as well as I do, and I have entire confidence in his not choosing any profession from which he will hereafter turn aside, or which might eventually become indifferent or wearisome to him. As soon, therefore, as I feel secure *on this point*, it is quite the same to me, what he may choose in this wide world, or how high or how humble his path may then be, if he only pursues it cheerfully! And as all agree in allowing him to make his own choice, and as he can now or never understand the serious aspect of life, and as this earnest feeling is the affair of his own heart, in which no one can assist him, or advise him, although it does affect each of us deeply, I believe he will not be found wanting in this respect, and will do well, what he settles to do; *that* would be my suggestion to him, but, otherwise, not to offer him the slightest approach to advice. It is the old story of Hercules choosing his path, which for several thousand years has always been acted once, at least in the life of every man; and whether the young maidens be called Virtue or Vice, and the young men Hercules or not, the sense remains the same.

In September, God willing, I intend to come to Berlin, and Paul has probably told you how seriously I am occupied with the thought of spending my life with you, my dear Sister and Brother, and residing with you, renouncing all other considerations. I wish to live with you, and never did I feel this more vividly than when the steamboat set off to Thun with Paul and his family, and Hensel; and, strangely enough (either for this reason, or in spite of it), it is almost impossible for me at this time to be with strangers. There is no lack of visitors here, both musical and others; scarcely a single day lately has passed without one, or several; but they all seem to me so empty and indifferent, that I, no doubt, must appear in the same light to them, so I heartily wish that we may soon part, and remain apart; and in the midst of all the phrases, and inquiries, and speechifying, one thought is always present with me,— the shortness of life; and, in fact, I hope we shall soon be together, and long remain together. Farewell, dear Sister, till we meet!

To Paul Mendelssohn Bartholdy.

Interlachen, August 3d, 1847.

Dear Brother,

We are all well, and continue to live the same quiet life that you enjoyed with us here. It was, indeed, most solitary the first days after you left us, when each of us went about with dismal faces, as if we had forgotten something, or were looking for something,—and

it was so, indeed! Since then, I have begun to write
music very busily ; the three elder children work with
me in the forenoon ; in the afternoon, when the
weather permits, we all take a walk together ; and I
have also finished a few rabid sketches in Indian ink.
Herr Kohl came here yesterday, the Irish and Russian
traveller, and spent the evening with us; also, Mr.
Grote,* whom I always am very glad to see and to listen
to; but I now feel so tranquil in this quiet retirement,
and so little tranquil with a number of people, that I
do all I can to avoid what is called society, and as yet I
have succeeded in this. Why were you not with me in
Boningen ? you would indeed have been pleased ! and
in Wilderschwyl, and Unspunnen besides ? This alone
would be a sufficient reason for your returning here as
soon as you can. We have not, however, *once* had fine
weather since the day of your departure, and often very
bad; there has been no further question, since then,
of sitting under the walnut-trees, and many days we
were unable to leave the house. Still we always took
advantage of the hours that were fair for all kinds of
expeditions ; and wherever you turn your steps here,
it is always splendid. If the weather becomes more
settled, I mean to go over the Susten, and to the sum-
mit of the Sidelhorn, which can be done from here in a
few days. But to carry this resolution into effect
seems by no means easy ; it is so lovely here, and we
so much enjoy our regular, quiet life. It has enabled
me once more to become often quite cheerful; but
when people come, and talk at random about commonplace matters, and of God and the world, my mood be-

* The author of the " History of Greece."
33*

comes again so unutterably mournful that I do not
know how to endure it.   You are obliged to surmount
such feelings, to the utmost extent; and I think of this
every day.   It must be hard on you, and I shrink from
the idea of it myself.   But it must be so, and it is
right: so, with the help of God, it can be done.   All
send heartfelt greetings; and ever continue to love
your

FELIX.

To General von Webern, Berlin.

My dear, kind Friend,

Interlachen, August 15th, 1847.

I send you a thousand thanks for your letter of the
14th of July, which had been much delayed, as I only
received it here a short time ago.   You have, no doubt,
seen my Brother since then, and he has probably told
you more minutely of my intention to visit Berlin this
autumn.   But I cannot delay sending you an immediate answer to your kind and friendly proposal about
the three concerts, but, indeed, I would rather not at
present agree to announce the three concerts (of
which two were to be "Elijah").   "Elijah" has not
yet been heard in Berlin, and it would not only appear
presumptuous, but would really be so, if I proposed to
the public to perform it twice in succession.   In addition to this, my present mood makes me so decidedly
disinclined for all publicity, that I have with difficulty,
and chiefly through Paul's sensible exhortations, resolved not to give up those performances to which I

had already agreed. I intend, also, to fulfil my promise to Herr von Arnim about the Friedrich Stift,* and the 14th of October seems to me a very suitable day. If the sympathy in the work is so great that a repetition of it is expected and desired within a short period, you may imagine that this can only be a source of pleasure to me, and then I would gladly see the receipts of the second performance applied entirely according to your wish. If, in spite of this very unsatisfactory and undecided answer, you will be so kind as to assist in promoting the first performance in October, and inspiring those who have to do with it, as soon as possible, with some activity, you will do me a great service, and I shall again owe you many thanks. For I know, as you say, the difficulties consequent on the state of things there, which is very similar to the sand, and must be desperately ploughed up before it brings forth any fruit.

Your letter to Cécile does not sound so cheerful as usual. We hope that this may have only been caused by some passing cloud, and that the sun of your gayer mood again shines as brightly as we are accustomed to see it with you. There are, to be sure, just now, very dense misty fogs, if not thunder-clouds, in our Fatherland, and many a day that might be bright and clear becomes thus sultry and grey, and all objects dim and dull; yet no one can strive against this, or maintain that they see the bright colours and forms which genuine sunshine brings; and, indeed, vivid lightning and loud thunder out of the black cloud are sometimes pre-

---

* To allow the "Elijah" to be performed for the benefit of that insti tution.

ferable to vague mists and foggy abysses. Every one
suffers from them, but these mists do not yet absorb
the light, and cannot fail to be dispersed at last. That
no personal reason, no illness of your family or yourself, or any other serious cause may exist for your de-
pression, is what we wish!

My wife and children are well, God be praised! We
walk a great deal, the children do their lessons, Cécile
paints Alpine roses, and I write music: so the days
pass monotonously and quickly. Preserve your regard
for me as I ever shall for you, for ever and ever.—Your
friend,

FELIX M. B.

To PAUL MENDELSSOHN BARTHOLDY.

Leipzig, October 25th, 1847.

Dearest Brother,

I thank you a thousand times for your letter to-day,
and for the hint you give about coming here, which I
seize with the utmost eagerness of heart. I really did
not know till to-day what to say about my plans. God
be praised, I am now daily getting better, and my
strength returning more and more; but to travel this
day week to Vienna (and that is the latest period which
will admit of my arriving in time for a rehearsal of their
Musical Festival) is an idea which cannot possibly be
thought of.* It is certainly very unlucky that they
should have made so many preparations, and that my
going there should be a second time put off. There is

---

* Mendelssohn was to direct the "Elijah" in Vienna.

no doubt, however, that my improvement in health is day by day greater and more sure, so I have written to ask if I may delay coming for a week; but, as I said, I place little faith in the practicability of the whole thing, and it seems to me I must remain here. In no case can I attempt to travel before eight days from this time; and as to the state of my expedition to Berlin, has not Herr von Arnim reported it to you in regular detail? If I cannot go to Vienna, the same reasons which prevent me going there must cause me to stay here for a fortnight or three weeks, and to put off the performance in Berlin till the end of November at the latest; and even if I do go to Vienna, this must of course still be the case.

After, however, these interrupted performances, which must now be carried through, that I positively undertake no new ones is quite settled. If it were not necessary to keep one's promise! but this must be done, and now·the only question is whether I shall see you again on Saturday? Say Yes to this; I believe you would do me more good than all my bitter medicine. Write me a couple of lines soon again, and be sure you agree to come. My love to you all! and continue your love for your

FELIX.

On the 30th of October his brother was summoned to Leipzig, in consequence of Mendelssohn being seized by another attack of illness. He died on the 4th of Novembe.

CATALOGUE

OF

ALL THE MUSICAL COMPOSITIONS

OF

FELIX MENDELSSOHN BARTHOLDY.

I. THE PUBLISHED WORKS, IN CHRONOLOGICAL
ORDER.

II. THE UNPUBLISHED WORKS, CLASSIFIED UN
DER DIFFERENT HEADS.

COLLECTED PRINCIPALLY FROM THE AUTHOR'S ORIGINAL
MANUSCRIPTS,

AND ACCOMPANIED BY A PREFACE,

BY

JULIUS RIETZ.

PREFACE.

In the first section of this Catalogue a few compositions are omitted, because the autograph notes, by which Mendelssohn was in the habit of recording the date and place of composition of his pieces, are wanting; the precise date at which these works were composed cannot therefore be given. They are as follows:—

Op. 6. Sonata for Pianoforte.
    7. Seven characteristic pieces for Pianoforte.
    8. Twelve Songs.
    9. Twelve Songs (with the exception of No. 3)
    10. Symphony No. 1.
    14. Rondo Capriccioso for Pianoforte.

These may all be placed between 1824 and 1828; the symphony, probably the earliest of all, about 1824; it was not published, however, till much later, and was then marked as Opus 11, that number happening to be vacant. In marking his works with Opus figures, both at that time and especially later, Mendelssohn invariably referred to the date, not of their composition, but of their publication; years not unfrequently intervening between the two. This fact is strikingly exemplified in the " Walpurgis Nacht," which, though composed in 1830, was not published till 1843, when indeed it was much over-elaborated. In his books of songs and other minor works, he was in the habit of selecting those which answered his purpose, out of a large number composed in *different years*. Thus, for example, the six songs in the first book of songs for men's voices (op. 50) were composed between 1837 and 1840. Dates are also wanting for

Op. 15. Fantasia for Pianoforte.

19. Six Songs, (with the exception of No. 6) undoubtedly written between 1830 and 1834.

44. String Quartett, No. 1.

66. Trio No. 2, for Pianoforte, Violin, and Violoncello.

72. Six Juvenile pieces.

13. Variations for Pianoforte.

All belonging to the last period, subsequent to 1840.

Besides these, the originals of many single songs, with and without words, are so dispersed, that with the most anxious desire to render the Catalogue complete, and notwithstanding all the efforts of the Editor, they have not yet been discovered. Still, even in its incomplete and imperfect condition, the Catalogue will be interesting to the friends and admirers of this immortal composer. It cannot fail also to be of great value to Mendelssohn's future biographer, for the striking picture it furnishes of his development, of which the Thematic Catalogue of Breitkopf and Härtel can give no idea, since in its compilation it was not possible to observe the chronological succession of the works.

This is the proper place to mention a widely-spread report, to the effect that Mendelssohn's sister, Fanny Hensel (who died on the 14th of May, 1847), had a share in the composition of many of his works. Thus, among others, she has been often named as the composer of the entire first book of " Songs without Words " (op. 19). This has been much exaggerated. We are now enabled to reduce it to its proper proportions,* and to state positively that Mendelssohn included six only of his sister's songs with words in his first four books of songs, *and beyond these not one of any kind whatsoever.* These songs are :—

    " Heimweh," No. 2

    " Italien," No. 3   } in Opus 8.

    " Suleika and Hatem," Duett, No. 12

    " Sehnsucht," No. 7

    " Verlust," No. 10   } in Opus 9.

    " Die Nonne," No. 12

We may further observe, that the song No. 12, " Die Blumenglocken mit hellem Schein," in the operetta " Heimkehr aus der Fremde " (Son and Stranger), was set to music by Carl Klingemann, the author of the libretto, Mendelssohn's most intimate friend, who died very recently. It had been already published by him in 1829, in a book of songs (Logier, Berlin), with other words, and was afterwards most charmingly and delicately instrumented by Mendelssohn for the operetta.

In addition to the list contained in the thematic catalogue of Mendelssohn's published works, the following have since appeared in Germany.

1. Two Pianoforte Pieces : (*a*) Andante cantabile, in B flat ; (*b*) Presto agitato, in G minor (Senff, Leipzig).

* In the tenth edition of Brockhaus's " Conversations-Lexicon," vol. vii., 1852, we read, " She felt great repugnance to publish, so that her brother *often*, in jest, allowed her compositions to appear under his name."

2. Two Songs for four Men's Voices: (*a*) "Schlummernd an des Vaters Brust;" (*b*) "Auf, Freunde, lasst das Jahr uns singen," in the "Repertorium für Männergesang" (Kahnt, Leipzig).

A "Te Deum," for a four-part chorus and organ, with English words, has been published in London.

Lastly, we must not omit to mention a published work of Mendelssohn's though not a musical one, namely a translation of the "Andria" of Terence. Its complete title is—

"The Maiden of Andros, a Comedy by Terence, in the metre of the original, translated by F——; with an introduction and notes, edited by K. W. L. Heyse. (Berlin, 1826, Ferdinand Dummler.)"

As the existence of this little work, or at any rate the fact that "Felix Mendelssohn Bartholdy" is concealed beneath the "F——," is not hitherto generally known, this notice will be received with some interest.

II. The second division of the Catalogue is intended to furnish a more ready means of reference to what Mendelssohn has accomplished in the most various styles of composition (beside the published works); it is not arranged chronologically, but under different heads,—Church Music, Dramatic, etc. etc. The immense number of the works it includes, bears testimony to the strict and conscientious manner in which Mendelssohn acted with regard to himself, and how many pieces he laid aside, which, if only revised, might have caused great delight and enjoyment to the world. The list also testifies to the caution of his representatives, and to their desire to act in the same spirit as himself, by not publishing anything among his papers which might be unworthy of his name, or of his importance in the history of art. Minor compositions for special occasions, songs for family *fêtes*, canons in albums, etc. etc., of which a vast number exist, are not included in the Catalogue, chiefly because it was impossible to make even an approach to a complete list. It may be mentioned, that Mendelssohn added full obligato organ parts to two of Handel's oratorios, viz. " Solomon " and " Israel in Egypt," as well as to the " Dettingen Te Deum." Those for " Solomon " and the " Te Deum " remain in manuscript; but those to " Israel in Egypt " are published in the edition of the Handel Society of London, for whom Mendelssohn edited the oratorio.

J. R.

34*

PUBLISHED WORKS,

1822.

Quartett for Pianoforte, Violin, Tenor, and Violoncello, in C minor, op. 1.   Berlin.*

1823.

Quartett for Pianoforte, Violin, Tenor, and Violoncello, in F minor, op. 2.   Berlin.

Sonata for Pianoforte and Violin, in F minor, op. 4. Berlin.

1824.

Quartett for Pianoforte, Violin, Tenor, and Violoncello, in B minor, op. 3. Berlin.

" Die Hochzeit des Camacho," Opera in Two Acts, op. 10. First Act.   Berlin.

Overture for a Military Band, in C Major, op. 24.   Dobberan.

Originally composed for the Band of the Dobberan Baths and subsequently arranged for a full Military Band.

---

* The name of the place invariably indicates where the Work was composed, or at all events finished.

1825.

"Die Hochzeit des Camacho," Overture and Second Act.

> This Opera was given once in the Berlin theatre, on the 29th April, 1827.

Capriccio for Pianoforte, in F sharp minor, op. 5. Berlin.

Octett for four Violins, two Tenors, and two Violoncellos, in E flat, op. 20. Berlin.

1826.

Quintett for two Violins, two Tenors, and Violoncello, in A, op. 18. Berlin.

> The Intermezzo, Andante sostenuto, in F major, was composed subsequently in Paris, in 1832. The Scherzo, in D minor, originally formed the second movement; the third was a Minuetto, in F sharp, Allegro molto; with a Trio, in D, Canone doppio.

Overture to Shakspeare's "Midsummer Night's Dream," in E major, op. 21. Berlin.

Song for Voice and Pianoforte, "Es lauschte das Laub," op. 86, no. 1.

1827.

Quartett for two Violins, Tenor, and Violoncello, in A minor, op. 13. Berlin.

Fugue for two Violins, Tenor, and Violoncello, in E flat, in op. 81.

Fugue for Pianoforte, in E minor. Berlin.

> No. 7 in a collection entitled, "Notre Temps," published by Schott, of Mayence.

1828.

Quartett for two Violins, Tenor, and Violoncello, in E flat, op. 12. Berlin.

> At the period of its composition, this Quartett appeared as "the first for stringed instruments."

Overture, "Meeresstille und glückliche Fahrt," in D, op. 27. Berlin.

Variations for Pianoforte and Violoncello, in D, op. 17. Berlin.

1829.

Song for Voice and Pianoforte, "Wartend," op. 9, no 3. Berlin.

Song for Voice and Pianoforte, "Der Blumenkranz." London.

> This appeared at a much later period, in an Album of Spehr's, Brunswick.

Three Fantasias or Caprices for the Pianoforte, op. 16. Coed Du, in Wales.

"Heimkehr aus der Fremde," Operetta in One Act, op. 89. London and Berlin.

> Composed for the celebration of the silver wedding-day of his parents. Performed in public for the first time on the 20th April, 1851, in Leipzig.

1830.

Overture, "Die Hebriden," in B minor, op. 26. Rome.

Psalm CXV., "Nicht unserm Namen, Herr," for Chorus, Solo, and Orchestra, op. 31. Rome.

Song for Voice and Pianoforte, "Reiselied," op. 19, no. 6. Venice.

Song without words, "Gondellied," op. 19, no. 6. Venice.

> A book of songs with words, and one of songs without words, are each marked as Opus 19.

Three pieces of Sacred Music for Solo and Chorus, with Organ, op. 23. Rome.

Three Motetts for Female Voices with Organ, op. 39.
Rome.
> Composed for the Nuns in Trinità de' Monti, in Rome; but
> not published till 1838, when it was partly re-written.

1831.

" Die erste Walpurgis Nacht," Ballad, for Chorus, Solo,
and Orchestra, op. 60. Milan and Paris.
> Re-written in Leipzig in 1842, and published in 1843.

" Verleih' uns Frieden," Prayer, for Chorus and Orchestra. No opus number. Rome.

Song for Voice and Pianoforte, " Da lieg' ich unter den
Bäumen," op. 84, no. 1. Düsseldorf.

Song for Voice and Pianoforte, " Die Liebende schreibt,"
op. 86, no. 3. Untersee.

1832.

Concerto for Pianoforte and Orchestra, in G minor, op.
25. Munich.

Capriccio Brillant, for Pianoforte with Orchestra, in B
minor, op. 22. London.

Fugue for Pianoforte, in B minor, op. 35, no. 3.

1833.

Symphony, in A major, op. 90. Berlin.
> Repeatedly mentioned in Mendelssohn's Letters from Italy
> as the Italian Symphony.

Overture, " Zum Mährchen von der schönen Melusine,"
in F, op. 32. Berlin.

Fantasia for Pianoforte, in F sharp minor, op. 28. Berlin.
> Entitled on the autograph, "Sonate Ecossaise."

Capriccio for Pianoforte, in F sharp minor, op. 33, no
3. London.

"Lied ohne Worte," in D, op. 30, no. 5. Düsseldorf.

Vocal Chorus, "Lord, have mercy," in A minor. No
opus number. Berlin.

> Published in an Album, by Bösenberg, Leipzig.

1834.

Rondo Brillant for Pianoforte, in E flat, op. 29.

Capriccio for Pianoforte, in A minor, op. 33, no. 1.

"Lieder ohne Worte :"—

    Op. 30, Nos. 1 and 4.

    Op. 85, No. 2.

Songs for Voice and Pianoforte :—

    "Minnelied," op. 34, no. 1.

    "Auf Flügeln des Gesanges," op. 34, no. 2.

    "Sonntagslied," op. 34, no. 5.

    "Jagdlied," op. 84, no. 3.

Romance for Voice and Pianoforte, "Schlafloser Augen,"
    No opus number.

> Published in an Album.   Breitkopf and Härtel, Leipzig.

Three "Volkslieder," for Soprano, Alto, Tenor, and
Bass, op. 41, nos. 2, 3, 4.

Commencement of the Oratorio of " St. Paul."

"Todeslied der Bojaren," from Immermann's Tragedy
of "Alexis," for a chorus of men's voices in unison,
and wind instruments; in E minor.

> First published as a contribution to the fourth volume of Im-
> mermann's works.   Schaub, Düsseldorf.

N.B.—All the works of this year were composed at Düsseldorf.

1835.

Oratorio of "St. Paul," op. 36. Düsseldorf and Leipzig.

> Performed for the first time at the Musical Festival of the
> Lower Rhine, at Düsseldorf, on the 22nd of May, 1836.

Capriccio for Pianoforte, in E major, op. 33, no. 2. Düsseldorf.

Fugue for Pianoforte, in A flat, op. 35, no. 4. Düsseldorf.

Song for Voice with Pianoforte, "Das Waldschloss." No opus number. Berlin.

1836.

Preludes for Pianoforte, op. 35 :—no. 2, in D ; no. 3, in B minor ; no. 5, in F minor. Leipzig.

Fugue for Pianoforte, op. 35, no. 6, B flat. Leipzig.

Fugue for the Organ, in G, op. 37, no. 2. Leipzig.

Étude and Scherzo for the Pianoforte, in F minor. No opus number. Leipzig.

Two-part Song, with Pianoforte, "Sonntagsmorgen," op. 77, no. 1. Leipzig.

1837.

Concerto for Pianoforte and Orchestra, in D minor, op. 40. Bingen and Horchheim on the Rhine.

Quartett for Two Violins, Tenor, and Violoncello, in E minor, op. 44, no. 2. Frankfort on the Main.

Psalm XLII., "Wie der Hirsch schreit," for Chorus, Solo, and Orchestra. Freyburg in Breisgau, and Leipzig.

Preludes for Pianoforte, op. 35 :—no. 1, in E minor ; no. 4, in A flat major ; no. 6, B flat. Leipzig.

Fugue for Pianoforte, op. 35, no. 2. Leipzig.

Three Preludes for the Organ, op. 37. Speyer.

Fugue for the Organ, op. 37, no. 1. Speyer.

Songs for Voice with Pianoforte :—

    "Suleika," op. 34, no. 4.

    "Reiselied," op. 34, no. 6. } Leipzig.

    "Suleika," op. 57, no. 3.

Songs for Four Male Voices :—
"Sommerlied," op. 50, no. 3.
"Wasserfahrt," op. 50, no. 4.
"So lang man nüchtern ist," op. 75, no. 3. } Leipzig.
"Geben wir Rath," op. 76, no. 1.
Song for Soprano, Alto, Tenor, and Bass, "Im Grünen,"
op. 59, no. 1. Leipzig.
"Song without Words," in A minor, op. 38, no. 5.
Speyer.

1838.

Serenade and Allegro Giojoso for Pianoforte, with Or-
chestra, op. 43. Leipzig.
Quartett for Stringed Instruments, in E flat, op. 44, No.
3. Leipzig.
Sonata for Pianoforte and Violoncello, in B flat, op. 45.
Leipzig.
Psalm XCV., "Kommt, lasst uns anbeten," for Chorus,
Solo, and Orchestra, op. 46. Leipzig.
Andante Cantabile and Presto Agitato, for the Piano-
forte, in B. Without any opus number. Berlin.
Appeared in an Album. Breitkopf and Härtel, Leipzig.
Song for Four Male Voices, "Türkisches Schenken-
lied," op. 50, No. 1. Leipzig.

1839.

Psalm CXIV., "Da Israel aus Egypten zog," for an
eight-part Chorus and Orchestra, op. 51. Horchheim.
Trio, for Pianoforte, Violin, and Violoncello, in D minor,
op. 49. Frankfort, Berlin, and Leipzig.
Sonata for the Organ, in C minor, op. 65, no. 2. Frankfort.

Overture to Victor Hugo's drama, " Ruy Blas," in C minor, op. 95. Leipzig.

Chorus for Two Female Voices, with Quartett accompaniment, from " Ruy Blas," in A, op. 77, no. 3.

> The foregoing two pieces were written for a performance of "Ruy Blas" for the benefit of the Theatrical Pension Fund, at the request of the Committee of the Fund.

Six Songs, for Soprano, Alto, Tenor, and Bass, op. 48. Frankfort and Leipzig.

Besides these :—

"Hirtenlied," op. 88, no. 3. ⎫
"Im Wald," op. 100, no. 4. ⎬ Frankfort.

Songs for Four Male Voices :—

"Liebe und Wein," op. 50, no. 5.
"Abendständchen," op. 75, no. 2.
"Ersatz für Unbestand." No opus number.
⎬ Leipzig.

Songs for One Voice with Pianoforte :—

"Frühlingslied," op. 47, no. 3.
"Volkslied," op. 47, no. 4.
"Wiegenlied," op. 47, no. 6.
⎬ Leipzig.

"Altdeutsches Lied," op. 57, no. 1. Horchheim.

"Hirtenlied," op. 57, no. 2.
"Herbstlied," op. 84, no. 2.
"Song without Words," in F sharp minor, op. 67, no. 2.
⎬ Leipzig.

1840.

"Hymn of Praise," Symphony Cantata, op. 52. Leipzig.

> Performed for the first time on the 25th of June, 1840, in the Thomas Church at Leipzig, at the Celebration of the Fourth Centenary of Printing.

A " Festgesang," for Male Voices and Brass Band,

35

"Begeht mit heil'gem Lobgesang." No opus number.

For the opening of the same Festival in honour of Printing.

Songs for Four Male Voices :—

"Der Jäger Abschied," op. 50, no. 2.

"Wanderlied," op. 50, no. 6.

Song for Soprano, Alto, Tenor, and Bass, "Der wandernde Musikant," op. 88, No. 6.

1841.

Music for "Antigone," op. 55. Berlin.

Performed for the first time on the 6th November, 1841, in the New Palace, at Potsdam, and in the theatre at Berlin, on the 13th of April, 1842.

Variations Sérieuses, for the Pianoforte, in D minor, op. 54. Leipzig.

Variations for the Pianoforte, in E flat, op. 82. Leipzig.

Allegro Brillant for the Pianoforte, arranged as a Duett, in A, op. 92. Leipzig.

Prelude for the Pianoforte, in E minor, for "Notre Temps." Refer to 1827. Leipzig.

Songs for Voice, with Pianoforte accompaniment :—

"Frische Fahrt," op. 57, no. 6. Leipzig.

"Erster Verlust," op. 99, no. 1. Berlin.

"Das Schifflein," op. 99, no. 4. Leipzig.

Song for Voice, with Pianoforte, "Ich hör' ein Vöglein locken." No opus number.

Appeared first as a contribution to a Collection of Poetry by Adolph Böttger.

"Songs without Words :"—

"Volkslied," in A minor, op. 53, no. 5. ⎫
"   in A major, op. 53, no. 6. ⎬ Leipzig.
"   in B flat, op. 85, no. 6. ⎭

1842.

Symphony, in A minor, op. 56. Berlin.
>   Called the "Scotch Symphony," in the letters of 1830.

Songs for Voice with Pianoforte :—
>   " Gondellied," op. 57, no. 5.
>   " Schilflied," op. 71, no. 4.

Song for two Voices, with Pianoforte, " Wie war so schön," op. 63, no. 2.

" Song without Words," in A major, op. 62, no. 6.

1843.

Music for the " Midsummer Night's Dream," op. 61. See year 1826. Leipzig.
>   Performed for the first time on the 14th of October, 1843, in the New Palace, at Potsdam ; and in the theatre at Berlin, on the 18th October, 1843.

Sonata for Pianoforte and Violoncello, in D, op. 58. Leipzig.

Choruses for Racine's " Athalie." Leipzig.
>   For female voices only, and with pianoforte accompaniment. This work was performed, in its later shape, for the first time on December 1st, 1845, in the Royal Theatre at Charlottenburg. See year 1845.

Concert Aria for Soprano with Orchestra, in B flat, op. 94. Leipzig.

Capriccio for Two Violins, Tenor, and Violoncello, in E minor, in op. 81. Leipzig.

Psalm XCI., " Singet dem Herrn ein neues Lied," for Chorus and Orchestra, op. 91. Berlin.
>   For the celebration of New Year's Day, 1844, in the Dom Kirche, at Berlin.

Psalm II., " Warum toben die Heiden ?" for an eight part Chorus, op. 78, no. 1. Berlin.

Anthem, "Herr Gott, du bist unsre Zuflucht," for a Chorus of Eight Voices, op. 79, no. 2. Berlin.

Hymn for a Contralto, Chorus, and Orchestra, op. 96. Leipzig.

> The elaboration of a work formerly published by Simrock of Bonn, without any opus-number, entitled "Three Sacred Songs for an Alto Voice, Chorus, and Organ."

Song for Voice with Pianoforte, "Es weiss und räth es doch Keiner," op. 99, no. 6.

Songs for Soprano, Alto, Tenor, and Bass:—

"Frühzeitiger Frühling,"
"Abschied vom Walde,"
"Die Nachtigall,"   op. 59, nos. 2 to 6.
"Ruhethal,"   Leipzig.
"Jagdlied,"

"Ich hab' ein Liebchen," op. 88, no. 2.
"Die Waldvöglein," op. 88, no. 4.   Leipzig.
"Lob des Frühlings," op. 100, no. 2.

"Songs without Words:"—

B, op. 62, no. 2.
E minor, op. 62, no. 3.
G, op. 62, no. 4.   Leipzig.
C, op. 67, no. 4.

1844.

Concerto for the Violin, with Orchestra, in E minor, op. 64. Leipzig.

Overture to "Athalie," in D minor, and March of the Priests, in F, op. 74. London.

Hymn, "Hör' mein Bitten," for a Soprano, Chorus, and Organ. No number. Berlin.

Sonatas for the Organ, op. 65 :—

F minor, no. 1.
C minor, no. 2.
A major, no. 3. } Frankfort.
D minor, no. 6.

Psalms for a Choir of Eight Voices, op. 78.

Psalm XLIII., " Richte mich Gott," No. 2.
Psalm XLII., "Mein Gott, warum hast } Berlin.
Du," no. 3.

Songs for Four Male Voices :—

" Wem Gott will," op. 75, no. 1.
" So rückt denn," op. 75, no. 4. } Berlin.
" Rheinweinlied," op. 76, no. 2.

Songs för Soprano, Alto, Tenor, and Bass :—

" Neujahrslied," op. 88, no. 1.
" Andenken," op. 100, no. 1.

" Songs without Words :"—

G, op. 62, no. 1. Berlin.
E flat, op. 67, no. 1. Leipzig.
B minor, op. 51. Berlin.

Songs for Two Voices with Pianoforte :—

" Gruss," op. 63, no. 2.
" Herbstlied," op. 63, no. 3. } Leipzig.

" Maiglöckchen und die Blümelein," op. 63, no. 6.
Berlin.

1845.

Music for " Oedipus von Kolonos," op. 93. Leipzig
and Frankfort.

> Performed for the first time on the 1st November, 1845, in
> the New Palace at Potsdam, and in the theatre at Berlin on
> the 10th November, 1845.

Quintett for two Violins, two Tenors, and Violoncello,
in B flat, op. 87. Soden.

35*

"Athalie," instrumentation and arrangement of the
Choruses for Soprano, Alto, Tenor, and Bass. See
the years 1843 and 1844. Op. 74.

Sonatas for the Organ :—
B flat, op. 65, no. 4. ⎱ Frankfort.
D minor, op. 65, no. 6. ⎰

Songs for One Voice with Pianoforte :—
"Tröstung," op. 71, no. 1. Leipzig.
"Frühlingslied," op. 71, no. 2. Frankfort.
"Wenn sich zwei Herzen scheiden," op. 99, no. 5.
Leipzig.

"Songs without Words :"—
B flat, op. 67, no. 3. Leipzig.
D, op. 84, no. 4. ⎱ Frankfort.
A, op. 84, no. 5. ⎰

Anthems for an Eight-part Chorus:—
"Frohlocket, ihr Völker," op. 97, no. 1.
"Herr, gedenke," op. 79, no. 4.

Commencement of the Oratorio of "Elijah."

1846.

Cantata to the "Sons of Art," Male Chorus and Brass
Band, op. 68.
Written for the first German-Flemish Vocal Festival at Co-
logne.

"Lauda Sion," for Chorus, Solo, and Orchestra, op. 73.
For the church of St. Martin, in Lüttich.

"Elijah," Oratorio, op. 70.
Performed for the first time at Birmingham, August 25,
1846.

Song for Four Male Voices, "Was uns eint als deutsche
Brüder," op. 76, no. 3.
For the Germans in Lyons.

Anthems for an Eight-part Chorus :—

"Erhaben, O Herr," op. 79, no. 3.

"Lasset uns frohlocken," op. 79, no. 5.

All the works of this year were composed in Leipzig.

1847.

Three Motetts for Chorus and Solo Voices, op. 69. Baden-Baden and Leipzig.

Recitative and Choruses from the unfinished Oratorio, "Christus," op. 97.

Finale of the first Act from the unfinished Opera of "Loreley," op. 98. Leipzig.

Besides this finale there are only extant, an Ave Maria for Soprano Solo and Female Chorus, a grand March with Chorus, and the beginning of three other pieces of music.

Quartett for Two Violins, Tenor, and Violoncello, in F minor, op. 80. Interlachen.

Andante and Scherzo for Two Violins, Tenor, and Violoncello, in op. 81.

Songs for One Voice with Pianoforte :—

"An die Entfernte," op. 71, no. 3. Leipzig.

"Auf der Wanderschaft," op. 71, no. 5. Interlachen.

"Nachtlied," op. 71, no. 6. Leipzig.

Song for Four Male Voices, "Comitat," op. 76, no. 4. Frankfort.

Song for Two Voices with Pianoforte, "Das Aehrenfeld," op. 77, no. 2. Leipzig.

Song for Voice with Pianoforte, "Altdeutsches Frühlingslied," op. 86, no. 6.

Mendelssohn's last composition, written on the 7th October 1847, in Leipzig.

II.

WORKS NOT PUBLISHED.

SACRED MUSIC.

"Magnificat" for Chorus and Orchestra, in D. 1822.

"Juba Domine" for Chorus and Soli, without Orchestra. 1822.

"Gloria" for a four-part Chorus and Orchestra, in E flat.

"Kyrie" for two Choruses and Soli, in C minor.

"Jesus meine Zuversicht," Chorale, four and five Voices. 1824.

"Ich bin durch der Hoffnung Band," Chorale and Fugue, for four and five Voices.

"Kyrie" for a five-part Chorus and Orchestra. 1825.

"Und ob du mich züchtigest, Herr," Canon for five Voices.

"O Beata," Chorus for three Female Voices and Organ.

"Te Deum Laudamus," for an eight-part Chorus. Eight movements. 1826.

"Tu es Petrus," for a five-part Chorus and Orchestra. 1827.

"Christe, du Lamm Gottes," Cantata for four Voices and stringed instruments.

" Ach Gott vom Himmel sieh darein," Cantata for four Voices and Orchestra.

" Vom Himmel hoch, da komm' ich her," Christmas hymn for four voices and Orchestra. Rome. 1831.

" Hora est de somno surgere," for four Four-part Choirs.

" Ad vesperas Dom. XXI. post Trinitatis. Responsorium et Hymnus," for three- and four-part Male Chorus.

" Beati mortui," for a four-part Male Chorus.

Two English Psalm-tunes for four voices. 1839.

Nine pieces in the Oratorio of " St. Paul," subsequently omitted :—four Choruses, three Chorales, four Recitatives, a Soprano Aria, and a Duett for Tenor and Bass.

" Herr Gott, dich loben wir," Chorale for double Chorus, Organ, four Trombones, and stringed instruments, for the celebration of the German Tausendjährige festival. 1843.

Psalm C., " Jauchzet dem Herrn," for a four-part Chorus. 1844.

The German Liturgy, for two four-part Choirs.

" Wir glauben all' an einen Gott," for Chorus and Orchestra.

> The most important of these works *a capella*, the "Te Deum," the " Hora est," etc., were written from 1826 to 1828 for the Berlin Singing Academy, at that time under Zelter's management, and were constantly sung there. The four last-named pieces were composed for the Cathedral Choir at Berlin.

SECULAR CANTATAS.

Grand Festival Music for the Dürer Festival. The Poem by Professor Levetzow. Performed in the

Hall of the Singing Academy at Berlin, on the 12th of April, 1828. Instrumental Introduction, and fourteen Numbers—Solos, Grand fugued Choruses, etc.

Festival Music, for a festival given in the Hall of the Royal Theatre at Berlin, by Alexander von Humboldt. The words by L. Rellstab. For Male Voices, with accompaniment of Clarionets, Horns, Trumpets, Kettle-drums, Violoncello, and Double Bass. Seven numbers, Solos and Choruses. 1827.

Festal Song at the uncovering of the statue of Friedrich August the Just, at Dresden, on the 9th June, 1842, for two Male Choirs and Brass Band.

DRAMATIC.

" Die beiden Pädagogen," Comic Operetta, in one Act, adapted from the French. Overture and ten numbers.

" Soldatenliebschaft," Comic Operetta, in one Act. Overture and fourteen numbers.

" Die wandernden Komödianten," Comic Opera in one Act. Overture and twelve numbers. 1821.

" Der Onkel aus Boston, oder die beiden Neffen," Comic Opera in three Acts. 1822–1823. Overture and fourteen numbers, with much Ballet Music.

Music to Calderon's Tragedy, " The Steadfast Prince." Two Choruses for Male Voices, Battle-piece, Melodrama. 1834.
  Written for a performance in Düsseldorf.

FOR VOICE, WITH ORCHESTRAL ACCOMPANIMENT OR STRINGED INSTRUMENTS.

Recitative and Aria, " Che vuoi mio cor," for a Contralto, accompanied by Stringed Instruments. 1824.

Scena and Aria, for a Soprano, with Orchestra. 1834.

<small>Much of this was afterwards made use of in the Aria, op. 94,
the only instance in which Mendelssohn's artistic energy permitted him so to do.</small>

Air for Barytone and Orchestra, with English Words,
written for Phillips, the singer, of London. 1846.

Songs for Voice, with Pianoforte Accompaniment.

Songs, finished ballads, several in Italian, chiefly from
Mendelssohn's earlier period to the year 1834. The
words are, with few exceptions, by unknown poets,
and the enumeration of the individual pieces can be
of little interest. Their number is from twenty to
thirty.

For Four Male Voices.

' A frischer Bua bin ich," for Immermann's " Andreas
Hofer." 1833.

" Der weise Diogenes war der erste der griechischen
Sieben," Canon for twice Two Voices. 1833.

" Musikanten Prügelei." 1833.

" Im Nebelgeriesel, im tiefen Schnee," Gipsy Song by
Goethe, for two Two-part Choirs.

" Worauf kommt es überall an," by Goethe. 1837.

" Auf ihr Herrn und Damen schön," Hunting Song.
1837.

Morning Song of the Thuringian Vocal Association,
" Seid gegrüsset, traute Brüder." For the Festival
in Eisenach. 1847.

For Full Orchestra.

Symphony, in D. 1822.

Grand Overture, in C. 1825.

<small>Performed at the Musical Festival in Düsseldorf, at Whit-
suntide, 1833.</small>

Sympnony for the celebration of the Reformation Festival, in D minor. 1830.

Performed in London and Berlin.

Marches for smaller Military Bands, composed for the use in Church Processions at Düsseldorf. 1833.

March for a full Orchestra, in D, in celebration of the visit of Cornelius the painter to Dresden.

FOR STRINGS.

Ten Four-, Five-, and Six-part Symphonies, in the years 1820 to 1823.

Concerto for the Violin, with accompaniment of Stringed Instruments, in D minor.

Quartett for Two Violins, Tenor and Violoncello, in E flat. 1823.

Many single Four- and Five-part pieces, Fugues, etc.

FOR PIANOFORTE, WITH ACCOMPANIMENT.

Concerto for Two Pianos, with Orchestra, in E. 1823.

Concerto for Two Pianos, with Orchestra, in A flat. 1824.

Concerto for Pianoforte and Violin, with Stringed Instruments, in D minor. 1823.

Concerto for Pianoforte, with Stringed Instruments, in A minor.

Sextett for Pianoforte, Violin, Two Tenors, Violoncello, and Double Bass, in D. 1824.

Quartett for Pianoforte, Violin, Tenor, and Violoncello, in D minor.

Trio for Pianoforte, Violin, and Tenor, in C minor. 1820.

Sonata for Pianoforte and Tenor, in C minor. 1824.

Sonata for Pianoforte and Clarionet, in E flat.

Sonata for Pianoforte and Violin, in D minor.

Sonata for Pianoforte and Violin, in F. 1838.

" Song without Words," for Pianoforte and Violoncello. For Fräulein Lisa Christiani.

FOR PIANOFORTE SOLO.

Grand Fantasia. 1823.

Fantasia, four hands, in D minor. 1824.

Sonatina, in B flat minor. 1824.

Sonata, in B flat. 1827.

Andante and Allegro, in E major and E minor. 1837.

A vast number of Songs without Words, Studies, Preludes, Fugues, Juvenile Pieces, etc., of all dates.

FOR CLARIONET AND CORNO DI BASSETTO, WITH PIANOFORTE ACCOMPANIMENT.

Two Concertos for the Royal Bavarian Kammer-Musiker, Herren Bärmann, father and son, composed in Munich, in 1832.

THE END.